D0855814

JAPAN'S
AMERICAN
INTERLUDE

JAPAN'S
AMERICAN
INTERLUDE

Kazuo Kawai

THE UNIVERSITY OF CHICAGO PRESS

CHICAGO AND LONDON

THE UNIVERSITY OF CHICAGO PRESS, CHICAGO 60637
The University of Chicago Press, Ltd., London

International Standard Book Number: 0-226-42774-9
Library of Congress Catalog Card Number: 59-14111

This book deals with the American interlude in the history of Japan during which time that country was not only occupied by American troops and politically controlled by American officials but was subjected to almost every conceivable variety of American influence. It does not attempt to tell the story of the Occupation itself, for that story has already been told many times by Americans who, as participants or close observers, were in a position to tell it well. Instead, this work deals only with selected controversial aspects of the Japanese reaction to American influence during the Occupation period.

This subject is one that bears recounting, particularly from the point of view of the Japanese themselves. Today the American interlude in Japanese history is over, and the Japanese seem to be repudiating much that the Americans tried to accomplish. But so great was the American impact—which, although of short duration, was the most powerful concentration of foreign influence ever to be exerted upon the eclectic culture of Japan—that its effect on the Japanese is not likely ever to fade completely away. Whatever they do will continue to reflect, even if obversely, some measure of this overwhelming intrusion into their lives.

At a time when a renascent Japan, recovering from her postwar debility, is looking more and more toward re-establishing herself in world affairs, the key to her future conduct may well be found in the long-range effects of the American influence that was once so powerfully exerted upon her. Although she can no longer hope to play a major independent role in world politics, her remaining potentialities may still enable her to be a decisive factor in a close balance of international alignments. What role she will be inclined to play in this balance—whether as a force for reaction, for radicalism, or for democracy—may be significantly conditioned by what her experience with the Americans meant in her national life.

Of course the definitive interpretation of the American interlude in Japanese history will not be possible until academic research turns up more empirical data about this period than are yet available. But public opinion and practical statesmanship cannot wait for scholarly monographs; resort must be made to reasonable guesses. The present work attempts to provide such a reasonable guess; it is admittedly subjective and tentative. But the writer hopes that his background as a newspaper editor in Tokyo, where by birth and social ties he was completely identified with Japanese life, has enabled him—despite his American academic experience—to contribute some insights into Japan which may have escaped the Western observer.

Grateful acknowledgment is made to Professor John W. Bennett, formerly of the Department of Sociology and Anthropology of the Ohio State University and now of Washington University, St. Louis, whose stimulating association helped sharpen many of the writer's ideas, and to the writer's colleague in the Department of Political Science, Frank O. Miller. Although they both read the entire manuscript and helped greatly with their constructive criticisms, they are not to be held responsible for any remaining errors of omission or commission, for, through mostly his own inadequacies, the writer was not able to respond adequately to all of their suggestions.

It is impossible to name the many other persons whose ideas, gleaned from conversations or through the reading of their works, strongly influenced the writer's own thinking. Some of these persons will undoubtedly recognize the specific points for which they were responsible. To all of them, the writer thankfully acknowledges his debt.

Contents

CHAPTER I

Attitudes

The peaceful beginning of the Occupation of Japan will always remain something of a mystery. A bitter war had prepared the Americans to expect treachery and resistance, the Japanese to expect rapine and pillage. In Japan, defiant diehards had tried by violence to obstruct the surrender. Wartime propaganda still gripped the minds of most Japanese. If their national tradition was any guide to what might happen, there should have been no dearth of fanatics to dash with swinging swords against the disembarking Americans.

Yet, after the first tense probings, both sides discovered to their amazement that the other was not what they had been led to believe. More than a decade later, after the inevitable misunderstandings, frustrations, friction, and reaction, it could still be said that, on balance, no occupation of an enemy country in all history had turned out to be such a happy surprise as this one for both the conqueror and the conquered.

What were the reasons for this unpredictable outcome? Why did the Japanese respond to the Occupation with such docility and with even such cordiality and co-operativeness? The Japanese themselves, puzzled by their own conduct, which went counter to their orthodox teachings, have engaged in considerable soul-searching. They could hardly dismiss the matter with a facile reference to the mysterious Oriental mind.

For policy reasons, both the Occupation authorities and the Japanese government adopted an official line which held that the Japanese people, freed by defeat from their militarist

1

masters, had become genuinely repentant and eager to redeem themselves through democracy. Although it contained a greater measure of truth than might be generally recognized, such an explanation was too naïvely sanguine to represent the whole truth.

Many Westerners, with the war still fresh in their memories, at first suspected that the Japanese attitude toward the Occupation was wholly insincere. The outward compliance was thought to be designed to lull the Americans into a false sense of security so that the Occupation might by devious means be eventually thwarted and nullified. Some thought they found definite proof—complete as to time, place, and names of participants—of secret meetings where the Japanese leaders had planned the strategy of this deep-laid conspiracy. But the more familiar the Americans became with the Japanese people and with Japanese conditions, the more implausible this "duplicity theory" appeared to be. While individual schemers might attempt to preserve their special interests by fair means or foul, the transparently spontaneous conduct of the great mass of the Japanese people ruled out the possibility that eighty million persons could be led by a few conspirators to practice perfect dissimulation.

Some attributed the Japanese conduct to the mystic power of the Emperor. When he commanded his people to accept the surrender, they co-operated with the Occupation unquestioningly, just as they had earlier unquestioningly obeyed his command to fight unto death. Unfortunately for this theory, however, Japanese history is replete with examples of wilful individuals who, in obedience to their own inner dictates, have defied imperial commands. Such dissidents could always claim that the Emperor needed to be saved from his false advisers. While the admonition of the Emperor to "endure the unendurable" undoubtedly contributed to the easy acceptance of the surrender, it certainly was not the sole key to the Japanese attitude toward the Occupation.

Some tried to explain the conduct of the Japanese on the grounds that they have an inordinate respect for authority. When their own rulers were discredited by defeat, it was supposedly only natural for the Japanese to transfer to the Americans, who had demonstrated superior power, the same respect and obedience they had previously manifested toward native authority. But this explanation places too much emphasis on the efficacy of naked power and ignores the factors of ideas, traditions, and sentiment which have often shaped the conduct of the Japanese. It does not explain why the Japanese, so amenable to authority under certain conditions, are also quixotically defiant of authority under certain other conditions.

Another theory held that the Japanese are easily susceptible to new ideas. They are imitators; their entire culture is essentially an eclectic one. When their old system was discredited by defeat, they lost no time mourning over their failure; they immediately sought to imitate the secrets of the success of their conquerors. It was not a blind worship of naked power and authority as the preceding theory would have it, but a sensitivity and responsiveness to new experiences. While true as far as it went, this explanation was still inadequate, as will presently be shown.

Seemingly the most sophisticated explanation held that the Japanese, as the result of their centuries of experience with despotic rulers, had learned how to protect themselves while bowing to authority. They were like a good boxer rolling instinctively with the punch. Without conscious duplicity and without orders from above, the Japanese instinctively responded to the Occupation with their age-old technique of bending without breaking, ready to spring back whenever the pressure was relaxed. The failure of Tokugawa authoritarianism to break the vitality of the bourgeoisie is often cited as a historic example. But even this theory, though valid in large measure, fails to explain fully the response of the Japanese to the Occupation.

While true in part, none of these theories is really adequate, for the reaction of an entire nation to such a complex and comprehensive experience as the Occupation was necessarily conditioned by an infinite number of factors. Some were to be found in the special circumstances of the moment, others in the underlying traits of the people as shaped by their history and culture. As many of these factors as can be identified need to be examined in order to find a reasonably adequate explanation.

The thoroughness of their defeat was one important factor in the receptivity of the Japanese to the Occupation. Their world, as they had known it, had collapsed. Not only were their cities in ruins, their economy shattered, and their manpower mangled and strewn over nearly half the globe, but the dreams of national greatness which had sustained their spirits had evaporated. They were disillusioned, demoralized, and paralyzed. Although traditional controls largely stifled overt expressions of defeatism, the horrors of the last few months of the war had reduced many of the Japanese to an inner state bordering on panic. The surrender came to them as a heaven-sent relief; the Occupation became a welcome symbol of deliverance from annihilation.

Their unpreparedness for defeat was another important factor in the reaction of the Japanese. Never having been successfully invaded in all their long history, they had never even imagined the possibility of an enemy occupation. When suddenly confronted with a situation for which their social conditioning had provided no preparation, they found themselves utterly bewildered. While they were thus off balance, they were easily susceptible to any new influence that might be directed upon them.

This extreme pliability of the Japanese in an unexpected situation can be explained further by what has been termed their "situational ethics." Whereas Western civilization has developed a universalistic ethic which regards all men as equal in the sight of God and before the law, Eastern civilizations with their polytheistic concept of the divinity and their pluralistic concept of society regard human relationships as particularistic and specific. That is to say, while in the West all relations between individuals must ideally be reconciled with the universal principle of a common humanity, in the East what is proper in the relations between two individuals in a given situation is considered intrinsically different from what is proper in another situation or between other individuals. This difference between Western and Eastern ethics has been accentuated for the Japanese by the Confucian emphasis on hierarchical categories in human relationships and by the comparative closeness of the feudal past when, as with all feudal societies, Japanese society was an interlocking complex of many specific personal relationships.

In a society made up of a difficult maze of special relationships, one cannot play by ear and trust to general principles to keep in harmony; one must closely follow the written score to avoid mistakes in social conduct. This is one of the reasons why the Japanese are so dependent on a rigidly formal code of conduct which reduces the risks of a complex social intercourse to a safe, conventionalized formula. So long as the situations which confront the Japanese are covered by prescribed rules, they are safe. But when a totally unexpected situation arises which is not covered in their book of rules, they become hopelessly lost and their conduct becomes uncontrolled and capricious. They have no eternally valid guides such as enable Westerners to improvise their conduct in unfamiliar situations.[1]

Accordingly, when the Occupation confronted the Japanese with a situation to which their traditional rules could not apply, they lost their bearings. In their undirected and highly fluid condition, it would conceivably have taken very little to turn the Japanese violently against the Occupation. But it also took very little to turn them to wholehearted co-operation. Whichever way they turned, they would have felt little consciousness of inconsistency. New situations called for new patterns of conduct.

Once they had turned to co-operation, moreover, it was furthered by the ingrained habit of the Japanese of always playing according to the rules of the game. Finding that their old rules no longer applied, they quickly began to yearn for the

[1] A normally gentle Japanese might, under unaccustomed conditions of combat, commit atrocities which would be unthinkable to him under ordinary conditions. Or a Japanese soldier, trained to regard capture as unthinkable, might upon being captured show wholehearted co-operation toward his captors whom he had recently been fighting. In unexpected situations for which he has no prepared rule, the Japanese has no universal ethic to fall back on to give consistency to his behavior. That this is a socially acquired, and not an inherent, trait is revealed by the fact that Japanese long resident in the West, and particularly the Nisei, react like Westerners.

security of new rules. Hence they turned to the act of surrender itself to provide them with new rules. In this new game of surrender, the rule to obey the conqueror's command appeared to be called for. In countless instances when they might have reasonably and successfully demurred, the Japanese therefore accepted unpalatable Occupation actions with the attitude: "It is only proper, since we have lost the war." This was a voluntary attitude quite apart from any deference to superior power. Some Americans mistook it for good sportsmanship; General MacArthur praised it as the "dignity" with which the Japanese bore their defeat. Elements of sportsmanship and dignity were no doubt present, but to the Japanese there was also a large measure of sheer self-gratification and comfort in conforming to an exacting set of new rules.

The situational ethics which permit the Japanese to adopt new rules with ease have also been augmented by their experience of the last hundred years. Since the opening of the country to Western intercourse, Japan has been in a state of virtually constant revolution. As in all Far Eastern countries, traditional ideas and institutions have been unable to hold their own against the overwhelming impact of the West. The overthrow of the Tokugawa Shogunate, the Meiji Restoration, the abolition of feudalism, constitutional government, Western education, modern technology, the rise of modern industry, the reshuffling of social classes, and a myriad other developments bespeak the speed and extent of Japan's transformation.

While their ancient history still inevitably exerts a strong conservative drag on their lives, more important is the fact that the bewilderingly rapid changes of the past hundred years have left the Japanese people with no deeply rooted convictions of their own. Cast adrift from their traditional moorings, some individuals struggle stubbornly to retrieve the past, while others cling hopefully to some new faith which they have found. But the vast majority, drifting aimlessly while troubled with feelings of instability and insecurity, clutch constantly at anything new that comes along in the hope that it can give them anchorage. In a sense, as the entire past century has been for them an unexpected situation to which their traditional book of rules could not apply, so the entire past century has been a hectic search by trial and error for new sets of rules. The Occupation represented only an intensified phase of this historic process rather than a wholly extraneous experience. As militarism was earlier, so was the Occupation in its turn eagerly welcomed by the Japanese as still another experiment that might yield them the truth which would rescue them from their uneasy flux. It was not simple fickleness or hypocrisy; it was the perennial quest of the modern Japanese for salvation. While this restless search might augur ill for the permanence of Japanese attraction to the Occupation program, at least it served to facilitate their initial acceptance of the Occupation.

The ready acceptance of the Occupation was also facilitated by the fact that the war had created little personal animosity among the Japanese toward the Americans. Feelings occasionally ran high, but there was a strong inclination to regard all the horrors of war impersonally as simply an inevitable part of the game. In an undemocratic country where the masses felt little sense of personal participation in public affairs, they could have no strong personal feelings about their enemies. They might fight fanatically, but they did so not out of inner conviction but only because they had been trained to do so.

But if the people could be trained to fight, could they not also be trained to hate? Certainly during the war official propaganda made every effort to whip up hatred in order to heighten the fighting spirit. But hatred simply did not take root. The Japanese people fought and worked hard enough, but they did so with an air of faithfulness to a bounden duty rather than with any spontaneous fervor. Although in their conscious mind they accepted the official propaganda—for they had access to no other information—in their subconscious mind did they not suspect that Japan was not really fighting a justifiable war of self-defense? Did they not somehow sense that the claim of Japan's "divine mission" was only a perverted compensation for the inadequacy their leaders felt in a world which was too much for them? In such a war, few Japanese could find reason to hate the enemy.

Japanese readiness to accept the Occupation was also aided by the fact that from the time of Commodore Perry to the outbreak of the war the United States had influenced Japan more

profoundly than any other foreign country. Japanese intellectuals might admire Europe more; political difficulties with the
United States and nationalist reaction in Japan might at times
and in some fields substantially curb American influence. But
in general America, popularly idealized as the model of progress and enlightenment, had continuously exercised the pre-
eminent influence in the making of modern Japan. Feelings of
inferiority and envy were not lacking; sometimes they erupted
into anti-Americanism in some sections of the Japanese public.
But the predominant attitude of the Japanese toward America
for nearly a century had been that of an eager pupil toward a
benevolent teacher. With the new demonstration of American
superiority which the war had given, it was easy for the Japanese to fall back into the familiar pattern of tutelage to
America.

The strong sense of hierarchy which prevails in Japanese
society further facilitated the Japanese acceptance of American
tutelage. In accordance with their native social structure,
strengthened by their Confucian training and their historical
experience, and sanctioned by the non-egalitarian bent of their
situational ethics, the Japanese think it natural and proper that
there should be differences in rank and status between nations
as well as between individuals. The circumstances of Japan's
relations with the United States after the war made it appear
more than ever proper to the Japanese to acknowledge their
subordinate rank and to act accordingly. The Japanese did not
regard this attitude as one of servile debasement. They tended
to regard it as somewhat akin to the fealty which bound a
knight to his liege lord, with obligations of honor on both sides.
Most Japanese were thus able to subordinate themselves to the
Occupation with little violence to their self-respect or to their
sense of propriety.

Acceptance of the Occupation by the Japanese was also
affected by the warmly emotional nature which lies close to
the surface of their rigidly formal behavior.[2] As the benevolent
character of the Occupation became quickly apparent to them,

[2] Perhaps it is to gain relief from the repressions which their code of
conduct imposes upon natural expressions of deep emotion that the Japanese often succumb to mawkish sentimentalism over trivial causes.

they responded with an outpouring of gratitude which was all the greater because they had been led to expect harsh treatment. Even their formalized conduct contributed in this case to their co-operation with the Occupation, for their code calls for a strict return of favors. Although a weakness for flattery on the part of some Occupation officials sometimes invited hypocritical Japanese expressions of gratitude, in the main the benevolent nature of the American policy elicited sincerely appreciative Japanese co-operation.

Many Japanese were also attracted to the Occupation program because a considerable portion of it represented the fulfilment of their own long-felt desires. Undistinguished as democratic development had been in prewar Japan, there had been in the past some spontaneous indigenous democratic trends. These had reached fairly substantial proportions in the comparatively liberal decade of the 1920's before interruption by the rise of the militarists in the 1930's. When it was seen that the Occupation program sought to restore and extend the trends which had existed in the 1920's, it naturally appealed to the Japanese elements which had supported them then. While some of the Occupation measures represented a forcible imposition of alien ideas which the Japanese did not welcome, enough of the Occupation's program coincided with desirable indigenous historic trends to enable the Occupation to ride on the wave of a substantial popular native support.

The Occupation program, moreover, created in Japanese society new vested interests which came to have a vital stake in supporting and perpetuating the new regime. While the former ruling classes naturally did not welcome the Occupation, the segments of Japanese society which felt themselves liberated and endowed with new power by the Occupation quickly came to constitute a pillar of support for the Occupation. Even when some of these new vested interests—like organized labor —clashed with specific Occupation policies and eventually turned against the Occupation, they comprised new countervailing forces in Japanese society which weakened the "Old Guard" and indirectly helped to advance the long-range democratic objectives of the Occupation.

Another factor which markedly aided the Occupation was

the strong inferiority complex which plagues most Japanese. Very few of them are aware they possess it; most of them would indignantly deny it. But the Japanese, in common with other Orientals struggling to get ahead in a world still largely dominated by the white peoples, often feel unsure of themselves. They thus waver between excessive shyness and excessive aggressiveness. What appears at times to be their over-assertiveness is really an attempt to compensate for secret fears and doubts. Their ultranationalistic megalomania of the wartime period was a perverted response to an inner compulsion to reassure themselves of their own adequacy. Their lawless international behavior before and during the war was in a sense a national tantrum over what they considered the world's unwillingness to accord them due recognition for their legitimate achievements. This aggressive phase was but a perverse hypersensitivity to world opinion.

The reverse side of the shield is the fact that the Japanese are pathetically grateful for any opportunity to win acceptance by the rest of the world. Defeat in the war curbed their aggressive phase; the benevolent nature of the Occupation appealed to their shy phase. Co-operation with the Occupation seemed to them to offer a way through which they could associate themselves with the aims of other democratic nations and thereby win acceptance into respectable world society. Such an opportunity was not one to be spurned. Hence there was often evidence of pride and eagerness in the Japanese response to the Occupation.

Finally, in addition to all the theoretical explanations of Japanese conduct was the simple fact that the Japanese were realistic enough to see that co-operation with the Occupation was the only practicable course open to them. While they might have had the power to sabotage the Occupation, they realized that no advantage could come to them through such action. Hence, turning necessity into a virtue, they made the best of the situation that confronted them.

While the principal explanations for the attitude of the Japanese toward the Occupation are thus to be found in the characteristics of the Japanese themselves, the characteristics of the Occupation and of the Americans also need to be noted.

In the first place, the Occupation policies were in general benevolent, constructive, and sound. Not all these policies were good, of course; in such an extensive and complex operation as the reshaping of an entire nation, mistakes were inevitable. The Japanese, as the direct victims of anything that went wrong, were acutely aware of these mistakes. But, after all, the over-all character of the Occupation was eminently good, and the Japanese could not help being impressed by it.

In the second place, there was the influence of the character and personality of General Douglas MacArthur. In the circumstances that surrounded Japan's surrender, the Japanese probably would have co-operated with any Occupation commander. But General MacArthur's personality so dominated the Occupation that, whatever the role of the impersonal official forces behind him, the Japanese saw the Occupation personified in his image. The special quality of their co-operation with the Occupation was therefore determined by their response to his personality, and the subsequent influence of his successors did not substantially alter this fact.

While Americans usually react to General MacArthur's personality with either extravagant admiration or violent repugnance, the Japanese view of him was much less controversial. At first most Japanese were swept into uncritical adulation of him; later virtually all of them became aware of his shortcomings. But insofar as his career in Japan was concerned, his brilliance far outweighed his shortcomings, and the Japanese continue to accord him a respect, gratitude, and admiration which have already made him a legendary figure in Japanese history.

One reason for his influence on the Japanese was his dedicated sense of mission. The egoism tinged with mysticism with which he regarded himself as the chosen instrument for the reformation and redemption of the Japanese people might sometimes be ludicrous and sometimes irritating, but there was no mistaking the sincerity and intensity of his idealism. To a remarkable degree he succeeded in infusing in his subordinates his own sense of idealism and dedication, and thus lifted the tone of the Occupation from a military operation to a moral crusade.

General MacArthur also provided the Japanese with strong personal leadership at a time when, disillusioned with their own leaders who had brought their world crashing down about them, they particularly needed someone whom they could trust and look to for inspiration. His viceregal manners were hardly democratic in spirit, but he did not neglect to give the Japanese as much democracy as they could initially absorb. To the degree to which he succeeded in imparting the lessons of democracy to them, his attitude and methods outlived their effectiveness, until eventually the simple friendliness of a successor like General Matthew Ridgway became more useful. But MacArthur's imperious aloofness and lordly graciousness did establish prestige and authority among the Japanese for the Occupation during its first critical years.

General MacArthur also was in a way a political genius. A supremely dogmatic man, with serious blind spots accentuated by his being surrounded by sycophantic subordinates, he nevertheless had a masterly grasp of broad historical perspective. This perspective gave him an intuitive feeling for political events which, while occasionally very wrong, usually enabled him to shape and time his actions with dramatic effect. Although his grandiloquent language was lost on the Japanese in translation, they were impressed by the sureness of his touch and felt assured that their political fortunes were in competent hands.

His first introduction to the Japanese was an example of this sure dramatic touch. Alighting from his plane at the Atsugi airfield with studied casualness at a time when the handful of American troops then present in Japan were virtually lost in a sea of still armed and excited Japanese, General MacArthur proceeded with uncharacteristic informality to deal with the Japanese as if inaugurating an Occupation were a matter of daily routine. It was an exhibition of cool personal courage; it was even more a gesture of trust in the good faith of the Japanese. It was a masterpiece of psychology which completely disarmed Japanese apprehensions. From that moment, whatever danger there might have been of a fanatic attack on the

Americans vanished in a wave of Japanese admiration and gratitude.

While it had nothing directly to do with Japanese attitudes, the confidence which General MacArthur commanded from the extreme conservative section of the American public was also an important factor in his success in Japan. Although American liberals might distrust him, they could generally be counted on to recognize his worthwhile achievements and to support them. Among the archconservatives in America, however, there might have been unreasoning opposition to Occupation policies had not the Supreme Commander been a man whom they trusted. Particularly such necessary but liberal Occupation measures as the land reform and certain economic reforms might have been wrecked by political opposition in the United States had it not been for the confidence General MacArthur commanded in conservative circles. He actually proved himself to be more liberal than those who swore by him. In this respect, no one else could have performed the role of Occupation commander more effectively than he.

Although General MacArthur's personality dominated the Occupation, the typically American characteristics of the nameless thousands who comprised the Occupation force also had much to do with the favorable Japanese response. With comparatively few exceptions, Americans apparently found it contrary to their nature to harbor their wartime hatred for long. Very quickly the officers and men of the Occupation came to look upon the Japanese as fellow human beings rather than as fiendish enemies and treated them with decency and consideration. Of course there were a few who raped, robbed, and beat up the Japanese. But the countless little demonstrations of spontaneous good will and kindness on the part of most of the American troops toward the Japanese more than counterbalanced the relatively few cases of American misconduct, and the Japanese attitude soon became unmistakably one of gratitude.

Missionary zeal also added to the benevolence and good will of most Americans. While few Americans can match the messianic drive of a General MacArthur, practically all seem to have a desire to impart the superior blessings of their way of life to others. Unlike some cultures which are exclusive, American culture is assimilative and proselyting. All Americans, even those who would deny any pretensions of superiority, seem to have some measure of the missionary complex.

This missionary spirit was saved from being too patronizing largely by the playful humor of the Americans. Even while they sought to enlighten the Japanese, most Americans did not take themselves very seriously. Their exuberant good spirits came as a welcome release to the Japanese, who had long been repressed by the humorless authoritarianism of their militarists. The enthusiasm with which Japanese children waved and shouted at passing GI's had little to do with gifts of chewing gum and candy, which generally were quite unexpected. The children must have been unconsciously responding to a kindred spirit of unspoiled youthfulness in the Americans which they failed to find in their own elders and for which they were starved. The elders also, laughing at the good-natured antics of the GI's, were charmed into letting down their suspicions against American influence. The Americans acted as the Japanese themselves would have liked to act but could not because of their social inhibitions, and thus the Americans became the envied models of a desired conduct. Finally, just as the Japanese were grateful to find that the Americans would not mistreat them, the Americans were delighted to discover that, contrary to wartime propaganda, the Japanese at home were not the fanatics they had encountered on the battlefield.

American soldiers might not recognize in the primitive peasants of the rural Philippines, for instance, the "little brown brothers" who were supposed to be so Americanized and who were supposed to share American tastes and American ideals. But in Japan, instead of the propaganda stereotype of the sinister, inhuman, feudalistic Japanese, the American soldiers found a people who seemed more Westernized than any other people they had encountered throughout the Pacific. Japanese Westernization might be superficial, but at least Japan had subways and elevated trains, neon lights, modern office buildings, and a white Christmas that reminded Americans of home. After months of fighting in jungles and on coral atolls, the homesick Americans experienced in Japan a rapturous return to a comparatively familiar civilization. The pleasure they felt at being in Japan reflected itself in their cordiality toward the Japanese, and the Japanese responded with flattered attentiveness. Perhaps the best way to get peoples to get along well with one another is to lead them first to expect the worst.

Today these attitudes, so pronounced during the early years of the Occupation, have come to seem strange and unreal. For reasons as complex as those responsible for the earlier attitudes, other factors which have recently come into operation have now wrought a radical change in Japanese attitudes toward the United States.

Even during the early postwar years, of course, not all Japanese shared the predominant attitudes. There were always a few unregenerate and incorrigible ones who never relented in their resentment against the Americans. There were many more who, while essentially friendly toward the Americans and their aims, held aloof in fastidious distaste from the unseemly obsequiousness of the majority toward the Occupation and recoiled particularly from the contemptible petty Japanese employees of the Occupation who appeared to think that working for the conqueror entitled them to lord it over other Japanese. But the predominant Japanese attitudes were those analyzed at length above, and, different as they were from the ones familiar today, they were the ones that conditioned the initial Japanese response to the Occupation.

CHAPTER II

The Character of the Occupation

The Occupation of Japan was nominally an Allied enterprise, as indicated by General Douglas MacArthur's being designated Supreme Commander for the Allied Powers. In effect, however, it was almost exclusively American. Having borne the brunt of the fighting in the Pacific and having come to exercise paramount power in that area, the United States logically assumed the major responsibility for the postwar disposition of Japan.

The machinery of the Occupation reflected this preponderant American authority. The Far Eastern Commission, set up in Washington by the eleven (later thirteen) most interested of the Allied nations to formulate general policies for the Occupation, arrived at its decisions by majority vote, but it was provided that the majority had to include the United States, the United Kingdom, the Soviet Union, and China. This provision in effect gave veto power to these four nations. There was further provision that, in case the Far Eastern Commission failed to act promptly enough to meet any particular exigency, the United States government could issue "urgent unilateral interim directives" which would have the same force as action by the commission.

During the first two or three years of the Occupation, despite occasional sharp exchanges between them, the Far Eastern Commission and General MacArthur apparently managed to work reasonably well together. But from the very outset the actions of General MacArthur tended to outrun the decisions of the Far Eastern Commission. Although in principle General MacArthur was merely to carry out the policies decided upon by the commission, in fact he often acted first and asked the commission later for its approval. In the fluid conditions of postwar Japan events undoubtedly moved too fast for a distant deliberative body to keep up, but this situation gave General MacArthur the opportunity to exercise more actual power than he formally possessed.

As the Occupation passed from its initial phase of reforming Japan to the subsequent phase of restoring her to normal status in the world community, differences between the United States and the other nations represented on the Far Eastern Commission increased. The United States thereupon resorted on several important occasions to the "urgent unilateral interim directives" she was empowered to issue. Much more frequently General MacArthur simply crossed over the thin and ill-defined line which separates execution of policy from formulation of policy and proceeded to put into effect whatever measures he deemed advisable. Although this independence on the part of General MacArthur probably irritated American officials in Washington as much as it did the members of the Far Eastern Commission, it nevertheless conveniently enabled American policies to prevail without the necessity of formally overriding the Far Eastern Commission. Later, as the Far Eastern Commission became increasingly paralyzed by disagreements, the United States began more openly to ignore this international body.

As long as the Far Eastern Commission functioned, its policy decisions were communicated to the United States government, which in turn translated them into instructions to General MacArthur. But General MacArthur held the dual role of theater commander of the American military forces in the Far East and of Supreme Commander for the Allied Powers. Inasmuch as all his instructions came down through the same channel of the regular American military chain of command, it was difficult—at least to the lay observer—to distinguish between the instructions which emanated from the Far Eastern Commission and those which originated from somewhere in the United States government. General MacArthur, moreover, interpreted his instructions, whatever their source, pretty much as he saw fit, and gave to his implementation of these instructions the unique color of his own personality. The effect, as far as the Japanese were concerned, was to make the Occupation appear to be primarily a MacArthur operation, secondarily an American operation, and only remotely an Allied operation. The Japanese were pleased, for they came to have confidence in General MacArthur's ability to understand their problems while they distrusted the unfamiliar figures in distant Washington.

The Allied Council for Japan, set up in Tokyo and composed of the representatives of the United States, the British Commonwealth, the Soviet Union, and China, contributed to this impression of MacArthur's predominance. The council's powers were merely advisory, but inasmuch as General MacArthur almost invariably chose to ignore its advice, it was a monument to futility. Periodically the Soviet representative would engage in propagandistic harangues against the American conduct of the Occupation, whereupon MacArthur's deputy would respond with long and bitter rebuttals. Occasionally the Australian who represented the British Commonwealth would relieve his frustration by supporting some of the Russian criticisms of MacArthur. Otherwise the meetings of the Allied Council on Japan remained painfully perfunctory.

General MacArthur ran the Occupation with a firm hand. "SCAP," which commonly came to refer more to the Occupation Command than to the person of the Supreme Commander for the Allied Powers, was a complex organization. Acting in some respects as the theater headquarters of the United States military forces, it included the standard staff sections common to any ordinary military headquarters, like G-1, Personnel; G-2, Intelligence; G-3, Operations; and G-4, Supply and Logistics. But acting in other respects as the administrative machinery for the Occupation, it also included a large number of special sections which paralleled closely, though not exactly, the various ministries of the Japanese government. Bearing such cabalistic designations as ESS (Economic and Scientific Section), CI&E (Civil Information and Education Section), NRS (Natural Resources Section), PHW (Public Health and Welfare

Section), and the like, they resembled the "alphabet agencies" of bureaucratic Washington in more ways than one.

Housed in dozens of commandeered office buildings, the thousands of Americans both military and civilian who manned these staff sections reproduced in Tokyo a fairly faithful replica of the atmosphere of Washington bureaucracy. There was a high degree of lofty statesmanship and dedicated labor, interlarded however with a conspicuous measure of petty red tape, jurisdictional rivalries, personal jealousies, and cocktail-party politics. Holding himself serenely aloof, General MacArthur seemingly allowed his subordinates to battle quite freely among themselves, apparently on the theory that in competing with each other they would vie in loyalty and service to him. The tactics of this bureaucracy seemed very familiar to the Japanese government officials who came in contact with it.

The most significant characteristic of the Occupation of Japan was the fact that it did not constitute in a strict sense a "military government." Unlike Germany, where the collapse of the native government had forced the occupation armies to assume governmental functions, Japan had surrendered while her own government was still intact. The Occupation was therefore set up merely as a supervisory superstructure over the existing Japanese government, which did the actual work of governing. The various staff sections of SCAP came into practically no direct contact with the Japanese public, but were designed to work through their respective "opposite numbers" among the ministries of the Japanese government.

The Japanese government, on its side, set up a Central Liaison Office to which a large part of the Foreign Office personnel was temporarily transferred. Although between SCAP and the Japanese government there could ostensibly be no "negotiation" as between equals, working arrangements between the two sides were in practice handled through the Central Liaison Office, which acted as an intermediary between the various SCAP sections and their Japanese government counterparts. Gradually as the officials on both sides gained experience in working with each other and direct operating procedures became established, the Central Liaison Office was increasingly bypassed until it eventually lost its originally great importance.

The permanent Occupation garrison force came to be comprised of the United States Eighth Army, subordinate to but administratively distinct from SCAP, and of some assorted air, naval, and marine units. After the initial task of establishing the Occupation physically in Japan, this force came to have very little to do officially with the Japanese, save for the military government teams attached to various Eighth Army units. "Military government teams" was a misnomer, later corrected by being changed to "civil affairs teams," for these groups did no governing. They were actually small inspection teams that checked on the activities of the local subdivisions of the Japanese government to see that the directives of SCAP to the national government were being properly carried out by the Japanese authorities at the local level.

Among the thousands of officers in SCAP, there was an occasional individual from one or another of the Allied countries other than the United States; and attached to the Eighth Army was a comparatively small British Commonwealth contingent, eventually composed mostly of Australians, garrisoned in the Kure area in the southwest. All others were Americans. Other nations were represented only by quasi-diplomatic missions accredited to SCAP.

Not only in organization and personnel but also in its program the Occupation was distinctively American. The United States had apparently started to prepare for its preponderant role in Japan from the very early days of the war. Various government agencies in Washington had worked on a variety of plans which, after innumerable conferences, had been coordinated into a master plan. In the absence of such planning by the other Allies, and in the absence at first of any inter-Allied organization for the control of Japan, the American plan was of necessity put immediately into operation upon Japan's surrender. The plan was outlined to General MacArthur in a directive called the "United States Initial Post-Surrender Policy for Japan," and elaborated subsequently in the "Basic Presidential Policy Statement" issued over President Truman's name. These two documents were essentially the same, save for somewhat greater detail in the latter. Later, when the Far Eastern Commission came into existence, it adopted this policy with but slight modification. In essence the policy called for the demilitarization and the democratization of Japan. These constituted, respectively, the negative aspect of the Occupation mission, which was to clear the ground, and the positive aspect, which was to reconstruct Japan on a new pattern.

The negative, or the demilitarization phase of the Occupation program, can be dealt with very briefly. Although the subject of intense interest at the time, it was to have relatively minor permanent significance. Real demilitarization, both in spirit and in the physical sense, had already taken place before the Occupation with the defeat and collapse of the Japanese war machine. All that was left for the Occupation was to dispose of the debris.

The Japanese Empire was reduced to the islands of Japan proper, and these were now formally occupied. The Japanese armed forces were ordered disbanded and abolished. This process involved not only the demobilization of the 2,200,000 troops in the homeland, some of whom simply took off for their homes immediately after the surrender with everything they could carry away from their barracks. It also involved the more complex task of bringing back 3,300,000 troops from overseas, collecting them from all over the Pacific, processing them through the separation camps, delousing them, paying them off, closing their records, and getting them back to their homes. Along with the troops, 3,200,000 Japanese civilians—including women and children and many who were sick—were repatriated from overseas areas now taken away from Japanese control; while of the Koreans and Formosans resident in Japan, 1,250,000 who wished to leave were shipped back to their homelands. This gigantic movement of peoples was handled by the Japanese authorities with remarkable speed and orderliness under the supervision of the Occupation officials.

The Occupation forces razed all Japanese military installations and destroyed all military equipment. Such military supplies as could be converted to civilian use were turned back to the Japanese government to be used for relief and rehabilitation; some of these, however, leaked into the black market. The

Occupation also ordered the Japanese government to prepare for shipment some industrial facilities which had been earmarked for reparations, although this work was eventually suspended for reasons which will be discussed later.

Among the demilitarization activities of the Occupation may be included the trial and punishment of war criminals, for these trials were intended, among other things, to ring down the final curtain on Japanese militarism by teaching the Japanese that "war does not pay." The International Military Tribunal for the Far East was created by the Allied Powers by special charter to try the high Japanese political leaders who were charged with responsibility for the policy decisions leading to Japan's "crimes against peace." These were the so-called "Class A" war criminals. Eleven judges representing as many nations sat in session almost every day from May 3, 1946, until sentence was passed on November 12, 1948. Seven persons, all generals except for one civilian, were hanged; sixteen were committed to prison for life; and two were given lesser terms of imprisonment. None was acquitted.

The "Class B" criminals were comprised of some twenty high-ranking military officers charged with command responsibility for troops who had committed atrocities. Two generals who were tried by *ad hoc* military courts in the fighting zone immediately after the surrender were quickly convicted and executed. The others of this class, given a more formal trial much later in special military courts set up in Tokyo by SCAP, were all acquitted.

The "Class C" criminals were small fry, the lesser officers and men charged with mistreatment of prisoners of war or with relatively minor atrocities. Some of these were tried overseas by British, Australian, Chinese, and other Allied military authorities. Most of the "Class C" trials, however, were conducted in Yokohama by military commissions of the United States Eighth Army. Of the approximately 4,200 in this category, approximately 400 were acquitted, approximately 700 were sentenced to death, and the remainder were sentenced to various terms of imprisonment.

It is not within the province of this work to delve into the legal, moral, political, and psychological implications of these trials. Experts can no doubt argue at great length concerning such questions as the legal competence of these unusual tribunals, whether or not they resorted to *ex post facto* law, the propriety of interested and aggrieved parties themselves sitting in judgment, the legitimacy of holding individuals personally punishable for official political acts of the state, and the reliability of testimony and evidence filtered through so many translators and interpreters between languages and cultures so different from one another. It is sufficient for the purposes of the present study merely to note that the war crimes trials did not have a major impact on the consciousness of the Japanese public.

At first most Japanese, disillusioned with their wartime leaders, were glad enough to see them brought to justice. As the trials dragged on month after month, however, the public lost interest. Finally, when the end of the trials brought on a renewed burst of publicity, the public was annoyed to be made aware that the trials had been going on so long. Why was further punishment necessary when history itself had already broken and discarded these old men?—such was the common attitude. With little sense of personal identification, most Japanese finally came to feel merely a mixture of mild pity for the culprits, or mild regret for their actions, and of mild irritation at being reminded at all of this distasteful subject.

The equivocal reaction of the Japanese was due not so much to moral callousness or to an attempt to run away from a subconscious sense of guilt. It was essentially just another manifestation of the "situational ethics" of the Japanese discussed in the previous chapter. War crimes may have been wrong, but they regrettably had seemed unavoidable in the circumstances of a desperate war. Punishment of the offenders, who had been trapped in those circumstances, might be tragic, but this also was unavoidable and therefore appropriate under the circumstances of Japan's surrender. If the circumstances had been different, the Japanese would not have committed atrocities and the Allies would not be meting out punishment. Both were predestined responses to particular situations. For the victor to claim that his punishment of the loser represented universally valid abstract justice, or that it would serve to deter all future wars, therefore appeared presumptuous to the Japanese. It seemed as futile as it would be for them to attempt to justify their past acts to the conquerors after the circumstances for those acts had disappeared. Whether because of "situational ethics" or of Buddhist fatalism, the Japanese feel that each act that occurs, being a product of its particular circumstances, has its own particular consequence which must be accepted without question as to rightness or justifiability. But already circumstances were again changing; the coming task was to build afresh for a new era. So why be bothered now with assessing blame for what was finished?

Thus, if the Allies had expected the trials to cause a change of heart among the Japanese, this expectation was not borne out. Yet the Japanese did experience, if not exactly a change of heart, at least a change of interest and a change of conduct. These resulted not from the trials that dug back into the past but from the Occupation's grandiose constructive program for the future. New situations called for new patterns of behavior. Far more important than the negative work of demilitarization, therefore, was the positive work of the Occupation of constructing a new democratic Japan. This work called for a program of sweeping reforms throughout many broad areas of Japanese life.

Politically, the Occupation sought to debar from power the individuals who had been responsible for the militaristic, ultra-nationalistic, and authoritarian character of the Japanese nation and to encourage the rise to power of more popularly representative elements who would presumably be liberal and peace-loving. To this end the Occupation, among other things, sponsored the adoption of a new constitution and encouraged its implementation through the development of an extensive new set of political institutions and practices.

Economically, the Occupation at first denied any obligation to help, but it soon realized that political democratization was impossible without a certain minimum basis of economic well-being. The policy hence came to be not only to aid in the physical rehabilitation of Japanese economy but also to promote the development of economic democracy. The latter objective was evidenced in the "zaibatsu-busting" program, the agrarian land reform, the encouragement of labor unions, and other important Occupation-sponsored reforms. These obviously had vast social as well as economic implications.

In the field of educational activities, the Occupation sought to influence the Japanese people to accept these democratic reforms. This objective was pursued—at least in theory—not so much through direct propaganda and indoctrination as through instituting a long-range educative process which would eventually cause the Japanese people to appreciate and cherish fundamental democratic values. To this end, the Occupation tried to bring about a change in the nature of Japan's formal educational system through such means as the reorganization of the school system, the revision of the curriculums, and the retraining of the teachers. It also placed much emphasis on reaching a wider public through the encouragement of adult education projects, libraries, community activities, and the like. Even more it sought to insure that the press, radio, theater, and other media of mass communication would contribute adequately to the formation of an enlightened public opinion.

All these reforms—political, economic, and educational—could naturally be expected to stir up a vigorous social and cultural ferment. The Occupation sought to utilize this ferment to induce the emergence of a changed Japanese society, with a changed set of habits, a changed pattern of behavior, and a changed scale of values.

Few, if any, Americans could have been so naïve as to believe that the Occupation could quickly transform the very nature of the Japanese nation. The Occupation did possess the physical power, in its military force, to impose any reform it desired; but as long as the Japanese themselves did not desire them, the reforms would inevitably lapse as soon as the Occupation pressure was removed. On the other hand, to educate the Japanese so that they would initiate and carry on the reforms themselves would take more time and effort than the Occupation could afford to expend. The Occupation nevertheless resorted to both these methods in combination: it used its authority to impose what it considered necessary reforms, and at the same time it engaged in as extensive an educational campaign as it could.

The theory underlying this procedure apparently was that, if the Japanese were forced to operate through democratic institutions even though they merely went through the motions at first without understanding or appreciation, this experience would eventually bring about understanding and appreciation. The educational compaign, although too slow by itself, might thus yield quick results if combined with forced practice. Just how effective this procedure was is a subject of controversy. The results naturally varied from field to field, but they undoubtedly turned out to be more generally successful than was expected. The Occupation itself was obviously highly pleased with the outcome. Certainly in its official pronouncements and publications, it claimed success in quite extravagant terms.

The combination of force and education called for in this procedure required the Occupation to use varied and complex techniques. Ostensibly everything was done by the Japanese government, with the Occupation offering only suggestions, advice, and assistance. Actually the Occupation manipulated the Japanese government through means ranging all the way from suggestion through cajolery, friendly persuasion, subtle intimidation, polite pressure, scarcely veiled coercion, to peremptory commands backed by demonstrations of military might. But however gentle and indirect the approach, it fooled no one, least of all the Japanese. The obvious possessive pride of the American officials and the conspicuous presence of American troops left no doubt as to where the inspiration and the authority for all the reforms lay.

The reforms were so sweeping as to take on the proportions of a revolution. Obviously it was not a spontaneous revolution, because the motivation for the changes did not well up from among the Japanese. Neither was it altogether an imposed revolution, for, although it was set in motion by American initiative, it was picked up and carried along at least in some measure by the Japanese. Occasionally the Occupation introduced altogether new changes, but more often it revived existing tendencies which had been thwarted in the past. Insofar as these revived tendencies became effective, they wrought a transformation which assumed the character of a national movement. The defeat which had caused the collapse of

Japan's old order would undoubtedly have brought about profound changes in any case; at the same time it was the Occupation which largely influenced the nature and the direction of the changes. This revolution might thus well be characterized as an induced revolution.

The pace and even the character of this revolution underwent considerable modification during the course of the Occupation's history. During the first two years or so, there appeared to be a frenetic effort on the part of the Americans to transform Japan in a hurry. Along with the messianic zeal, there could be discerned some indications of an unconscious punitive motivation. There was certainly a sternly didactic tone to the exhortations of the Occupation officials as they pressed the Japanese for reforms and yet more reforms.

Sometimes the Occupation officials expressed exasperation at the readiness of the Japanese to go off half-cocked without attempting to learn what the reforms were intended to accomplish. On other occasions the Occupation officials impatiently accused the Japanese of deliberately raising obstacles to the necessary reforms. Undoubtedly there was as much justification for one as for the other of these seemingly contradictory criticisms, for Japanese reactions were not always consistent. But, in the main, the mood of the Japanese people at this time caused most of them to be highly receptive to the American efforts; and within the limits imposed by their capacity and by the natural speed of their social processes they responded with notable alacrity.

Along toward the end of 1947 or the beginning of 1948, the emphasis of the Occupation shifted from that of reforming a vanquished enemy to that of building him up as a potential ally of the United States. The intensification of the Cold War obviously was primarily responsible for this change. As the drift of China toward the Communist orbit became unmistakable, Americans began to conceive of Japan, rather than China, as the new major force in the Far East for peace, democracy, and friendliness toward the United States. Some feared that the new emphasis would cause Japan's democratization to be sacrificed to sheer expediency in power politics. Fear, suspicion, and jealousy caused some nations that had suffered from

Japanese aggression to protest that the United States was showing more favor to an undeserving former enemy than to her old friends. But, in any event, the Occupation effort came to be concentrated on making Japan—in the words of American spokesmen—the "workshop of the Far East" and the "bulwark of democracy" in that part of the world.

It should not be forgotten, however, that no matter how important the considerations of the Cold War, the Americans probably would not have so readily conceived of Japan as a possible ally if the Occupation had not been proceeding with eminent success. To a great extent it appeared that Japan had already been remarkably reformed and converted to a democratic orientation. Not only did Japan now seem qualified to be America's ally, but it also seemed that identifying her as an associate of the United States would be the best way to insure her continuing development in the desired direction.

Long before the actual shift in policy, a psychological shift had begun to take place in the personal relations between the Japanese and Occupation personnel. The hectic atmosphere of the early months of the Occupation gave way to a more relaxed mood of geniality as the Americans found the Japanese generally responding much more satisfactorily than had been expected. After they had worked together for a while in intimate daily contact, the Americans and the Japanese became less aware of their contrasting status and more conscious of their common interest in a common endeavor. Of course there continued to be some gentle arm-twisting from the one side countered by some polite blackmail from the other, accompanied by uncomplimentary mutterings on both sides, but it was well understood that these proceedings were part of a friendly game between partners. This warm rapport between the Occupation and the Japanese was something which Americans at home—much less other Allied nationals—could hardly comprehend, but it undoubtedly played an important part in facilitating the shift in Occupation policy.

Gradually, as the rehabilitation and rebuilding of Japan proceeded, the policy of the Occupation underwent still another shift. In Japan the Occupation began to taper off its activities sharply; more important, the United States strove to get Japan reinstated into normal international relations and to have her accepted as a respected member of the world community. Encountering disagreements in the Far Eastern Commission, the United States turned increasingly to bilateral negotiations with each of the other Allies to persuade them to adopt more or less the American attitude. Finally, as the result of these efforts, the stage was set for the peace treaty signed in San Francisco on September 8, 1951, which restored Japan to legal independence and full standing in the family of nations. Thereupon on April 28, 1952, the Occupation was technically ended. With hardly a perceptible break the Occupation force slipped into its new role as the supporting force of an ally supposedly requested by Japan, under the terms of a mutual security agreement, to stay on to help protect her.

Now that the passage of time since the end of the Occupation affords some perspective, it should be possible to appraise how successful the Occupation really was in winning its objectives and how permanent its effects are likely to be. Widely differing opinions have already been voiced. Those who were caught up in the hectic, exciting changes of the early Occupation years will find it difficult not to believe that they were participants in one of the momentous episodes of history. Those who have been observing the "reverse course" of recent years will find it equally difficult not to believe that the Occupation's work was mostly just sound and fury signifying, if not nothing, very little at best.

This difference in appraisal stems not only from a difference of focus in time but more fundamentally from a difference in conception of what democracy, and democratization, really implies. Except among a few intellectuals, this ideological problem seems to have received little attention in relation to Japan. The officials who formulated policy in Washington were not primarily reflective thinkers but practical politicians. Even more, the men in the Occupation who carried out the policies were soldiers or civil servants, strong on action but weak on theory.

Although they shared with all Americans a general notion of what democracy implied, with rare exceptions they had never formulated in their minds precisely what were the essential principles of democracy apart from their specific manifestations under American conditions. Hence, like most Americans they tended to equate democracy uncritically with the American way of life, which all too often carried connotations of central heating, big autos, and PX privileges. Thus they blandly assumed that the only way to democratize Japan was by making Japan over in the closest possible imitation of the United States. This explains why, for example, a distinguished American police expert insisted, at a time when cloth was in critically short supply in Japan, that the old policemen's uniforms with stand-up collars must be replaced immediately with new uniforms with roll collars and neckties because the latter were more "democratic."

Many Occupation officials were bewildered when they discovered that some American practices, suitable for a large and wealthy country like the United States, just would not work in a small and poor country like Japan. Familiar only with particular applications but not with the basic principles of democracy, such people did not know how to make democracy work under Japanese conditions. They could only fall back on the platitude that democracy was something that could not be taught, that it was something that the Japanese would have to learn for themselves—through mystic enlightenment, presumably. Some Japanese welcomed a democracy that could be so subjectively interpreted, under which they could, for instance, construe taxes as being an infringement on the freedom of the individual. But for exactly the same reason other Japanese recoiled from such a democracy as dangerously anarchic nonsense.

It is unfortunate that for many Americans the only alternative to a complete equation of democracy with the American way of life was a retreat into pious obscurantism. Even if they possessed no theoretical knowledge of democratic principles, with a less provincial outlook they might have made use of many western European—and particularly British—models of democracy more appropriate to Japan's circumstances than examples from America. There is no estimating what setbacks democracy received from attempts to foist American ways too completely and too quickly upon Japan. Much sounder progress could have ensued from the encouragement of other forms of democracy which were perhaps more modest but also more suitable. It is a tribute to American good sense and practical ability that, despite such ideological deficiencies, the Occupation officials floundered no more than they did and generally left as creditable a record as they did.

But to return to the matter of appraising the effectiveness of the Occupation, it is natural that those who equate democracy with their own Americanism should be disillusioned, for the Occupation could not possibly make Japan over into a little America. Those who hold to a strict ideal of pure democracy are also likely to be disappointed, for, in view of the shortcomings of both the teachers and the pupils, it is unrealistic to hope that the Japanese could acquire within a few years, even through imitation, what took the West centuries to develop.

Those who take a more pragmatic approach, however, and who are more concerned with the process of democratization than with the ultimate goal, might appraise the Occupation in a much more favorable light. The most that any military occupation can hope to accomplish in a conquered enemy country is to remove the obvious physical obstacles in the way of the desired conduct, set that country in the desired direction, and guide its first faltering steps. From there on, progress can be made only by the independent efforts of the nation itself. By this standard of what was possible, the Occupation did about all it could have done, and in many respects it did more than could have been expected. In this sense the Occupation was justified in the pride it took in its accomplishments.

It is obvious that General MacArthur himself conceived of the Occupation's mission in this limited sense. For all his messianic dreams and grandiloquent pronouncements, his astute practical political sense enabled him to see clearly the natural limitations of the Occupation's functions. As early as March, 1947, in an unprecedentedly uninhibited talk to foreign correspondents, he argued that the time had already come to start drawing up a peace treaty and to prepare to liquidate the Occupation. Japan had, he said, faithfully fulfilled the requirements of the Potsdam Proclamation under whose provisions she had surrendered. The Occupation had already done all any military force could do. Prolonging the Occupation would only give rise to a "colonial" psychology injurious to both the occupier and the occupied. If deprived of effective power for too long, the Japanese would either fall into the irresponsible habit of relying on the Americans for everything or else in frustration they would build up nationalistic resentment. The Americans, on their side, would be gradually corrupted by unaccustomed absolute power over a subject people and would fall prey to insidious moral decay leading to arrogance and delusions of both grandeur and infallibility alien to American ideals.

Coming at a time when many people still believed that a twenty-year—or even a hundred-year—occupation would be necessary to reform Japan, General MacArthur's arguments generally met with incredulity. But within a few years the injurious effects he had predicted began to be discernible: some of the Occupation personnel were beginning to act like carpetbaggers, and the Japanese were getting restive. By the time most of the world came around to his point of view and agreed to a peace treaty, it was none too soon, for the effects of the Occupation were already beginning to turn a little sour.

But this sourness was not enough to damage the Occupation's achievements seriously. However inadequate by ideal standards, by practical standards these achievements were significant. A historical objective can seldom be attained in one prodigious jump; three steps forward and two steps backward still add up to substantial progress toward a goal. Despite the "reverse course" that now seems to be undoing some of the work of the Occupation, Japan is hardly likely to slip back completely to the past. The shock of defeat and the impact of the Occupation were too overwhelming an experience for the Japanese ever to be able to slough off completely. In some respects the present reaction may even be interpreted as a healthy movement to correct the Occupation's undue Americanizing effects in order all the better to consolidate its more legitimate democratic achievements.

Whether such an interpretation seems reasonable or not depends to a large extent on what one conceives the proper democratic objectives of the Occupation to have been. As long as no general agreement on such a basic premise exists, no conclusive judgment can be rendered on the success of the Occupation. But some tentative opinion should be possible, and an important factor contributing to the formation of a reasonable opinion should be the reactions of the Japanese themselves to the Occupation efforts. A common-sense examination of these Japanese reactions may help to make possible the formulation of a sound criterion for evaluating the lasting influence of the Occupation.

CHAPTER III

The Background for
Democratization

The Occupation's objective of democratizing Japan seemed likely at first glance to be almost insuperably difficult. In view of that country's recent record of dictatorial rule characterized by fanatic militarism, imperialism, and ultranationalism, the Japanese people appeared poor prospects for democracy.

Democratic government rests essentially on the consent of the governed. The principle of consent assumes the equality of all individuals—not in the patently absurd literal sense that all men have equal talents, powers, and positions, of course, but in the sense that common human dignity entitles all persons to an equality of public opportunity to prove their own worth. The principle of consent also requires guarantee of the safety and security of all persons whether they participate in the ruling power or whether they choose to oppose it and to seek to supplant it, for without such guarantee, free consent could not exist. By such a criterion, no Japanese government in the past, obviously, had ever qualified as a democracy.

At the same time, even an essentially undemocratic regime may have some democratic features. All undemocratic regimes are not the same; some are more nearly democratic than others or show more democratic potentialities than others. In this sense, discouraging as the record of Japan had generally been, it was not without some rays of hope; there had been some quite respectable incipient democratic tendencies. If the Occupation could recognize them, and nurture and invigorate them sufficiently, the successful accomplishment of the task of democratization might be found to be within the bounds of possibility. In order to judge what success the Occupation had in this regard and why the Japanese responded as they did to the Occupation efforts, it is necessary first to identify the latent democratic factors that existed in Japanese experience and to note their limitations as well as their potentialities. Such identification calls for the examination of a considerable historical background.

Some incipient trends toward democratic development were evident even before the influx of Western influence. Starting in the early seventeenth century, the Tokugawa Shogunate had begun to forge a considerable degree of national unity out of a welter of petty feudal states. But because it operated merely through ingenious manipulation of institutions that remained essentially feudal in character, the more closely it approached national unity, the more incompatible its feudalistic institutions became with the very conditions they had helped to create. The internal contradictions of this paradoxical feudal-national state gave rise to strains—some of which had democratizing effects—that by the nineteenth century threatened to rend this regime asunder.

Specifically, the peace and order resulting from unification enabled the baronial subsistence economies to be supplanted by a nationwide money economy which gave rise to a new class of wealthy merchants. This burgher class, straining at the feudal social order that subordinated them to the aristocrats, aspired to political influence and social status more commensurate with their actual strength and ability. The aristocrats, finding the economic basis of their power being cut away from under them, sought to preserve their position artificially through legal contrivances, but they found themselves being forced into compromising deals with the merchants.

The peace and order brought about by national unification also deprived the samurai, or gentry, of their traditional function as warriors. Those who could not be absorbed into administrative functions were thereupon encouraged by the Tokugawa authorities to work off their restless spirits in the sedate field of scholarship where, it was believed, they would

have the least opportunity to raise mischief. But these con-
verts to scholarship unexpectedly used their new intellectual
weapons to develop the disturbing theory that the Tokugawa
Shogunate itself was essentially a usurpation, that it was a
feudal power exercising a national authority which should
rightfully be restored to the long-overshadowed Emperor.

As these and other political, social, economic, and ideological
anomalies eventually strained the Tokugawa regime, the re-
bellious ambitions of the rival feudatories were stirred; and
these feudatories now made common cause with the long-
neglected imperial court which, like them, had hitherto been
forced to bend to Tokugawa hegemony. Dissension within the
Tokugawa house over succession to the Shogunate and appre-
hension over the Tokugawa's passive policy of seclusion in the
face of approaching Western encroachment added to the general unrest. It needed only the triggering action of Commodore
Perry's arrival to set off an upheaval which resulted in the
Meiji Restoration of 1868 and the subsequent chain of extensive reforms that transformed Japan into a modern state.

Caused thus by a multiplicity of factors, the Restoration
movement included some clearly reactionary elements, but it
also included other elements at least potentially democratic in
character. The upthrust of the bourgeoisie and the bankruptcy
of the aristocracy obviously were among the democratizing
forces that now found release. In the abolition of feudalism,
which logically followed the Meiji Restoration, the aristocrats
lost their privileged status. While the former feudal nobility
salvaged enough to retain a reduced but still advantageous
position in the new society, most of the samurai suffered disaster. Although the more enterprising among them managed to
carve out profitable new careers, as a class the samurai were
plowed under among the commoners and lost their distinctive
identity.

As if their disappearance as an aristocratic class were not in
itself a sufficient democratic phenomenon, the samurai before
disappearing altogether sought to save themselves by demanding the democratic right of representation in the new regime.
Some of the former feudal lords also, as well as the adherents
of the now shattered Tokugawa regime, discovered that in-

sistence on a widening of the base of government and on respect for minority interests provided one way in which they might protect themselves from the oppressions of the new ruling oligarchy. In their adversity the former aristocrats thus became advocates of democratic rights. They were joined by the more articulate of the farmers, who sought relief from the heavy taxes on agricultural land required to subsidize the modern industry and commerce which the new regime was so eager to develop. Rationalization for these special interests was found in the ideological resources provided by the intellectuals who, out of purer motives themselves, were discovering and expounding the democratic doctrines of the West. The period of extensive changes following the Meiji Restoration therefore saw a considerable democratic ferment.

The small oligarchy which maneuvered itself into power in the Restoration, however, eventually blocked off these democratizing tendencies. Most of the oligarchs themselves, rising from comparatively modest gentry origins, represented in a sense the democratic triumph of individual ability over a hereditary power structure. As former samurai they must have felt some sympathy for the great number of their fellows who were faring ill in the new era. But as practical statesmen and uncompromising patriots, they held above all other considerations the task of transforming Japan as quickly and as effectively as possible into a modern nation-state strong enough to hold its own in the dangerous international arena into which it had been drawn. In this light, democracy was regarded as a debilitating and distracting influence; the intellectual advocates of democracy were seen as radical dreamers, while the more practical advocates of democracy were viewed as utilizing the arguments of democracy only for selfish or even reactionary ends. The oligarchs, trusting only their own patriotic intentions and their own ability, eventually immobilized one by one all the elements that competed with them, both democratic and reactionary, until political power was gathered completely into their own hands. They resurrected and reinterpreted the half-forgotten emperor myth of antiquity, devised the Meiji Constitution of 1889, and utilized them both as means by which to consolidate their own power behind the façade of the restored authority of the imperial throne.

The resulting power structure, while authoritarian, did not constitute a continuation of traditional authority. It rested on a different foundation from that of the preceding feudal regime. It was no longer the shogun at the top, the feudal nobles at the second level, the samurai next, and the commoners at the bottom with the merchants ranking lowest among the commoners. Instead, it was now these oligarchs at the top manipulating the Emperor; supporting them were industrial and financial magnates created out of the former lowly merchants or out of the few exceptionally adaptable former feudal nobles; then came the bureaucrats, who were qualified administrative technicians of whatever origin; and at the bottom were all the others, whether former commoners or former aristocrats, who failed to secure a place higher up on the new ladder. Although this was not a democratic society in the sense of representing an upthrust of the masses or of representing egalitarianism, it did signify a considerable reshuffling of class distinctions and a considerable increase in social mobility. To a much greater extent than the old regime, it favored an aristocracy of talents rather than an aristocracy of blood; and to the degree that it offered opportunity to all men of ability, it constituted democracy of a sort.

For the first thirty years or so of the operation of the government under the Meiji Constitution, the oligarchs maintained their monopolistic control over this system. As advisers of the Emperor, they were the power behind the throne; as the founding fathers of the new constitutional regime, their prestige and influence were sufficient to insure that only their direct protégés would succeed to vital posts in this political system. Their power and status came to be formalized in the extra-constitutional institution of the *genro*, or elder statesmen. But for all their power, they could not completely destroy the democratic forces that gravitated toward the political parties in the Diet. Although the oligarchs maintained their dominance, they did so only by constant struggle, sometimes simply beating down the parties, sometimes cajoling them by conciliatory gestures, and sometimes seducing their leaders into apostasy.

From about the time of World War I, however, a distinct shift in the locus of power began to take place. By the so-called "liberal decade" of the 1920's, seemingly popular political parties came to dominate the government in a manner quite closely approximating the functioning of the democratic parliamentary governments of western Europe. Although this pattern of political procedure was still very precariously established, it seemed so naturally desirable to most Japanese of this period that they idealized it as *kensei no jōdō,* or "the normal course of constitutional government."

The causes of this change were of course complex. For one thing, the oligarchs were beginning to die off and the *genro* was approaching extinction as an institution. Despite efforts to find a substitute, no new group could fill the shoes of the founding fathers. Moreover, a new generation had grown up who had no direct memories of the historic work of the founding fathers and therefore stood in no compelling awe of them. This generation, having acquired experience at playing with the mechanics of parliamentary government, could see no reason why they should not go on to take control over the substance of government as well. Educated in modern schools, they had assimilated a considerable portion of the Western tradition as a part of their own intellectual heritage.

But perhaps most important of all, World War I had wrought a significant change in the nature of Japanese society. It was not only that Japan, as one of the Allied Powers in that war, had absorbed some of the then current utopianism about "making the world safe for democracy." Japan's industry and foreign trade had expanded spectacularly as the war forced the Western Powers to relinquish their Asian and Pacific markets to Japan and as some of the Allies even became dependent on Japanese industry for their military supplies. This meant a tremendous rise in the power of Japanese big business and a great shift of the working population from the agricultural countryside to the urban industrial centers. Big business came to look beyond mere partnership with the declining oligarchs; it sought dominance over the government so that the bureaucracy might be made to serve its interests. It calculated that it could achieve this dominance through the political parties. Through providing financial support to the parties, which would then be strengthened enough to make the executive branch of the government responsible to the Diet, big business would be able to wield dominant power while appearing to be championing democracy against the autocrats.

Although eventually the conflicting interests of big business and of organized labor would come to the surface, for a while the new urban proletariat could be expected to identify themselves with their employers. Not only did the factory workers share in the business prosperity, but the relatively emancipated urban population, unlike the conservative peasants rooted to tradition, were likely to be attracted by the seemingly enlightened and progressive nature of big business' support of democratic parliamentarism. For a while a sense of liberation and visions of new democratic horizons exhilarated the nation as the power of the oligarchy and of its subservient bureaucracy receded before the advance of the political parties.

This period of comparative liberalism did not, however, last very long. An overwhelming mood of disillusionment soon set in, giving rise to a trend toward military dictatorship. To resist this new common threat, the political parties, most of the bureaucracy, and the one surviving *genro* joined forces, but by the 1930's they found themselves in full retreat. Although they fought stubborn rear-guard actions, they were unable to stop the drive of the militarists to power.

The complex causes of this turn of events can only be briefly suggested. Basically, despite the new economic and social conditions which had elevated big business and the parliamentary parties to power, the culture of Japan in a wider sense still had not changed sufficiently to provide the general environmental conditions which would enable democratic party government to flourish. There was yet no widespread conception either of the essential equality of all men or of the supreme worth of the individual. There still prevailed the Confucian notion that all men were not essentially equal, that the individual could not be an end in himself but that society was the end, and that the individual found his own worth as he completed the unity of society in the role in which his endowments had cast him. Such concepts supported the organic theory of the state, in which all components of society were conceived as having interdependent functions in the all-embracing state organism. Although there were not a few independent thinkers who tended toward individualism, even the political parties that sought to limit governmental powers could not quite bring themselves to do so as independent forces in competition with the state authority. While many of the activities of the political parties in effect challenged traditional authority, a large measure of ambiguity and consequent weakness was inherent in the position of the political parties, for, regarding themselves as a part of the state organism, they sought merely to ameliorate arbitrary government action instead of attacking the very basis of state power from without, which would have been the most thorough way to curb state power. Although it might have been possible, as many Japanese contend, to attain a practicing democracy under a proper interpretation of the Meiji Constitution and of the organic theory of the state on which it was based, it seems undeniable that both the organic theory of the state and the specific provisions of the constitution tended to inhibit the latent tendencies of the political parties to attack the bases of state power from without.

Insofar as big business spearheaded the party movement of the 1920's, there were additional special reasons for weakness. While big business admittedly did have its enlightened and progressive aspects in its advocacy of constitutional parliamentary processes and a peaceful foreign policy, these were motivated not so much by principle as by the selfish desire for conditions conducive to the greatest business profits. Democratic parliamentary processes were regarded primarily as just a means for taking over power from the oligarchs. Big business had no real quarrel with the idea of an all-powerful state, just so long as it could control the state. It did not conceive of itself as an outside challenger to the power of the state; it did not advocate laissez faire except in a very limited sense; it favored a close alliance between business and government so long as business was not subordinated to government. Big business, furthermore, shared with the oligarchs the national aim of making Japan a strong contender among the major powers of the world, and to this end it was willing to countenance a considerable measure of disciplinary authority to impose unity in the national effort. In the pursuit of its aims, big business showed no real concern for the interests of the little man; it had no appreciation of economic or social democracy.

It has been suggested by one astute American scholar that the democratic movement of the 1920's might have eventually succeeded with the forces at hand in Japanese society had the timing been more propitious.[1] For instance, even big business might have evolved into a truly democratizing force had there been sufficient time. But Japanese business elements did not have the time to develop the doctrine of laissez faire with its democratic implications as the English business class of the nineteenth century had done; while English commercial interests of that period had the leisure to oppose governmental power in the absence of serious foreign rivals, Japanese business in its period of growth was constantly pressed by powerful Western competitors so that it never dared to venture very far beyond the political prop of a nationalistic neo-mercantilism with its restrictive controls. Also among the factors involved in this matter of timing was the unfavorable general climate of the world as indicated by the declining vigor of liberalism and the rise of fascism in the West at the very time when the Japanese were making their most ambitious stab toward democracy.

Although basic conditions still prevailing in the Japanese cultural environment were undoubtedly primarily responsible for the failure of democratic parliamentarism, in the popular mind the obvious faults of big business provided inviting targets for attack on the political parties. The cry was raised that the old-line political parties were too much the tools of big business and that they were consequently not democratic. Organized labor and its sympathizers among the intellectuals put their faith in new proletarian parties now making their appearance. They were joined by large numbers of peasants who had failed to share in the industrial and commercial prosperity and who blamed the business-controlled government for neglecting their interests. Yet, while disillusioned with the major parties, the masses were not ready to support the proletarian parties

[1] Robert A. Scalapino, *Democracy and the Party Movement in Prewar Japan* (Berkeley and Los Angeles: University of California Press, 1953).

adequately. Lack of financial resources, lack of experienced leadership, doctrinaire ideological dissensions, and harassment by the business-dominated government rendered these proletarian parties ineffective. A sense of crisis arose when the great depression, soon to become world-wide, first hit Japan at the end of the 1920's and discredited the efficacy of the regime of big business. Thus neither the proletarian nor the big business parties appeared capable of meeting the needs of the time.

At this juncture the army stepped forward with the claim that it alone was qualified to serve as the savior of the nation. It had some peculiar reasons for claiming such a messianic role. Heretofore a military career had been a gentleman's vocation, and the higher officers generally had had close social connections with the oligarchs and with the important business families. But since the 1920's a revolutionary change had been taking place in the character of the professional officer corps. Attracted to the great opportunities opening up in the burgeoning world of industry and business, the sons of the more privileged families began to spurn military careers. The army then had to recruit its officer cadets increasingly from among less privileged farm boys, until a steadily growing proportion of the officer corps represented the same social class as the rank and file, who came mostly from the depressed agricultural countryside. These young officers were bitterly resentful of the big business interests which, they believed, were sacrificing the welfare of the masses for the sake of capitalistic profits. They also had a professional interest in opposing the conciliatory foreign policy of the business-motivated government, which, they thought, was sacrificing national security in favor of trade relations based on ephemeral international good will.

Contributing to this resentful mood of the young officers was a xenophobia stemming from the fact that this group came from the sector of society that had been left behind by the rapid modernization and Westernization of the dominant urban portion of Japanese society. The young officers and the class they represented no longer felt at home in their own country. But instead of recognizing that their sense of alienation was due to their own anachronistic orientation, they accused the

supposedly corrupting, decadent Western influence of destroying the puritanical, Spartan-like, native virtues and of transforming Japan into a profit-mad, materialistic, compliant lackey
of the West. They conceived of themselves as patriots called
upon to save the nation from this degradation.

The program which they came to espouse was threefold.
They advocated, first, a system of "national socialism," for they
wanted an anticapitalistic society which would serve the
masses but which would be untainted by the democratic soft-
ness they distrusted. They advocated, secondly, a system of
regional autarchy, for they distrusted the international commercial dealings of big business and felt that only the creation
of a closely integrated bloc of neighboring nations centered
upon Japan could achieve for the Far East the economic self-
sufficiency necessary to assure security from Western imperialism. They advocated, thirdly, what they termed a return to the
"native spirit," which they never clearly defined but which
they preached in confused mystic terms. So fanatically did
they believe in these goals that they were willing to resort to
terrorism, mutiny, or revolution to establish a military dictatorship which would advance their aims.

Because most of the advocates of this program had only a
sketchy education except along narrowly professional military
lines, and because they were moved more by seething emotion
than by reason, they were not capable of thinking out very
clearly either their program or the ideology behind it. Although their movement was purported to represent a return to
Kōdō, or the "Imperial Way" of ancient Japan, it was actually
based on a fantastic jumble of notions lifted from Marxism,
fascism, Naziism, Haushoferian geopolitics, Malthusianism,
Confucianism, Shintoism, Pan-Asianism and other widely divergent sources, all pieced together with wild imagination.

This militarist resurgence no doubt bore essentially the
nature of a traditionalist revival. The nation's martial traditions,
popular habits of docility in the face of authority, the emperor
myth, and other such historic factors provided an environment
which offered little natural immunity to the appeals of the
militarist agitators. Even more, the militarist resurgence effectively blocked for the time being the recent trend toward

democratic development and sought to revive traditional cultural ideals and social patterns. The very fact of its military character seemed to represent a return to the kind of military dominance characteristic of the feudalism which had prevailed in Japan for almost eight hundred years.

At the same time, however, it should not be overlooked that the program of the militarists did not imply a simple, atavistic reversion to the historic past. In its inclusion of strong Marxist, fascistic geopolitical, and other modern concepts, and in the demagogic appeal of its purported concern with the welfare of the masses, this movement, while antiliberal and antidemocratic, contained elements that were far removed from anything traditionally Japanese. Moreover, although the extremist military officers who pushed this movement loved to pose as the modern samurai, they themselves were mostly peasant upstarts. The actual descendants of the samurai were now prominent among the ranks of their enemy—in industry and commerce, in party politics, in the civilian bureaucracy, and in arts and letters—while many of the descendants of the feudal nobility were now capitalist magnates. Despite its self-conscious display of pseudo-historic trappings, the militaristic, imperialistic, ultranationalistic movement of the 1930's was in many ways a modern phenomenon arising out of an essentially modern situation.

By the end of the 1930's military dictatorship finally won out, aided greatly by the disappearance of the *genro*. Although it is true that during the lifetime of the *genro* the divisive issues had not yet become so acute as they were to become later, so long as these oligarchs were alive they had been powerful enough to keep in check the bureaucracy, the plutocracy, the political parties, and the militarists alike, and had forced them to work more or less together as a team. Upon the extinction of the *genro*, however, there was no longer a superior power to restrain them, whereupon the various rival forces began to clash openly. For a while big business was in the ascendancy, but in the end the militarists prevailed because they were more fanatic, more desperate, more ruthless, and were willing to resort to the ultimate force of arms. The dictatorship they then established lasted until it was discredited by impending defeat in the war into which it had carried the nation, whereupon the moderates staged a partial resurrection and prepared the way for eventual surrender and peace.

This review of the historical background suggests some conclusions concerning the nature of the democratic movement in prewar Japan. On the face of it, this democratic movement had been a resounding failure. It had failed to prevent the rise of the oligarchy; it had failed to prevent the miscarriage of parliamentary rule by the plutocracy; it had failed to prevent the establishment of military dictatorship. Oligarchy, plutocracy, and military dictatorship, by their essentially authoritarian and unegalitarian character, deny the principle of the consent of the governed, which is the basic requisite of democracy.

But in the sense that even undemocratic regimes can have some democratic features or some tendencies that incline toward democracy, the Japanese record was not devoid of some encouraging aspects. Compared with the feudal regime which it succeeded, the government under the Meiji Constitution, even though devised by the oligarchs more out of expediency than out of principle, contained features that marked it as a great advance toward democracy. Although this constitution rested on ordained authority rather than on popular consent, it did recognize—other than for members of the imperial family—the equality of all persons before the law. As concessions rather than rights and therefore subject to serious conditions, such personal liberties as freedom of speech, freedom of association, freedom of movement, and the like were nevertheless guaranteed within fairly broad limits. In matters outside the constitutional field, the regime provided for even more equality—for instance, a system of compulsory, universal, uniform education and a civil service based solely on merit as measured by competitive examinations.

Under the governmental system set up by the Meiji Constitution, moreover, even though the substance of policy was controlled by the oligarchy or the plutocracy or the military, the people gained the experience and acquired the habit of participating at least in the mechanics of parliamentary representative government. From 1890 for the national government and even earlier for local governments, the people at the least went through the motions of holding regular elections to choose representatives who interpellated and criticized the authorities and who scrutinized and exercised some supervision over the annual budgets. The people during all that time supported political parties which fought to make these popular political activities more than merely gestures and to make them the real controlling factors in government. In fighting for this goal, thousands of party adherents periodically scuffled with the police and went to jail; newspapers at times even maintained "jail editors" to assume the penalties so that the regular editors could continue without interruption to criticize the government in defiance of censorship laws. From one point of view these happenings of course indicate the oppressiveness of the ruling powers; but from another point of view they prove the persistence and tenacity of the democratic elements. Such experiences, sustained through almost three generations, comprise a record rare among any people not born to the western European–American democratic tradition.

These endeavors, moreover, had not always been quite in vain. Although full victory for democracy was never attained, there were occasions when the government not merely granted concessions but came fairly close to responding directly to the will of the people. Examination of the legislative record, and even more of the political climate, of the comparatively liberal decade of the 1920's will reveal that there were more promising developments then than is now generally recognized. A surprisingly large proportion of the reforms sponsored by the Occupation will be found to have revived and elaborated reforms the rudiments of which were initiated by the Japanese themselves in the 1920's. Although later events were to render it abortive, the slogan *kensei no jōdō,* or "normal course of constitutional government," was perhaps not so inappropriate for that time as it might now seem.

Even during the period of the military ascendancy mitigating aspects were not altogether lacking. While big business was being discredited by its selfishness and the militarists were gaining considerable popular favor for their sincere if misguided patriotism, the majority of the people were never thoroughly converted to the ideas of the militarists. The tenacity of the democratic tendencies is evidenced by the fact that in every legal election the properly constituted parliamentary parties continued to win. The militarists were able to advance their power only by intimidation exerted through assassinations, military *Putsches,* and artificially created war emergencies. It was only after the militarists had taken the nation into global war that they were finally able, by utilizing abnormal wartime pressures in the "Tojo election" of 1942, to remove the opposition of the popularly elected Diet. But even in this notoriously controlled election 20 per cent of those voted in by the electorate were "unindorsed" candidates whom the military authorities had tried their utmost to defeat.

The 80 per cent majority which the militarists managed to gain for their hand-picked candidates was more than sufficient, of course, to enable them to ram through their policies, but it was a far cry from the virtually unanimous votes that truly totalitarian regimes characteristically muster. Although during the war the public perforce had to put up with it, Japanese militarism, unlike fascism and Naziism, never succeeded in developing a broad mass base; it remained a conspiracy of a military clique associated with a relatively small group of civilian collaborators. The militarists may have controlled the substance of governmental policy, but they found it politic to retain intact both the formal structure and the procedural forms of the legitimate government under the Meiji Constitution. It was the fact that this dictatorship was less than totalitarian which enabled its opponents to escape total liquidation. Hence, once the army extremists were discredited by the turn in the tide of war, with surprisingly little dislocation in government it was possible for them to be quietly jockeyed out of power in 1944 by the moderate elements who had managed to survive.

The significance of the democratic elements in Japan should not, of course, be exaggerated. After all, their actual accomplishments were meager; not much more can be said of them than that they had managed to persist against heavy odds. Why, however, had they thus managed to persist against such heavy odds? Some recent students of Japanese social history suggest that, while the formal organization of Japanese society and the official norms of social behavior have been rigidly hierarchical and authoritarian, there has paradoxically always been a tacit acceptance, or sometimes even an open idealization, of certain trends which were in apparent opposition to the official norm. Thus, in Japanese social history there has been a tradition of glorifying such trends as the defense of their own rights by dissident groups, defiance of authority, individual action, and open personal achievement. These have significantly modified the dynamics of the social process in Japan in contrast to the outward forms of Japanese social organization. If this view is valid—as recent studies,[2] which cannot be reviewed here, increasingly indicate it is—then it is not surprising that certain democratic tendencies have shown such tenacity as they have. To be sure, democracy as a political system, as defined at the beginning of this chapter has hitherto never existed in Japan; but some democratic features, as a social tendency, were always just around the corner, if not actually present, most of the time. The fact that such democratic tendencies existed was an asset, for they offered a possibility that the Occupation might succeed in nurturing them to eventual vigor and dominance. In any event, it meant that there were in existence materials with which the Occupation could attempt to work.

Examination of the history of political change in Japan would also seem to offer additional grounds for hope. The periods of comparative success and of comparative failure in the democratic efforts in Japan have been less related to the nature of Japanese institutions and traditions than to the imponderable demands of the moment. There does not seem to be any such entity as the "Japanese soul" or the "Japanese temperament" which innately predestines the Japanese to any particular pattern of behavior. Of course habit and tradition exert strong influences, but these relatively constant factors have been less decisive than the more variable factors of circumstances. History can be cited to argue that the Japanese are a revolutionary people as well as to argue that they are a conservative people. The determinant is to be found in the prevailing mood of a particular time as shaped by the circumstances of the moment.

The same formal political institutions and historical traditions were in existence at the time the oligarchy exercised a

[2] See Robert Bellah, *Tokugawa Religion* (Glencoe, Ill.: Free Press, 1957), for an example of such recent interpretation in which there is attributed to Japan what is equivalent to the "Protestant ethic."

monopoly of power, at the time the oligarchy gave way to the rise of the political parties, and at the time the political parties succumbed to the military dictatorship. The Meiji Constitution was not amended during all these shifts in actual power; there was no change in the official doctrine concerning the nature of the Japanese state. The oligarchy rose to power because the times called for a strong, tight leadership to modernize and strengthen the nation upon its sudden exposure to the outside world. The political parties came to power in their turn because by that time the chief aim of the oligarchy had already been attained and the political parties had come to reflect more accurately the prevailing concerns of the nation. The military dictatorship succeeded the parties because the parties eventually failed the new expectations of the nation, expectations which the military claimed to be better able to fulfil. While the contributing role of ideological principles, moral doctrines, sentiment, habit, and other such subjective factors should not be minimized, it would appear that the external factor of social, economic, and political circumstance has been the most direct determinant in shaping modern Japanese historical development.

These factors mentioned above indicate, of course, only that the Japanese are not wholly lacking in the potential for democratic development; there is no assurance that this potential is likely to be successfully realized. In view of their past failures, it would be unwarranted indeed to hold any optimistic hopes regarding the prospects of the Japanese for democracy. If, however, it is admitted that the Japanese are not precluded from democracy by inherent incapacity, and if it is admitted that external circumstance has been a significant determinant of Japanese historical development, then the Occupation provided the most likely circumstance ever yet provided for the Japanese to make a successful democratic experiment. A catastrophic war leading to unprecedented defeat and prolonged enemy occupation constituted without doubt an external circumstance of potent magnitude. It is not unreasonable to assume that an unprecedented circumstance might possibly be sufficient at last to bring about an unprecedented result. It remains to examine the various sectors of Japanese life to see whether in fact this turned out to be the case.

CHAPTER IV

The Constitution

The making of the new constitution for Japan was the most notable political achievement of the Occupation.[1] It was, however, by no means the most felicitous in its results.

The official version of the story is simple. The Japanese government, aware that the Meiji Constitution of 1889 was not viewed with favor by the victorious Allies, undertook on its own initiative to make a thorough revision. In so doing, although it closely consulted SCAP officials and received much advice and many specific suggestions, the Japanese government itself was responsible essentially for the work of drafting the new document; and the Japanese Diet freely adopted the new constitution after full and open debate. The old undemocratic constitution was thus replaced properly and legally with a model new constitution which would virtually assure the satisfactory democratization of Japan. Such in brief was the fiction outwardly maintained by both the United States and the Japanese governments.

The actual story was quite different. As was apparent from the outset to almost everyone, the new constitution was drafted in secrecy within General MacArthur's headquarters, sprung upon a distraught Japanese Cabinet, and forced through a reluctant Japanese Diet after a few minor changes had been per-

[1] This chapter is an expansion of the author's article "Sovereignty and Democracy in the Japanese Constitution," *American Political Science Review*, Vol. XLIX, No. 3 (September, 1955).

mitted to the Japanese.[2] So obvious was the American inspiration that one American news magazine parodied the opening
words of the preamble as "We the mimics . . ." while a rival
news magazine even more aptly told of a Japanese who, when
asked what he thought of the new constitution, replied: "Oh,
has it been translated into Japanese already?"

Although many Japanese realized that the Meiji Constitution
required drastic revision, there were probably even more who
felt this constitution itself to be essentially satisfactory and the
fault to be in its interpretation or enforcement. Soon after the
beginning of the Occupation, therefore, within the government,
within the political parties, and in intellectual circles, a wide
variety of plans and proposals were discussed concerning what
should be done or not done about the constitution. All of them
assumed that, although SCAP would have to be consulted
about the minimum limits of what would be acceptable to the
Allies, any revision of the constitution would be the result of
the thinking of the Japanese themselves.

Suddenly on March 6, 1946, however, while it was known
that nothing like a consensus had yet been reached among the
Japanese, the newspapers appeared with the full text of a
completed draft of a new constitution. It was in awkward Japanese; it was full of expressions and ideas that were quaintly
alien. Accompanying it was a statement by General MacArthur
graciously praising the Japanese people and their government
for having produced such an exemplary document which so
coincided with his own notion of what was best for the country.
Accompanying it was a statement by the Emperor dutifully
indorsing the draft as coinciding with his desires. While poker-
faced Occupation officials parroted General MacArthur's praise
of the supposed Japanese action, American intelligence agents
alerted themselves to the reactions of the Japanese. Meanwhile,
the American military censors suppressed all except laudatory
comments in the Japanese press.[3]

[2] The official version of the story is presented in SCAP, Government Sec-
tion, *The Political Reorientation of Japan* (2 vols.; Washington, D.C.:
Government Printing Office, 1950). The most scholarly analysis of the
actual happenings is provided in Robert E. Ward, "The Origins of the
Present Japanese Constitution," *American Political Science Review,* Vol.
L, No. 4 (December, 1956).

[3] Some of the present author's own editorials were thus suppressed.

Rumors quickly spread concerning the specific individuals at SCAP headquarters who were supposed to have written the draft, the manner in which the finished draft had been presented to Prime Minister Shidehara without previous warning, and how a high Occupation official had used picturesque methods of intimidation to force the dismayed Japanese Cabinet into swallowing their objections. Recently revealed evidences and testimonies which are gradually filling in the actual details of the story indicate that the original rumors were not far wrong.

The inevitable effect upon the Japanese was an uneasy apathy born of impotence. SCAP officials apparently quickly discerned the unfortunate effects of their heavy-handed machinations. Soon an inspired publicity campaign urged the Japanese to discuss the draft constitution freely and to propose modifications. A mild flurry of discussion ensued. One old unregenerate member of the House of Peers peevishly denounced the draft constitution from beginning to end, proving at least that freedom of speech existed in the Diet. But, in the main, although the members of the Diet—and particularly the House of Peers—conducted some searching interpellations, they obviously felt considerable restraint. The government, on its side, was too ready to resort to any expedient argument which would allay the Diet's embarrassing questions. It was obvious that, regardless of what assurances they had been given, the Japanese believed that under the circumstances of the Occupation they had little practical choice but to approve the draft which General MacArthur had already so vigorously indorsed.

So, after the government had made a few minor changes, the Diet amid funereal gloom voted for the adoption of the draft constitution over the opposition of about half a dozen dissenters, mostly Communists. On May 3, 1947, when the new constitution went into effect, only five thousand people braved the drizzle to attend the rally held in the plaza fronting the palace to celebrate the occasion, and they were obviously much more interested in getting a close view of the Emperor and Empress than in cheering the beginning of a supposedly bright new era in their political life. Three days earlier at the same spot, with better weather but without the attraction of the Emperor and

Empress, four hundred thousand persons had turned out for a Communist-inspired labor demonstration.

These circumstances of the origins of the new constitution give rise to the following questions: Was it necessary for SCAP to have thus forced this new constitution upon the Japanese? In the conditions prevailing at the time, would not the Japanese, left to their own devices, have come up with a constitution of their own which would have satisfied the requirements of the Allies? Were there not more subtle ways for SCAP to influence the results so as to leave the Japanese with a sense of responsibility and pride in their own work? Would not such a product of their own efforts be more enduringly taken to their hearts by the Japanese than an obviously alien imposition? Today the movement in some Japanese circles to get rid of the "MacArthur Constitution" as a humiliating symbol of alien domination bears upon the answer to these questions.

It would not be fair, however, to ignore the probable reasons why General MacArthur decided on the course that he did. The wide disparity of views prevailing in Japan made it likely that it would take a long time for the Japanese to reach agreement among themselves. The conservative character of the government then in power indicated that it would try to get by with the minimum of constitutional changes and that hard bargaining would be necessary for SCAP to persuade this government to produce a satisfactory new constitution.

But time was of the essence. The program of democratic reforms envisaged by SCAP would be delayed and hampered unless there was first an adequately democratic constitutional foundation. Certain Allied nations represented in the Far Eastern Commission were advocating dangerously doctrinaire ideas concerning constitutional revision which were unsuited to the realities of the Japanese situation and incompatible with American aims. There might even have been jealousies between General MacArthur's staff, who felt they were in a position to understand Japan best, and certain government agencies in Washington whose notions of what was desirable for Japan were regarded by those on the spot as being too theoretical. It is understandable why General MacArthur, confronted by these seemingly dangerous obstacles to the practical conduct of the

Occupation, should have suddenly come up with a *fait accompli* of his own making.

On the face of it, this new constitution was an eminently good one. Although in places its turgidly MacArthurian language was annoyingly un-Japanese and although it was loosely organized and redundant, its provisions did conform to the best standards of a true parliamentary democracy.

Under the old constitution the Emperor, as the sovereign, had been the fountainhead of all authority. To be sure his powers were almost purely nominal, for he could take no official action except through his ministers, whose advice was in practice mandatory. But this concentration of such extensive theoretical powers in the person of the Emperor, with the practical requirement that he follow the advice of his ministers, had been rendered dangerous by the multiple nature of the executive, in which the civilian component and the military component had enjoyed virtually independent and co-ordinate power. On civil matters the Emperor was bound to take the advice of the Cabinet, while on military matters he was bound to take the advice of the Supreme Command. In the realm of high policy, the line of demarcation between civil and military matters could seldom be clear-cut, with the result that there was inevitably conflict of jurisdiction and conflict of advice.

Inasmuch as the Emperor was constitutionally bound to accept both sets of mutually contradictory advice, the Japanese government in times of greatest crisis tended to go off in two different directions at once. In this intolerable situation, the military had finally resorted to the powers of coercion it characteristically possessed to establish its dominance. Throughout this struggle within the executive, the Diet or legislature, which only inadequately represented the people, lacked sufficient power to influence the outcome.

The new constitution produced under the aegis of the Occupation corrected these fundamental defects. While it retained the general organization of its predecessor and purported to be no more than an extensive amendment, it was in actuality an entirely new and much longer document.

It transformed the Emperor from sovereign and theoretical fountainhead of authority into a mere "symbol of the State . . .

deriving his position from the will of the people in whom resides sovereign power." It made both houses of the Diet directly elective by and representative of the people, and it raised the Diet from its former position of relative impotence to the unchallengeable position of the "highest organ of state power." The several competitive components of the multiple executive were streamlined so as to leave only the Cabinet, and this Cabinet was made directly responsible to the Diet in a manner identical to that in Western parliamentary democracies.

In addition, the new constitution transformed the "bill of rights" from a group of concessions conferred by the sovereign under certain conditions into an extensive body of inalienable God-given rights not to be infringed upon by any human authority under any circumstance. These rights included the most meticulous safeguard of the basic individual liberties as well as of some surprisingly advanced notions of social welfare. The new constitution also enhanced the independent position of the judiciary as a guardian of these new rights and introduced the doctrine of judicial review—an innovation for Japan—which tends to uphold the immutable majesty of the law as against political expediency. The new constitution also called for a wide extension of local autonomy to nurture the development of a grass-roots democracy as a check to the dangers of national regimentation. It also provided for the permanent demilitarization of the nation. So far as the letter of the law could do so, the new constitution thus effectively corrected the shortcomings of the old one and provided the most impressive basis for a liberal and democratic state.

From the point of view of Western thinking, therefore, the substance of the new constitution is beyond reproach. Most Americans hence seem to assume that the degree of Japanese acceptance of and continuing support for this constitution is an index of Japanese acceptance of the democratic ideals fostered by the Occupation. If the Japanese continue in the future to retain this constitution, the Occupation supposedly has been a success; if the Japanese abandon this constitution, the democratizing efforts of the Occupation supposedly have been in vain. Such a simple equation, however, would be far from the truth.

From the Japanese point of view, complex difficulties hardly imaginable to the Western mind are involved.

Easily understood, of course, are the difficulties caused by the peculiar origins of this constitution. However desirable the contents, this constitution suffers from the fatal stigma of being an alien-imposed document. As the Occupation recedes further and further into history, it is inevitable that the revival of national independence and self-respect will give increasing rise to the demand for a truly indigenous constitution.

A more serious difficulty from the point of view of the Japanese, which Westerners may find hard to understand, is to be found in the fact that the new constitution arbitrarily changes the fundamental nature of the Japanese state. Traditionally, the essential nature of the Japanese state—the unique characteristic of Japan which makes it Japan—has been considered to lie in the fact that this nation has been and shall be "reigned over and governed by a line of Emperors unbroken for ages eternal." In the jargon of Japanese political theory, this is what is known as *kokutai,* or "national polity," a term which to most Japanese has an almost mystic significance.

Japan had traditionally been a theocratic-patriarchal state in which the Emperor had occupied the position of god-father. While such a god-father was not divine in the sense Westerners conceive of divinity, the Emperor did occupy in the eyes of the Japanese a position of unique pre-eminence which was considered ordained in the natural order of things and which therefore enjoyed divine sanction. The Meiji Constitution of 1889 had therefore accurately reflected dominant Japanese belief in its declaration that "the Emperor is sacred and inviolable" and that "the Emperor is the head of the Empire, combining in Himself the rights of sovereignty."

The new constitution, as already noted, proclaims that "sovereign power resides with the people" and that the Emperor shall be a mere symbol whose position is derived from the will of the people. Such an explicit expression of the doctrine of popular sovereignty is completely alien to Japanese thought. It is true that there has hardly ever been a time in all of Japan's history when the Emperor has actually ruled. The exercise of authority has always been intrusted to, or usurped by, advisers who relieved the Emperor of the risk of committing political mistakes incompatible with his sacred character. This assumption of responsibility by his advisers had given rise to the doctrine that the Emperor must never act except in accordance with their advice. Nevertheless, the Emperor had been the theoretical source of all authority. Thus, while the new constitution only recognized an established historical fact in characterizing the Emperor as "the symbol of the State," it did introduce an unprecedented idea in attributing sovereignty to the people. In so doing, it arbitrarily violated the *kokutai*, the "national polity," which was the essence of the Japanese state.

The naturally ordained supremacy of the Emperor was not only a matter of political theory. It was inextricably imbedded in the social organization of Japan, whose orderly hierarchical structure logically calls for a capstone at the top. The functioning of this hierarchical system requires a chain of authority extending from the apex to the bottom layer, and a chain of loyalty from the bottom layer to the apex. Even the complex lateral relationships within the layers of this pyramid are kept in order by their linkage to the clearly defined vertical relationship. In such an integrated social organization, in which each unit fits so neatly into its logically defined niche, the whole scheme appears to be ordained by the inherent nature of things. It is inconceivable that the capstone should owe its position to any free-will decision of the lower strata, for there can logically be no other choice.

Hence the doctrine of popular sovereignty with its implication of the social compact theory, as embodied in the new constitution, did violence to Japanese social reality as well as to Japanese political theory. Although this social hierarchy has in modern times been undergoing rapid change, it has not yet by any means entirely disappeared. The doctrinal basis of the new constitution, so out of keeping with the facts of Japanese life, could hardly appeal to the Japanese.

This inconsistency between the "national polity" and the new constitution, moreover, did not lie solely with the American authorship of the constitution but was compounded by the fact that its roots go back to the confused circumstances of Japan's surrender. Japan's first formal offer to surrender was made explicitly on the basis of the Potsdam Proclamation of July 26, 1945, in which the Allied leaders had rather liberally defined the "conditions" of their earlier demand for unconditional surrender. One of the features of this Proclamation which appealed to the Japanese was its implication that the victorious Allies would not interfere with the institution of the emperorship. Desiring more specific confirmation of this point, the Japanese government in its note of August 10, 1945, offering to accept the Potsdam Proclamation as the basis for surrender, asked for further assurance that "the said Declaration does not comprise any demand which prejudices the prerogatives of His Majesty as a sovereign ruler." The Allied answer was: "From the moment of surrender, the authority of the Emperor and the Japanese Government to rule the state shall be subject to the Supreme Commander for the Allied Powers, who will take such steps as he deems proper to effectuate the surrender terms."

The highly ambiguous nature of this answer was obviously intentional. In order to induce the Japanese to surrender, the Allies hoped to convey to them the impression that their request regarding the Emperor had been granted. At the same time, in order to remain free to impose whatever changes in the imperial institution might later seem desirable, the Allies carefully avoided making any definite commitment.

This ambiguity posed a problem for the Japanese. The opponents of surrender argued that if the Emperor were to be "subject to" the Allied Supreme Commander, his prerogatives would obviously be prejudiced. The advocates of surrender argued that the prerogatives of the Emperor would remain intact, since the exercise of his authority would be limited by the authority of the Allied Supreme Commander only temporarily and then only insofar as necessary "to effectuate the surrender terms." The question was resolved only by the Emperor's arbitrary ruling that in his opinion the Allied terms did not prejudice his prerogatives as the sovereign ruler.

This ruling, however, overlooked the fact that the Potsdam Proclamation had also stated that the Allied occupation force would be withdrawn from Japan only after "there has been established, in accordance with the freely-expressed will of the

Japanese people, a peacefully-inclined and responsible government." If the nature of the Japanese government, including the
status of the Emperor, was to depend on "the freely-expressed
will of the Japanese people," obviously there was implied a
fundamental shift in the locus of sovereign power from the
Emperor to the people. In the face of this provision in the
Potsdam Proclamation, the Allies could hardly have assured
the Japanese government that the Emperor's prerogatives as
a sovereign ruler would not be prejudiced. Thus the Allied
answer, while misleading in intention, was correctly noncom-
mittal in fact. The Japanese official interpretation was therefore made, not on the basis of fact, but as a matter of expediency to facilitate the necessary surrender. By thus accepting
the Potsdam Proclamation as the basis of the surrender, Japan
had actually acceded to a fundamental change in her "national
polity."

Having lightly acceded to a fundamental change in the
"national polity" in this casual manner, the Japanese government was then inevitably forced to continue to pretend that
there had been no essential change in the historic character of
the Japanese state. In this course the Japanese government was
unconsciously abetted by SCAP, which, although probably un-
interested in the problem of "national polity" as such, was
anxious to endow the new constitution of its own creation with
the appearance of legitimacy. Accordingly, SCAP insisted that
in the adoption of the new constitution the regular procedure
for the adoption of amendments as provided for in the Meiji
Constitution be followed as closely as circumstances would
permit.

The inconsistencies and ambiguities in this situation were,
however, clearly discernible to the more perceptive among the
Japanese. The members of the Diet therefore searchingly questioned the government whether the new constitution did not
in fact alter the "national policy." The government compounded
the vulnerability of its position by giving less than honest
answers, which trapped it further in the mire of contradictions.

At first the government sought to soften the impact of the
doctrine of popular sovereignty by making a euphemistic translation of the original English draft. The unlegalistic, literary

quality of the Japanese language lends itself particularly well to such treatment. Thus, for example, the English original, "We, the Japanese people, acting through our duly elected representatives . . . do proclaim the *sovereignty of the people's will*," emerged in an ambiguous Japanese form which, while not actually a mistranslation of the original, might also be translated back into English as, "We, the Japanese people, acting through our duly elected representatives . . . do proclaim *in accordance with the supreme will of the people*," which, of course, has a different connotation.

The Allied Powers, through the Far Eastern Commission, apparently finally put a stop to such contrivances by the Japanese government and insisted on the adoption of the following form: "We, the Japanese people, acting through our duly elected representatives . . . proclaim that *sovereign power resides with the people. . . .*" Such blunt honesty was welcomed by the members of the Diet, who had been seeking clarification.

But the government next sought to interpret the word "sovereignty" in a special sense. The people are sovereign, but "the people" means, not the people as opposed to the monarch, but the corporate body comprising all the individuals in the state, including the Emperor. In such an organized corporate body, the Emperor naturally stands at the apex. Thus the government argued that popular sovereignty did not alter the traditional "national polity."

When many members of the Diet protested against this sophistry, the government shifted its ground and resorted to still another sophistry which was inconsistent with the first. It admitted that there had indeed been a legal change but insisted that it was a "mere" legal change. Historically, the Emperor of Japan had been more a moral ruler than a political ruler. Hence, the government could assert with some show of plausibility that sovereignty in Japan is a moral, not a legal or political, concept and that the moral position of the dynasty, which is the essence of the "national polity," therefore remains intact.

These arguments had little practical effect on the adoption of the constitution, for, as has already been made obvious, the course of events was really dictated by the overriding argument of MacArthur's occupation army. But the obscurantism of the government's tortured explanations and the attempts of SCAP to retain for the new constitution an appearance of historical continuity, while designed to surround the new constitution with an aura of legitimacy, actually permeated it with the odor of chicanery and unreality.

From the foregoing account, it might appear that the objections of the Japanese to the arbitrary change in their "national polity" sprang from a blind resistance to any change and particularly from an opposition to democratic development. Many Western critics have assumed that the equivocal character of the Japanese government's interpretations of the new constitution stemmed from a reactionary conspiracy to water down the constitution's democratic objectives and to salvage as much of the authoritarian position of the Emperor as possible. By the same token, the Diet's criticisms of the government's position have been assumed to represent a still more reactionary position which regarded even the government's apparently equivocal sponsorship of the new constitution as going too far.

The truth, however, was quite to the contrary. The government was sincerely anxious to get the necessary task of adopting the new constitution over with as expeditiously as possible. If its attitude seemed questionable, it stemmed from a willingness to use any argument that would serve to mollify the critics of the constitution in order to get the constitution adopted. The government clutched at fallacious arguments which confused its stand, but it did so in an attempt to defend the constitution, not to subvert it. Also, as for the critics, some of the severest attacks upon the new constitution came from staunch liberals who had distinguished themselves in the difficult earlier struggles for the democratization of the Japanese government.

One group of liberals, more prominent outside the Diet than within, objected to the fraud of pretending that the "national polity" remained unchanged, not because they objected to the change, but because they welcomed the change and thought that it should be openly proclaimed. Not only had the defeat and the Occupation demonstrated the necessity of a clean break with the past, they thought, but they further believed that the changing character of modern Japanese society had by now brought the Japanese people to a point where they would willingly accept a fundamental change in their political ideology as natural and even inevitable. What was needed was a frank acknowledgment of this situation; then the Japanese people would be prepared to accept the basic ideology of the new constitution for what it really was.

More prominent among the liberal critics of the government's position, however, were those who feared that the new constitution tended to defeat its own democratic ends. What was needed to insure the successful democratization of Japan, they believed, was neither a sudden, clean break with the past nor a clumsy attempt to disguise a break but a more natural and logical transition from the past to a steadily more democratic future. What was needed was not a repudiation or even a disguised alteration of the "national polity" but a steady development of democratic practices within the framework of the historic "national polity" through a natural evolution in its interpretation. The tremendous prestige of the "national polity" could then be brought to bear in support of democracy instead of in opposition to it. The logic of this point of view can be seen through an examination of the Japanese historical background.

The Meiji Restoration of 1868, which inaugurated the modernization of the Japanese government, obviously did not represent a democratic movement. It was engineered by a relatively small elite group. Although it abolished the dual government of the feudal Tokugawa Shogunate and restored unified government directly under the throne, it did not fundamentally alter the nature of the traditional Japanese state. The Emperor had always been the theoretical source of all authority, even in the feudal period of imperial eclipse; and this imperial authority had in practice always been delegated to advisers who assumed responsibility for all official acts. The Meiji Restoration in essence merely effected a change in the clique of advisers.

Yet it was of utmost significance that the Restoration was in another sense much more than just a palace revolution. For, although there was no mass movement, the new set of advisers owed their rise to power at least in part to the upsurge of new economic and social forces which coincided with the influx of Western influence. These factors had to be given recognition in the new government. At the same time, the new set of imperial advisers, while singularly free from motives of personal self-seeking, did have a strong belief in their own indispensability to the nation and therefore sought to assure for themselves as much power as possible.

The Meiji Constitution of 1889 was designed to meet these requirements. It sought to mollify the new social forces by conceding to them some of the trappings of representative government; it sought to satisfy Western standards of acceptability by setting up governmental institutions resembling in form those of the West. But it also sought to preserve and even to strengthen the oligarchic rule of the new group of imperial advisers. This it did by formalizing the exalted powers of the Emperor in such a way that they had to be exercised by these advisers, who, being responsible only to the Emperor whom they advised, were in effect responsible only to themselves.

The Meiji Constitution, in other words, was designed to safeguard the power of the clique that had engineered the Restoration. But the very fact that this clique owed its power in part to new social forces meant that these social forces would tend to assert themselves. And the very fact that a written constitution had been adopted at all provided an entering wedge for these new social forces to work for the democratization of the Japanese government.

No one, of course, could directly challenge the fact that, in theory, the Emperor in his sovereign capacity had conferred the constitution upon his people. But it could be argued that the Emperor had been constrained to grant the constitution in response to the pressure of the new social forces which could no longer be ignored. It could also be argued that, extensive as were the Emperor's powers, the fact that these powers were defined at all in the constitution signified that they were subject to limitations. Finally it could be argued that the Emperor, by having granted a constitution stipulating that his powers were to be exercised through duly constituted executive, legislative, judicial, and advisory bodies, was now himself bound by the provisions of the constitution.

The theoretical justification for this limitation on the exercise of the Emperor's powers, and thus on the arbitrary actions of his advisers, was provided by the corporate theory of the state, which conceives of the state as a corporate entity possessed of a legal personality. Although this theory was of Western origin, picked up by Japanese constitutional lawyers studying in Europe, it could easily be assimilated into the stream of Japanese thought, for it was quite compatible with the concept of the nation as an integrated organism inherent in the Japanese view of their theocratic-patriarchal state. It was thus much more acceptable to them than the doctrine of popular sovereignty, with its corollary—so completely alien to Japanese thought—of the social compact.

This theory of the corporate state had liberalizing implications for Japan, for in a corporate state the Emperor is not himself the state but is merely one of its components. The Emperor is sovereign, to be sure, but only in the sense of being the bearer of sovereignty as an organ of the state. As such, the Emperor, even though he is the supreme organ, cannot act arbitrarily, but can exercise his powers only in consonance with the other organs of the state. This concept could lead logically to making the Emperor's advisers responsible not solely to the Emperor, and thereby in effect only to themselves, but responsible also to such other organs of the state as the legislature.

The beauty of this "organ theory" of the emperorship, as the Japanese term it, lay in the fact that it provided a rationale for the democratization of the Japanese government which, while not wholly indigenous, was nevertheless comprehensible to the Japanese in terms of their own ideological pattern. At the same time, it weakened the notion of the mystic uniqueness of the Japanese "national polity" by explaining the nature of the emperorship in rational, universalistic terms. It provided an unbroken bridge between tradition and modern democratic government over which the Japanese could advance under their own motive power.

The traditionalists quickly discerned the democratizing implications of the "organ theory" and denounced it as a heresy. The leading traditional theorist, Professor Shinkichi Uesugi of

the Law Faculty of the Tokyo Imperial University, charged
that the "organ theory" was incipient republicanism in disguise,
that it was the product of the European movement from absolute monarchism to popular sovereignty, and that hence it was
subversive of Japan's "national polity." Professor Tatsukichi
Minobe of the same institution, who was the chief exponent of
the "organ theory," replied that the corporate theory had
nothing to do with monarchism or republicanism as such but
merely elucidated the true nature of all states, and that, far
from being inimical to monarchical sovereignty, the "organ
theory" in no way conflicted with the "national polity."

The public controversy between the two, which started in
1912 and raged for two decades, developed into the most bitterly fought issue in the constitutional history of modern Japan
and eventually involved the entire Japanese political and academic worlds. Minobe at first appeared to emerge victorious.
While Uesugi's supporters steadily dwindled, Minobe was
loaded with official honors, his works became the authorized
handbooks for public school teachers, his disciples filled most
of the important government offices, and the general public
swung behind him. All this was accompanied by a steady
growth in parliamentary government that, while feeble by
Western standards, held promise for the further democratization of Japan.

The significance of Minobe's success, however, did not lie
wholly in the general acceptance of his "organ theory" as such.
Although the rationality of this theory appealed to the new
generation educated in the scientific atmosphere of modern
Japan's Westernized school system, there were many among
Minobe's supporters who harbored doubts as to the validity of
the "organ theory" itself. Yet they supported him because of
the character which the controversy had assumed; Minobe had
become the symbol of progress, enlightenment, and democracy
as opposed to the dead hand of tradition. As new times created
new social classes which strained at the immobility of the traditional hierarchical social structure, Minobe appeared to
these classes as the standard-bearer of their assault on the
ideological underpinnings of the old order. Although Minobe
himself was hardly a thoroughgoing democrat by tempera-

ment, his "organ theory" became the battle cry of democracy.[4]

If Minobe prevailed in the comparatively liberal atmosphere of the 1920's because he had become a symbol of liberalism, it was precisely because he was such a symbol that disaster later struck him. As Japanese liberalism succumbed to a trend toward military dictatorship in the 1930's, the forces of reaction concentrated their fury on the popular liberal symbol. Unable to best Minobe in argument, in 1935 they coerced the government, by then already susceptible to militarist intimidation, into arbitrarily proscribing the "organ theory." Such an act could not permanently resolve the controversy over the "national polity," however, for it was a decision imposed virtually by military fiat. Military fiats may produce outward compliance, but they do not change men's minds. Whenever the reactionary movement should wane, it was to be expected that at the first opportunity the "organ theory" would be raised again as the symbol of a reviving liberalism.

In the light of this historical background, it is easy to see why, when the establishment of the Occupation opened the way for the resumption of democratic growth, the sudden appearance of the "MacArthur Constitution" struck many of the Japanese liberals with consternation. While this constitution was intended to establish democracy in Japan, it ran counter in almost every way to the means by which the Japanese liberals had been trying to make democracy palatable to their countrymen. It proclaimed the alien doctrine of popular sovereignty, with which the reactionaries had tried to smear the liberals and which the liberals had striven so hard to deny. It cast doubt on the "national polity," whereas the liberals had tried very hard to show that increasing democratization was in keeping with the "national polity." It imposed these ideas virtually by military fiat, just as the reactionaries had imposed their ideas in 1935. This did not look like the way to vindicate the historic struggle for democracy in Japan.

It should be possible to appreciate why many of the Japanese liberals were reluctant to write off their own struggles of

[4] The author is indebted to his colleague, Frank O. Miller, for much of the foregoing material concerning Minobe. For a further theoretical interpretation of the reasons for Minobe's popularity, see chapter xii.

half a century and to accept instead a ready-made foreign gift.
Except for their setback in the 1930's, they had had heartening
success in the past in slowly but steadily adapting democracy
to the Japanese environment. What they had cultivated so
arduously and so long seemed to them to hold greater promise
of further growth in the native soil than a sudden new trans-
plantation. What they had fought for so hard had more value
to them than something handed to them by an alien, if benevolent, conqueror. Minobe himself thought that the Meiji Constitution, properly interpreted, would be sufficient to assure the
full growth of democracy. Others favored some revision of the
Meiji Constitution, but only such revision as would facilitate
the evolutionary democratization of Meiji institutions. Few had
faith in innovations that ignored the Japanese historical background.

The issues could not be openly and honestly debated at the
time of the adoption of the "MacArthur Constitution" because
of the restraints inherent under Occupation conditions. The
government, as has been noted, further muddled the issue by
trying to pass the new constitution off as being more in accord
with what most Japanese wanted than in fact it was. Inevitably, as the Occupation fades into the past, inhibitions surrounding discussions of the constitution will fall away and the
likelihood of revision will steadily grow. Some restoration of
the theoretical authority of the Emperor, but with such popular
controls as are called for by the "organ theory," appears to be
a natural prospect.

In the practical politics of today, however, the central issue
in the problem of constitutional revision has come to be overshadowed by the lively controversy over the demilitarization
provision of the constitution. This is an unfortunate development, for the issue of demilitarization or rearmament, despite
its seemingly liberal versus conservative overtones, is really
quite irrelevant to the problem of the future of democracy in
Japan. Even such other controversial constitutional questions
as the exact circumstances under which the prime minister may
dissolve the lower house of the Diet, the spelling-out in practice of the relations between the national authority and autonomous local authorities, the specific implementations of the bill

of rights, and all the rest are completely subsidiary to the basic problem of "national polity," the essential nature of the Japanese state.

Should Japanese democracy be based on new revolutionary concepts bodily imposed by the Occupation, or should Japanese democracy be based on more modest but familiar traditions evolved by the Japanese themselves out of their own travail? Which stands the better chance of success as a foundation on which to continue to build Japanese democracy? Was the native foundation so hopelessly inadequate that it had to be scrapped in favor of the imported model, or was the imported model the product of a shortsighted capitulation to expediency? These are the questions that will be answered by what the Japanese proceed to do with the sections of the new constitution that deal with the matter of sovereignty—and hence by implication with the "national polity"—which is at the crux of the problem of the constitution.

At the moment, the left-wing groups are adamantly opposed to any revision of the present constitution on the theory that any tampering with it, no matter how apparently justifiable, carries the danger of opening the floodgates to a stream of changes which might sweep away its desirable democratic substance. These groups fail to realize that, in view of the legitimate questions which so many Japanese have about the constitution, such an inflexible stand may only dam up the opposition until it accumulates enough sheer weight to sweep this constitution away, democratic substance and all.

The reactionaries, on the other hand, obviously want to discredit the present constitution in order to make way for a return to the past. But the advocacy of change by the reactionaries should not be allowed to obscure the fact that many sincere advocates of democracy also believe that some modification of the present constitution is highly desirable. In fact, some judicious modification might be the only way to protect the essential democratic features from being swept away in a general reaction against the anomalies of the constitution.

It is unfortunate that the present constitution contains these weaknesses, for they will make future controversies over revision almost inescapable. If the American authors of the constitution had had a better appreciation of the Japanese historical background, which was too much to hope for, or if the Japanese had not been so submissive, which also was too much to expect in view of their mood during the early years of the Occupation period, a different constitution might have taken shape and might have avoided these difficulties.

But with the constitution, as with so many other matters, the Occupation tried to go too far and too fast in conferring democracy from above. As a result, much of the handiwork of the Occupation was left dangling in mid-air, with no contact with the foundations that had been laid earlier by the painful efforts of the native pioneers of democracy. A change in the present constitution, therefore, need not necessarily mean a retrograde step from democracy. On the contrary, it might well prove to be a necessary step toward strengthening Japanese democratic development by re-establishing it upon a sounder historical foundation.

CHAPTER V

The Emperor

What the constitution has to say about sovereignty is important, of course, but probably even more important for the future of democracy in Japan is what the common people now think about the Emperor.[1] The popular attitude has recently undergone great changes, but because of its long history the imperial institution unquestionably continues to exercise a powerful influence.

According to the national mythology, the Emperor is directly descended from the Sun Goddess; the Japanese people are all in some degree descended from the same line; hence the entire Japanese nation comprises a great patriarchal family of which the Emperor is the father and his subjects the children. This unique relationship supposedly constitutes an essential part of the *kokutai* or "national polity." On January 1, 1946, however, the Emperor formally renounced his divinity, while the constitution of 1947 declared him to be a mere "symbol of the State . . . deriving his position from the will of the people in whom resides sovereign power."

The myth implies an undemocratic system embodying such concepts as a divine ruler, a chosen people, and a hierarchical relationship between ruler and ruled fixed by indissoluble hereditary ties. The new dispensation, on the other hand, im-

[1] A portion of this chapter has appeared previously as an article, "The Divinity of the Japanese Emperor," *Political Science,* Vol. X, No. 2 (September, 1958), published by Victoria University of Wellington, New Zealand.

plies a democratic system in which the throne has theoretically come to have no more authority than the British crown, so that the Japanese people now possess as much opportunity for popular government as the people of any Anglo-Saxon country. The question is, do the Japanese still cling to their old myth, or have they accepted the new dispensation?

Common sense would indicate that official pronouncements and a few years of American influence could hardly be expected to bring about a sudden reversal of ancient folkways. But common sense would also indicate that even ancient folkways cannot remain forever immune to the inexorable march of historical change. The present attitude of the Japanese people toward the imperial institution must therefore lie somewhere between the two extremes, ancient myth and the new doctrine. The problem is to determine just where.

The problem is complicated by the lack of perspective of the Japanese in judging their own position and by the inability of other peoples to comprehend an institution so alien to their own experience. The Japanese, reacting strongly to the changes which they are now undergoing, probably tend to exaggerate the magnitude of these changes. Westerners, finding even the changed Japanese attitudes to be so different from their own, probably tend to underestimate the significance of the changes.

An attempt at clarification might well start with an analysis of the traditional attitudes. Much of the Westerner's inability to comprehend the Japanese attitude toward the Emperor stems from a misapprehension of what the Japanese mean when they speak of the divinity of the Emperor. Questioning the Japanese on this point does little good, for most Japanese even today are as likely as not to affirm that they really believe the Emperor to be a god. This confounds the Westerner from the outset, for he cannot imagine how any rational person can regard a flesh-and-blood being as a god. To the Westerner, a god is a supernatural being characterized by powers of omnipotence, omniscience, and omnipresence. A god is the opposite of finite man. The Westerner imagines even a heathen idol to be an attempt at representation, however distorted and inadequate, of some aspect of the Absolute.

To the Japanese, as with many Orientals, however, the dis-

tinction between god and man, the supernatural and the natural, the divine and the secular, is not so clear. Rather than a
fact to be defined and comprehended, it is regarded as a matter of feeling lying in the realm of poesy and symbolism.
Whether he be a Buddhist or a Christian in his formal beliefs,
the Japanese with his folk background of animistic and pan-
theistic Shintoism tends vaguely to feel that every material
phenomenon in the universe is permeated with a spiritual character; that along with the hard physical fact of a stone exists
the spiritual reality of a stone which might be termed the
spirit or the god of the stone, and that along with the wet physical fact of a river exists the spiritual reality of a river which
might be termed the spirit or the god of the river. The physical
aspect of any entity is mundane while the spiritual aspect of
any entity is divine. All things are therefore both secular and
divine. To the extent that man has an entity beyond his physical body, he has a divine spark that makes him in some degree
a god. The easy apotheosis of a hero or the war dead or even
any ancestor into a Shinto deity is therefore not a transformation at all, but a continuation of their true entity, for they had
all always been gods as well as men. The death of their physical body means that only their spiritual entity or their entity
as a god remains.

Not only the Emperor, not only the Japanese, but all human
beings are thus gods in varying degrees. What is so strange,
then, about regarding some individuals as being more spiritual
or divine than others if they are more dedicated to sacerdotal
functions than others? The Emperor is divine in the sense that,
as the ex officio chief high priest of the nation, a greater degree
of sanctity attaches to his person than to others. The difference
between him and his subjects is not so much a difference in
kind, between a supernatural being and a human being, as a
difference in degree and rank among fellow gods or fellow
men.[2]

At the risk of appearing sacrilegious in Catholic eyes, it
might be said that a somewhat similar Western example may

[2] The writer's anthropologist colleague informs him that this idea of the
divine ruler is indigenous to the whole Indonesian-Oceanic region and
does not occur in this particular form anywhere else.

be found in the position of the Pope. As an individual, he is a mortal man with all of man's frailties and limitations, but when he acts in his official capacity he is the vicegerent of God, whose pronouncements ex cathedra are infallible. The Emperor as an individual is a mortal man, but in his official capacity as emperor-patriarch-priest he is the symbol of supreme authority, spiritual as well as temporal, and thus enjoys a higher degree of sanctity than ordinary men. In this sense he is more of a god than other men.

No Japanese, even the most ignorant and superstitious, has ever believed the Emperor to be a god in the Western sense of possessing powers of control over natural phenomena or that he necessarily possessed even superior human qualities. It was an open secret that the long "illness" of the Emperor Taisho, who reigned from 1912 to 1926, was mental. How on one occasion he rolled up a scroll from which he was reading a ceremonial message to the Diet and peered through it as through a telescope at the assembled legislators, and other similar stories of his deranged behavior, were quite common knowledge. Yet this knowledge had no more effect on the Japanese veneration of the Emperor as an institution than the immorality and rascality of some of the Popes of the Middle Ages affected the authority and sanctity of the institution of the papacy. The Emperor as a god in the Japanese sense is a symbol rather than an actual deity. An insane Emperor is as much a national god as a heroic Emperor, in the same way that a flag made of cheesecloth is as much a national emblem as a silken flag.

It is illuminating that visiting Japanese often note with amazement that in America the people make a veritable emperor of their flag. The Japanese, possessing an animate flag in the person of the Emperor, regard their inanimate flag as not much more than decorative bunting. The carelessness with which they handle the flag, even in the armed forces, often allowing it to drag on the ground when raising or lowering it, shocks Americans. But Japanese are equally puzzled by the elaborate ceremony which Americans accord to the flag, like the public ritual of pledging allegiance to the flag, for such acts represent the kind of respect which Japanese show only to the Emperor and his portrait.[3] Essentially, however, there seems to be little difference in the wellsprings of the attitudes of the two peoples.

This conception of the Emperor as a symbol also underlies the historic Japanese doctrine that the Emperor may hold no political opinion of his own and may take no official action except in accordance with the advice of his ministers, who assume all responsibility. To say that the Emperor is too sacred to be sullied with politics is only another way of saying that he must remain nonpartisan in order that he may serve as the symbol of the entire nation. He should be nothing other than a flag carried aloft by those in power—a flag which can also be waved just as fervently by the opponents of those in power. It is this essential neutralism of the imperial institution that caused the responsible Allied authorities to permit the retention of the Emperor despite the fact that the war had been waged in his name. There was no reason why democracy, any more than militarism or ultranationalism, should not make use of the prestige value of this banner-in-the-flesh.

But while this concept of the innocuous political neutralism of the imperial symbol is valid, it must be admitted that this symbol seems to lend itself more easily to manipulation in support of authoritarian goals than in support of democratic ones. At least it has been so manipulated in the past. The very origin of the official mythology is the prime case in point.

It is quite evident that Amaterasu, the so-called Sun Goddess, was in fact a woman chieftain whose tribe established hegemony over other tribes in south-central Japan during the protohistoric period. A descendant of hers five generations later was Jimmu, who, upon considerably enlarging the territory under his control, assumed the title of Emperor, an act which took place on February 11, 660 B.C., according to prob-

---

[3] When the new constitution went into effect, General MacArthur rescinded the orders heretofore restricting the use of their flag by the Japanese and informed them that the flag might now be flown over the principal government buildings. This gesture of concession by the Occupation merely puzzled the Japanese, for they had never flown flags over their government buildings before. Now they dutifully erected flagpoles atop the government buildings on the assumption that this was another American custom which they had to adopt in order to satisfy their conquerors.

ably inaccurate legend. The early empire, however, was no more than a loose confederation of virtually autonomous tribes over which Jimmu's tribe claimed a shadowy pre-eminence which was contested by rival groups. In order to strengthen their tribe's claim to pre-eminence, Jimmu and his descendants identified their illustrious ancestor Amaterasu with the sun, the indisputably most dominant of natural phenomena. A genealogy was elaborated which projected Amaterasu's ancestry to heavenly progenitors and also traced her progeny through Jimmu to the tribal chieftains who succeeded him and from whom all the Emperors of Japan are supposedly directly descended.

This easy apotheosis of human beings into Shinto deities resulting from the indistinct demarcation between the mundane and the spiritual in Japanese thought has already been discussed. It was also facilitated by the fact that a single word, *kami*, in ancient usage stood both for god and for anything high or superior, indicating the characteristic Japanese lack of differentiation between the divine and the secular. It was easy for *kami*, the superior chieftain, to be identified with *kami*, the god. This identification was further facilitated by the fact that the tribe of this early period consisted of a patriarchal clan (*uji*) together with inferior non-related individuals organized in occupational guilds or corporations (*be* or *tomobe*) attached to the clan in a subsidiary relationship. In such a society, the same individual served politically as the chieftain of the tribe, socially as the patriarch of the clan, and religiously as the priest in the worship of the household gods. By reason of his function as priest, the patriarchal chieftain enjoyed a greater measure of sanctity than other individuals, which in turn led easily to the concept of his divine character. As the dominant tribe eventually consolidated its control over rival tribes and the loose confederation was welded into a centralized monarchy, the claims of the ruling house to supremacy by reason of divinely ordained authority became formalized into the familiar national mythology perpetuated in literature and in political propaganda.

Although this myth thus glorified the position of the imperial family, the actual political potency of the myth should not be overestimated. Whatever its influence on the primitive people of the tribal period, it is debatable to what extent the myth was literally believed and to what extent it was merely an aesthetically satisfying imagery fancied by a poetic people unconcerned with political analysis. Certainly by the time a centralized monarchy took firm shape in the seventh century A.D., the imported Confucian doctrine of a social and political order based on the moral authority of the virtuous ruler had overshadowed the native myth completely as the ideological justification of the existing governmental system.[4]

Furthermore, neither the imported Confucian ideology nor the indigenous Shintoist myth was potent enough to assure anything more than the emptiest of lip service to imperial authority throughout the greater part of Japanese history. In the eighth century the occupants of the throne became puppets in the hands of the ambitious Buddhist clergy. From the ninth to the twelfth centuries, the Emperors were mostly *rois fainéants* manipulated by the Fujiwara family of courtiers. During the long Feudal Age which followed the decline of the monarchy in the late twelfth century, the Emperors were so neglected that one of them had to peddle his own verses for a living; another lay unburied for six weeks after his death for lack of funds for a funeral; the coronation of still another had to be postponed twenty years because of lack of means. It is significant that the futile attempt of Toba II to assert his power over the Hojo Regent is known as the Imperial Conspiracy of 1221, as if assertion of imperial authority against a domineering feudal lord were an act of rebellion. In the period of the Tokugawa Shogunate, which immediately preceded the opening of Japan to the West, most of the peasants were probably not even aware of the existence of the emperorship, while Townsend Harris, the first American minister to Japan, did not realize until several years after his arrival that "a sort of pope" whom he had vaguely heard of as living in the ancient capital of Kyoto was in reality the Emperor.

Although some intellectuals of the late Tokugawa period in-

[4] The myth of divine lineage did, however, persist sufficiently to prevent the adoption of the Chinese concept of a Mandate of Heaven which could be transferred for cause to new dynasties.

voked the imperial myth in their attack upon the Shogunate, it was not until after the Meiji Restoration that the political potency of the myth was finally exploited to the full. Then the "Westernized" government of modern Japan systematically resurrected and refurbished this half-forgotten myth as an inspiration for a new nationalism which would overcome feudal particularism and create a unified nation-state capable of taking its place among the nations of the West. Through such modern instrumentalities as public schools, printing presses, and readily indoctrinated conscript armies, the government disseminated this official propaganda so effectively that within a few decades both the Japanese people and the outside world were led to believe that the imperial institution had always been the dominating force in Japanese life. Actually this belief was a largely synthetic modern product. While some of its elements can undeniably be traced back to antiquity and while it has a strong emotional hold upon the Japanese people, the relative neglect of the imperial myth as well as of the imperial institution itself throughout much of Japanese history would indicate that their great influence in modern times— until 1945—was an anomalous phenomenon of an exceptional and not necessarily permanent character.

The religious sanction which the myth gave to the authority of the imperial government undoubtedly carried great weight with the common people, who for several decades before 1945 had been intensively subjected to official indoctrination. There were even some well-educated people who became fanatic believers and advocates. But it is unlikely that the leaders who calculatingly cultivated the myth as a matter of state policy were taken in by their own concoction. Furthermore, even while the official myth was being taught in the schools, the essentially rational and scientific bent of Japan's modern educational system could not help creating a constantly growing skepticism. Although the human mind is capable of strange compartmentalization—individuals otherwise highly sophisticated may often remain quite uncritical in matters of politics or religion—it is certain that many Japanese never accepted the imperial myth as literal fact. Yet, in the face of official pressure and a general political situation which called for united patriotic effort, few Japanese cared to express doubt openly con-

cerning the orthodox mythology; and indeed many who silently rejected the literal accuracy of the myth nevertheless found
emotional satisfaction in it as a patriotic allegory. Not all
Christians are fundamentalists; many who do not accept literally the biblical stories of the Creation or of the miracles as
empirical fact find it possible to be faithful members of orthodox evangelical churches. A similar attitude characterized the
modernist Japanese with respect to the mythology of state
Shintoism.

From the foregoing account it should be clear that the
change instituted by the Occupation in the official doctrine
concerning the Emperor did not entail quite so revolutionary a
change in the thinking of many Japanese as might have been
expected. To a greater extent than was probably generally realized, there were many Japanese whose earlier thinking had already prepared them to accept the new doctrine without difficulty. Even in the case of those to whom the new doctrine
came as an unexpected new idea, the ambiguous and ambiva-
lent Japanese concept of the relation between the secular and
the divine rendered the change less upsetting than Westerners
might imagine. To the Japanese it was as easy to demote a god
to a man as to elevate a man to a god; it required no real
change, only a slight shift of focus.

With this background of basic Japanese attitudes toward the
Emperor in mind, it should be possible to view in a meaningful
perspective the reactions of the various groups of Japanese to
the postwar changes in the imperial institution.

The first indication of the forthcoming changes, and the one
which moved the Japanese people the most, was the role assumed by the Emperor at the time of the surrender. Although
the people had no way of knowing the exact part the Emperor
had played in the secret maneuvers for peace, the unprecedented radio broadcast by which he personally announced his
decision to surrender made evident the importance of his role.[5]

[5] The Emperor's seemingly personal decision to surrender did not, however, violate the historic constitutional principle that the Emperor should
be free from all political responsibility. Even in this case he merely accepted the advice of the overwhelming majority of his ministers against
the advice of an obdurate but small minority.

The momentous character of this event shook the nation to its very depths.

Months of devastating bombings climaxed by the two atom bombs and the declaration of war by the Soviet Union, on whom they had pinned their last hopes for a mediated peace, had left the Japanese people with an awful sense of desolation and loneliness. While outwardly stoic, they clung inwardly to each other in terror of impending doom. Suddenly came instructions not to miss an important radio message from the Emperor. All activity came to a halt as the appointed hour approached; hardly a person throughout the land failed to listen. Soldiers, factory workers, and office employees were drawn up in mass formation before loudspeakers; family groups huddled around their radio sets. Over them all fell a hush so tense as to be almost physically painful. Was this to be the final call to fight unto death, as most fearfully expected, or was this the announcement of surrender as some suspected and few actually knew?

Exactly at noon on that fateful fifteenth of August, 1945, the recorded broadcast began. First came a squawk and a sputter, then a band playing the national anthem, then the hoarse, strained voice of aged Prime Minister Kantaro Suzuki in a few words of introduction. In a moment followed the voice of the Emperor. It was a surprisingly musical voice; somewhat high-pitched, but gentle, liquid, and mellow; a little tired and pathetic, but very clear and very sincere. The measured cadences of the classically phrased rescript which the Emperor read were not easy to follow, but there was no doubt about their general import. It meant surrender; the call was not to arms but to restraint and fortitude in enduring the pangs of defeat.

The response of the listeners was practically uniform throughout the whole nation. In virtually every group, someone—generally a woman—broke out in a gasping sob. Then the men, who with contorted features had been trying to stay their tears, also quickly broke down. Within a few minutes almost everyone was weeping unabashedly as a wave of emotion engulfed the populace. It was a sudden mass hysteria on a national scale, but a hysteria held to a strangely subdued, muted, minor key. Hardly had the broadcast ended than crowds began pouring into the plaza fronting the imperial palace. Instinctively hundreds of thousands were drawn there, hushed and reverent, to bow and to weep before the palace and then to stumble away. For hours the people kept streaming into the plaza as if in a trance; only after a day or more did the spell gradually fade. Never had so many Japanese undergone such a simultaneous emotional experience; never had the nation been spiritually so united as in this response to the Emperor's voice.

What did this demonstration of the evocative power of the Emperor mean? Why was it touched off by the surrender, which ironically was to lead to at least a theoretical curtailment of the Emperor's authority? Did it mean that the strength of traditional attitudes would foredoom to futility all changes in the imperial institution?

The people probably responded as they did for many reasons. They were of course overwhelmed by the sense of historic tragedy. Twenty-six centuries of the nation's proud history had ended in unprecedented surrender, and theirs was the generation fated to suffer ignominy for this catastrophe. Their grief was inconsolable. The dramatic nature of the climactic broadcast which suddenly released long-accumulating tensions undoubtedly added to the effect. There surged up in the people a deep sorrow over the pain the Emperor must have endured in calling upon them to bear with him this national humiliation.

But most powerful of all was the feeling of profound relief, and with this relief welled forth gratitude toward the Emperor for making possible the ardently desired peace which no one had been able to bring until now. The Emperor had acted to spare his people from destruction. He had at last come down from the awesome heights upon which the national myth had secluded him, to talk directly now to each listening individual. In sharing with him the common sorrow over the nation's tragedy, the people felt as never before an intimate bond of understanding and sympathy toward him.

The paradoxical significance of this event was prophetic. It revealed the unifying power of the imperial institution to be so strong that a crisis vitalized rather than weakened it. But it also indicated the emergence of a new attitude in which the people identified the Emperor with themselves so that he be-

came a personification of the popular will instead of a manifestation of authority from on high. At the moment when the
personal popularity of the Emperor thus reached its height, he
necessarily became less a remote deity and more a democratic
symbol.

In the light of this situation, although the Allied leaders did
not fully realize it then, their decision to permit the Japanese
to retain their Emperor was not only wise but necessary. Any
other course would have spelled irretrievable disaster for the
Occupation and for Japan.

It is understandable that, during the war, there was widespread feeling in Allied countries that the Japanese Emperor
should be overthrown. This sentiment was undoubtedly based
on the misapprehension that the Emperor was actually responsible for Japan's policy of militaristic aggression. Not only
should he therefore be personally punished, but it was assumed
that the institution of the emperorship was the basic cause of
the evils of Japanese life and that therefore only the overthrow
of this key institution with attendant revolutionary turmoil
could enable a new democratic and peaceful Japan to emerge.

Westerners who knew Japan most intimately, however, did
not share this popular notion. They correctly understood the
essential neutralism of the imperial institution and the Emperor's lack of personal responsibility for the political decisions
of the government. They also realized that, however modern
and artificial was the extreme form which the emperor myth
had assumed, it did exercise a powerful influence on the contemporary Japanese, having as it did historical roots imbedded
deep in the national consciousness. Even those Japanese who
did not hold to the orthodox belief nonetheless felt almost invariably a strong attachment to the imperial institution as a
patriotic symbol. Any attack on the Emperor or the imperial
institution by the conquerors, far from facilitating the emergence of a more democratic Japan, would inevitably have
united the Japanese solidly in desperate resistance against the
conquerors and their aims. It would have resulted in a reactionary fanaticism which would have swept away any possibility
of democratic development. As a *New York Times* editorial a
few days before the surrender rather crudely but so aptly

noted, "a discredited god" would be more useful to the Allies than "a martyred god."

The Japanese are not sure who were most influential in shaping the final American decision. They suspect that Joseph C. Grew, the last prewar American ambassador to Japan, and General Douglas MacArthur, together with some of their close aides, were primarily instrumental. But, in any case, despite the skepticism of a large section of the American public and over the opposition of some of the Allied governments, the United States eventually persisted in allowing the Japanese to retain their emperor system, subject to a few necessary modifications.

Very early in the Occupation, General MacArthur took steps to reassure himself that his views concerning the Emperor were correct. After a searching personal conference with the Emperor, he emerged with a warm commendation of the Emperor's integrity, sincerity, and good intentions. Subsequent meetings between the two men apparently increased their mutual respect and appreciation. Immediately after the surrender, a few Japanese had voiced the opinion that the Emperor should abdicate in favor of the crown prince. Although fully cognizant of the Emperor's freedom from political responsibility, they felt that abdication would nevertheless be an appropriate gesture of national contrition. But, to the relief of most Japanese, General MacArthur's attitude caused this view to disappear.

With the immediate fate of the Emperor thus settled, the necessary next step was to develop the latent democratic potentialities of the emperor system so that it would serve the aims of the Occupation and of the now compliant Japanese government. Admittedly these potentialities did not seem very promising. The emotional outburst evoked by the surrender broadcast bore undeniable religious overtones. Even as an expression of public will, the adoption by the people of the Emperor as their popular symbol contained elements of unhealthy charismatic irrationality. These were hardly compatible with a sound democracy. But it was also true that in the attitude of the people there could be discerned some hopeful incipient trends toward a desirable concept of a democratic constitutional monarchy. These had to be carefully nurtured.

The formal renunciation of his divinity by the Emperor, already alluded to, was obviously the first order of the day. Ostensibly initiated by the Emperor himself, it was undoubtedly inspired by the Allied authorities. It seems to have aroused far more interest abroad than in Japan. Some foreign commentators hailed it as a revolutionary transformation of an ancient institution, while others deprecated it as an insincere gesture designed merely to deceive the world. Neither view was correct, for both stemmed from Western notions of divinity which, as earlier explained at length, simply were not relevant to Japanese thinking.

The Japanese had known right along that the Emperor was a mortal man. So what, thought they, was the point in formally announcing the obvious? At the same time, the Japanese know that all human beings are also in a sense divine. No formal proclamation could divest the Emperor of this kind of divinity any more than a formal proclamation could divest any other human being of his own lesser measure of this same kind of divinity. Therefore, although some literal-minded conservatives undoubtedly deplored the proclamation while some literal-minded liberals welcomed it, the vast majority of Japanese remained comparatively indifferent and mildly puzzled. They felt that no fundamental change had taken place; neither did they regard the announcement of change as being insincere. Depending on the context of a given situation, any person could call attention to whichever aspect of his being he pleased.

The formal renunciation of divinity by the Emperor did, however, have some limited degree of usefulness. It practically eliminated the possibility of the emperor myth ever being revived as an instrument of reaction. It facilitated uninhibited public discussion of the constitutional problem of sovereignty. Even if it had done no more than to give emphasis to the human side of the Emperor's nature, by so doing it at least accelerated the process of developing the rational, progressive aspects of the emperorship which could be made to serve democratic ends.

Of more practical importance than the formal disclaimer of divinity or the constitutional provision of popular sovereignty was the campaign to "humanize" the Emperor in the eyes of the people. Again the initiative ostensibly came from the court, but the plan obviously had the approval of the Occupation authorities, if it was not in fact inspired by them. It took the form principally of having the Emperor go on extensive tours of inspection throughout the country and attend concerts, art exhibits, sports events, and other public gatherings so that he could observe at first hand the condition of the people and in turn be seen at close range by them. The Communists promptly denounced the plan as a reactionary plot to strengthen the influence of the imperial institution, but the results were by no means predictable. Although in the main the Emperor emerged with an enhanced personal popularity, the public reactions were not uniform.

Almost everywhere the officials in charge, as in the past, caused the points to be inspected to be specially cleaned and furbished, the frock-coated local dignitaries to recite set speeches of welcome, and the crowds to be drawn up at a respectful distance. Many of the older people bowed in awe and with obvious gratitude at the honor conferred on the locality by the Emperor's visit. But in many places the crowds, showing a spontaneity of conduct unimaginable in earlier years, ignored the official arrangements. They were clearly dominated by curiosity rather than respect; they scrambled for vantage points as they trooped after the Emperor and pressed in close to him. The Emperor, on his part, dutifully clambered over rubble-strewn areas, poked into damaged factories, went down into mine shafts, and asked questions of workers and bystanders picked at random. In acknowledging their replies the Emperor, obviously ill at ease, hardly ever seemed able to respond with anything but a vacuous "Ah, so!" The observing crowds tittered and nicknamed him "Ah-so San," meaning "Mr. Ah-so." While it shocked the more respectful, many individuals took to referring to the Emperor as "Ten-chan," which was like contracting "His Imperial Majesty" to "Impy."

In an ill-fitting suit and a rumpled felt hat instead of in uniform on a white steed, the Emperor cut an unimpressive figure. On one occasion a newspaper photographer caught the matronly Empress reaching over to straighten the Emperor's necktie as the two walked along the street on some tour of inspection, and the next morning the entire nation chuckled over the picture. On another occasion when the Emperor and the Empress visited an art exhibit at a department store, a disorderly swarm of reporters and cameramen pushed the imperial couple into a corner and made them strike pose after pose to the accompaniment of peremptorily shouted directions. Although the most aggressive were the foreign correspondents, Japanese photographers were not far behind, while a crowd of Japanese spectators looked on the rowdy proceedings with no signs of embarrassment. Such disrespectful behavior toward the Emperor would have been unthinkable in the past.

Most revealing was the incident early in the Emperor's tours when he descended into a coal mine in the northern part of the country. A miner suddenly pushed his way past the attendant officials, stuck out his hand, and said he wanted to shake hands with the Emperor. The startled Emperor managed to stammer, "Let's do it the Japanese way; you bow to me and I'll bow to you." The two thereupon bowed to each other. But the miner was obviously dissatisfied and later told newspaper reporters that the Emperor was a poor sport, that he had not yet learned to be the symbol of a democratic nation if he were not willing to shake hands with a representative of the toiling masses. A lively newspaper controversy ensued, some editorials supporting the attitude of the miner, others criticizing him for his presumptuousness and holding that he should be more than satisfied with a bow from the Emperor. That such an incident could take place was a revolutionary change in Japanese attitudes. In the past, not only would the miner's conduct be considered lese majesty, but any debate in the newspapers over the Emperor's behavior would have been a sacrilege and therefore taboo.

The worst indignity took place on the campus of the University of Kyoto, where a crowd of several hundred students stopped the Emperor's automobile and noisily demanded that the Emperor explain the government's rumored plans for rearmament in violation of the new constitution. The fact that these students represented only the relatively small Communist-influenced minority among the 10,000-member student body, or that they chose to ignore the Emperor's lack of connection with the government's political actions, was less significant than the unprecedented fact that the Emperor was held virtually a prisoner for almost half an hour by a shouting, heckling, unfriendly mob until the police could come to his rescue.

The mixed reactions of the public to the humanized Emperor who now walked in their midst were nowhere better reflected than in the tactics of the Communists. At first they denounced the emperor system and called for its overthrow. They had some measure of success in marshaling support for their point of view, as evidenced by such examples as the University of Kyoto incident. But on another occasion, when the Empress happened to drive by a Communist demonstration agitating against the emperor system, the demonstrators quickly lowered their red banners and fell into embarrassed silence until her automobile had passed out of sight. Even the Communists could not free themselves completely from traditional attitudes. Eventually, although they never formally changed their stand, the Communists gave up agitating openly for the abolition of the emperorship; they found that their agitation created more unpopularity for themselves than for the Emperor.

In this process of humanization, the imperial family apparently took to their new role with relish. Although heretofore shielded from the gaze of the multitude, the Emperor had always been reputed to be a shy, gentle person, more at home with his hobby of marine biology than with state ceremonials. Now, as the people frequently saw him at close range, this reputation was confirmed. They saw a slight, stoop-shouldered figure, often with a startled or bewildered look in his thick-bespectacled eyes, embarrassed by the attention he attracted but obviously delighted with the somewhat greater freedom and informality with which he could now move about. The Empress also seemed more like a competent, motherly, family soul than a public social figure. As for the Emperor's brothers, while all of them were quite approachable, the youngest, Prince Mikasa, especially caught the public fancy. Now a history teacher in a women's college, for a while he used to ride the crowded commuter trains, hanging from a strap like everybody else. His enthusiasm for square dancing delights his students as much as his unconventional social and political views discomfit the elders.

The greatest change in the public's image of the imperial

family is typified, however, in the person of the crown prince, who is almost completely a product of the postwar era. While Occupation officials were still hesitating to suggest such a course, the Emperor and the Empress of their own volition asked for an American tutor for the crown prince. How he developed under the wise influence of the remarkable Mrs. Elizabeth Gray Vining and how he eventually went on to the university, where he led an active campus life with ordinary student companions instead of being tutored in seclusion within the palace like his forbears, is by now a well-known story. More recently, how he wooed a commoner whom he met on the tennis court and how he is supposed to have insisted on marrying her over the objections of some of the court officials, has become an international legend. The frenzied squeals of delight with which the Japanese bobby-soxers of today greet the young prince and his bride are a far cry from the awe and trepidation with which the past generation greeted his grandfather. However glamorous royalty may continue to appear to the public eye, with the education and experience which the prince and his contemporary public have by now both received, it is hardly likely that his people will ever regard him— or that he will ever regard himself—as a mysterious presence behind the clouds of a Japanese Olympus.

The conclusion to be drawn from these evidences of the contemporary popular attitude toward the imperial institution is not a simple one. An observer can find almost anything he wishes to find. There are many who still regard the Emperor with almost religious veneration. Not all who flock to the shrines of the former state cult are holiday excursionists; many among the crowd must undoubtedly be true pilgrims. There was no dearth of volunteer groups from small-town women's clubs who considered it a high honor to be allowed to help clean up the war-damaged palace grounds and who were quite overcome with joy if the Emperor so much as gave them a word or two of greeting as he strolled by. Even among those who have no firm devotion to the emperor system, there are many who feel vaguely uncomfortable over the growing freedom and informality toward the Emperor and suspect that the new trend is somehow improper.

On the other hand, an observer can find plenty of evidences of the opposite attitude. Much discussion, some serious but some quite irreverent, goes on concerning the pros and cons of the emperor system. The debate is now hardly ever over the truth or falsity of the imperial myth; most articulate expressions now take it for granted that the myth is just a myth. The argument is simply whether or not the imperial institution under modern conditions continues to have a political utility which renders it worthy of being cherished. Although the weight of the argument generally seems to favor those who would honor the imperial institution, it is significant that the arguments are now couched in rational terms. Although some mystic devotees of the emperor cult undoubtedly continue to exist and may yet in certain circumstances find opportunity for a militant resurgence, they have at present been reduced to nurturing their belief virtually in silence while the rationalists and the skeptics dominate the arguments. Even magazines most favorable to the imperial cause now seek to exploit the human interest angle in their portrayal of the imperial family in order to cater to the mass demand for vicarious glamor and romance. Treatment of the imperial personage with awe and veneration no longer carries a popular appeal. To a Westerner, particularly to one from a republican country, respect toward the imperial institution may still seem to be a prominent Japanese attitude; but to one who has known Japan in earlier times, the casualness and freedom with which traditionally taboo subjects are now bandied about appear in startling contrast to the past.

As might be expected, it is among the more elderly, among the peasants, and among the petty bourgeoisie—the bulwarks of conventional respectability in any nation—that the traditional attitudes are still found most prominently. It is conspicuously, but not exclusively, among the younger elements of the population, among the urban workers and "white collar class," and among the intellectuals that the newer attitude is found. In Japan's population, the young far outnumber the old, the urban industrial and commercial elements outnumber the rural elements, and universal literacy makes for a widespread and vigorous—though not necessarily wise—intellectual activity.

The continued presence of traditional elements in the population undoubtedly has a retarding effect, but there can be little question as to the direction of the prevailing trend.

At the same time, the lingering influence of the imperial tradition helps to provide a valuable sense of continuity, legitimacy, and stability in Japan's democratic development. Without this stabilizing factor chaos might have ensued in the upsetting period following the surrender and have given rise to the extremism of a mass authoritarianism more dangerous than the extremism of the old emperorism. As it is, the attitude of the Japanese people is by peaceful evolution steadily moving in the direction of the attitude which prevails among the peoples of the constitutional monarchical democracies of Europe. This process of evolution might be even more natural and assured were it not for the constitutional anomalies concerning the "national polity" and the status of the Emperor discussed at length in the preceding chapter. These anomalies might yet invite extensive amendment of the constitution. Such amendment might restore the status of the Emperor to a sounder historical position and thereby assure a sounder democratic growth in the long run, but again the amendment could take a reactionary turn. In any case, it might interrupt and confuse, at least temporarily, the present trend in the popular attitude toward the Emperor. But theoretical and constitutional questions interest only the sophisticated minority; unless deliberately blown up into a political issue such matters have little chance of stirring the masses. There is therefore at least good likelihood that the present popular trend will continue to mold the Japanese Emperor into a true symbol of a democratic nation.

CHAPTER VI

Political Reorganization

The democratization of the Japanese government obviously involves much more than the new constitution and the new popular attitude toward the Emperor. More significant are how the political system decreed by the new constitution is being implemented and in what manner the formal institutions have been working out in practice.

A vital key to the operation of any political system is of course the nature of the leadership. Recognizing this fact, as soon as the Occupation had fairly got under way and long before any definite move had been made toward a new constitution, SCAP ordered "the purge." SCAP was apparently determined that the new Japanese regime, whatever constitutional or legal bases it was to have, should not be prejudiced by the baleful influence of the persons who had been responsible for the previous regime. The purge was intended to bar these undesirable individuals from public office so that a new group of leaders could come to the fore.

Like almost all Occupation activities, the purge was ostensibly carried out by the Japanese government, although in reality it was closely directed by SCAP officials. "Public office" from which undesirable persons were to be excluded was very broadly defined to include not only all government employment at any level and all elective offices in any public organization but also all teaching and administrative positions in both public and private educational institutions and the higher editorial and executive positions in newspapers, magazines,

91

and other media of mass communication. One year later the definition was further broadened to include executive positions in some two hundred or so designated business corporations.

Certain categories of persons were automatically debarred from these "public offices." Such categories included all former commissioned officers of the regular army, navy, and volunteer reserves; all former members, whether commissioned, non-commissioned, or civilian, of any military police or naval police or secret intelligence organizations; those who had held important official posts in occupied territories; former officers of business organizations that had been involved in overseas exploitation; and former officers of certain designated "undesirable" organizations. In addition to these automatic purgees, any individual who had played a prominent part in "the Japanese program of aggression or who by speech, writing or action has shown himself to be an active exponent of militant nationalism and aggression" was subject to the purge. In practice, the latter individuals, although handled with somewhat more flexibility, were designated much like the automatic purgees on the basis primarily of the kind of posts they had held in the government or in public or political organizations.

Literally millions of people were required to fill out book-sized questionnaires probing into minute details of their life history—these questions, incidentally, had to be answered in English, creating a frantic run on the inadequate available supply of English translators and typists. On the basis of the questionnaires, which were screened by Japanese government committees closely supervised by SCAP officials, approximately 220,000 persons were purged, of whom about 180,000 were former military officers. Virtually no appeals were allowed for many years, and then, for a while, only a slowly growing trickle. But with the approach of the peace treaty, a sudden mass "depurge" was permitted in 1951.

While the purge was on, it stirred lively discussion among both the Japanese and the Occupation people. Some held that the purging of only 220,000 individuals was too mild a measure to have any appreciable effect on the democratization of the country. Others held that this number, including as it did a large proportion of the most capable leaders of the country, was enough to endanger the necessary task of reconstruction. Some argued that in a dictatorial regime like that of pre-surrender Japan, only fifty or a hundred men had any real responsibility for policy and that all the others in even seemingly important posts were not much more than technicians who had no choice but to go along with the established policy. The latter might have been readily won over to support the new regime, whereas instead the purge unnecessarily alienated and embittered these potentially valuable people. Even more argument raged over the inflexible character of the predominantly automatic purge. Many rascals were said to have escaped because they happened not to have held positions that fell within the designated categories, while on the other hand many fine individuals were caught in the purge on mere technicality. There were not a few individuals, fundamentally liberal and unsympathetic toward the wartime policy, who had deliberately stayed at their official posts in the belief that they could more usefully help to moderate the government's actions from within than by attacking the government from without. The automatic purge made no distinction between such persons and the others.

SCAP's attitude was revealed in the case of the unsuccessful appeal carried to General MacArthur by some American missionaries on behalf of a retired admiral who had long been president of a Methodist university. Even though this Christian educator had resigned from the navy before the war out of lack of sympathy for the official military policy, as a former career officer he was ordered ousted from his position. General MacArthur is reported to have explained that, while there undoubtedly were many cases of obvious injustice like this one, individual exceptions to general rules could not be allowed without danger of causing the whole program to bog down—that in removing gangrenous infection it is often impossible to avoid cutting away some good flesh along with the bad.

This rigidly impersonal policy was not, however, always manifest. Just before the general election of 1947, the government in power suddenly purged two prominent Opposition candidates, only to clear them on grounds of insufficient evidence soon after the election from which they had thus been effectively removed. The case of Finance Minister Tanzan Ishibashi, who eventually became prime minister some time after Japan's recovery of independence, also looked suspicious. Ishibashi admittedly had written two or three articles praising some aspects of fascism soon after a visit to Italy, but as editor of a liberal economics journal he had consistently opposed the authoritarian and imperialistic policies of the militarists. No question was raised of his fitness for office when he became finance minister, but later when he began making disdainful remarks about the professional competence of the Occupation's economic planners, SCAP suddenly ordered that he be purged. SCAP officials maintained that he was purged for his articles on Italian fascism and not for his views on postwar economic policies for Japan, but the Japanese public remained highly skeptical, while even some American correspondents circulated petitions and agitated on his behalf. Much later, after the start of the Korean war, SCAP also reinterpreted the purge regulations in such a way as to apply them to Communists, virtually driving the Japanese Communist movement underground for a while. Drastic action against the Communists at that time was no doubt justified, but the use of the purge in this context certainly was not in accord with its original purpose.

In fact, many Japanese believed that the purge was not used in a perfectly objective manner in accordance with fixed criteria but that it was applied by SCAP officials in accord with the varying considerations of the moment and even in accord with varying personal predilections. Thus, it was widely believed that within SCAP itself there was sharp disagreement with regard to the application of the purge between the Government Section, which was interested primarily in internal reform, and the Civil Intelligence Section, which was more concerned with Japan's potential role in the Cold War. Indeed, although it was always officially denied, it was a well substantiated open secret that a running feud extending over a wide range of activities existed between the two generals who respectively headed these two SCAP sections. Some Japanese were caught in the cross fire between the two sections, while others tried to play one against the other to their own advantage.

Despite some injustice and irregularities, however, in relation to the tremendous scope and complexity of the operation,
the purge was conducted with about as little abuse as could
practicably be expected. It seems to have worked out better
than the "de-Nazification" procedure in Germany, where the
semiautomatic purge soon gave way to judicial judgments that
carried sentences of stiff fines and other punishments. Whereas
the court trials in Germany apparently afforded opportunity
for much inconclusive wrangling over questionable testimony
inspired by political bias or personal spite, the virtually automatic administrative character of the Japanese purge allowed
the intrusion of a minimum of petty politics or subjective influences. Unlike the war crimes trials, it carried practically no
punitive connotations; it was primarily a constructive political
measure to facilitate the emergence of fresh national leadership.

Despite cynicism in some quarters, the purge seems to have
successfully served its purpose. No doubt some of the purgees
tried to continue exercising their influence from behind the
scenes, but working through puppets could not be as effective
as working directly in the open. As the handicaps of the purgees became increasingly evident, the erstwhile puppets tended
to follow their own natural ambitions, until most of the purgees
soon found themselves left behind in the backwash of rapid
new developments. How effective the purge really was can be
judged from the atrophied vitality revealed by the depurgees
after the rescinding of their legal disabilities. Despite the
notable comeback staged by some individuals, the proportion
of those who have succeeded in returning to positions of prominence is relatively small. Most of those who were important
enough to have been purged—other than junior military officers
—were comparatively old men. Six years or more of enforced
inactivity apparently left them so far behind events as to
render them incapable at their age of catching up and competing with the vigorous new generation.

The leaders of the reactionary ultranationalistic movements
have shown the least signs of revival. In their case, however,
the purge was among the least important of the reasons for their
disappearance. They had been so completely discredited by

the catastrophic collapse of their schemes that the Japanese public gladly dropped them into oblivion. With no crisis in sight of a kind that would offer a fertile field for their kind of activity, they have shown only the slightest stirrings of resuscitation. The purgees who used to hold executive positions in government or in private corporations have also recovered only slightly. In their case, apparently, technological and administrative changes during their enforced absence have been too great to allow them to catch up, and there have been too many capable successors who have already firmly established themselves.

The greatest success in returning to active public life has been experienced by the purged party politicians. Apparently political techniques have not changed so much as to make six years away from the hustings an insuperable handicap. The seasoned experience of the veteran political tactician evidently still counts for enough to make him a respectable rival of the less experienced postwar politician. The average depurged politician, moreover, fits better into the postwar environment than the average depurged administrator or soldier, because such a politician represented about the most liberal element in the active public life of the prewar era. Although now considered quite conservative by contemporary standards, he is not so different from postwar politicians as to be altogether an anachronism in postwar society. Even then, however, the success of the ex-purgee politician has not been overwhelming. In the first general election following the mass depurge, about one-third of the successful candidates were ex-purgees, and these comprised about one-third of all the ex-purgees who sought office. In subsequent elections the ratio of successful ex-purgee candidates has been steadily falling. And while these ex-purgees have been the moving spirits of the "reverse course" which seeks to correct the supposed excesses of the Occupation, and although a few of them have attained very high office, they have made no more than limited headway against the resistance of the new generation of politicians who have come to have a vested interest in the new order. The ex-purgees are furthermore a dwindling generation; despite their brief season of revival they are already moving inevitably toward extinction.

These results indicate, therefore, that despite its relatively brief duration and other inadequacies, the purge performed its intended purpose. By removing from the scene many of the older undesirable leaders during the first critical formative years of the new regime, it enabled a new generation of leaders at least to gain a foothold. With such a foothold, the new leaders have for the most part been able to resist being displaced by the returning purgees. Although the purge could not of course insure the good quality of the new leaders, nevertheless by eliminating most of the undesirable old leaders it made what must be considered an essential contribution to the process of democratization.

As the purge helped to eliminate undesirable leaders, so the new constitutional guarantee of civil rights helped to eliminate undesirable practices. The "bill of rights" of the Meiji Constitution, while quite enlightened in relation to the time and circumstances of its origin, was nevertheless basically defective in its inability to hold the government to liberal practices. As has previously been intimated, while the enumerated personal liberties could not arbitrarily be flouted, as a grant from the sovereign authority they were specifically conditional on their being exercised within limits not prejudicial to public order. This condition provided a loophole through which these liberties might in effect be nullified at times under the guise of seeming legality.

As also previously mentioned, the "bill of rights" of the new constitution corrects this fundamental defect by proclaiming basic civil rights and individual liberties as inalienable natural human rights which may not be infringed upon under any circumstance. In addition to all the standard civil rights familiar to the constitutions of the older democratic nations of the West, it also includes many provisions of a social and cultural nature which seem to imply a commitment to the concept of the welfare state. It proceeds to spell out the particulars in thirty-one articles comprising the longest section of the constitution. Thus there are included such unusual provisions as the guarantee, not only of free compulsory and equal education, but also of academic freedom; of the right to "maintain the minimum standards of wholesome and cultural living"; and of the right of workers to organize and to bargain collectively. It provides of course for universal suffrage and secret ballot, bans censorship, prohibits the state from religious activity, and guarantees that there shall be no discrimination in political, economic, or social relations because of race, creed, sex, social status, or family origin. There is a particularly detailed group of provisions affording protection to the individual in case of arrest, including the principle of habeas corpus.

These provisions are not very logically or succinctly stated; and they are often wordy and repetitive. There is much that sounds strange to Japanese ears, being a close paraphrasing, or even outright reproduction, of portions of the United States Constitution and of the constitutions of several American states. But all imaginable contingencies are provided for in considerable detail. Insofar as the letter of the law can do so, this constitution provides for the strictest and most extensive protection of democratic rights that anyone could wish for.

Far more important than the letter of the law, of course, is its implementation. In this regard the Japanese record has been much better than might have been expected. The masses of the people have obviously no real comprehension of the change from conditional privileges to inalienable natural rights. No inspired thinker has as yet worked out a completely satisfactory reconciliation of the doctrine of natural rights with traditional Japanese thought. But, as in all matters, the ideological rationalization will no doubt appear in due time once the practice has come to be sufficiently desired. From this point of view, the prospects are encouraging. Not only had the intellectuals been interested in the theory of natural rights off and on over a long period of time, but from the standpoints of both ethics and of practical political consequences they had been disturbed over the violation of civil liberties. Therefore, although the new doctrine was merely thrust upon them without effort on their part, it was eminently welcome to them, and they soon proceeded to give it much prominence in their writings and discussions. Although without much comprehension, apparently in reaction to the oppressiveness of the wartime regime, the masses responded surprisingly favorably to the prominent attention given to this matter by the writers, so that the term "human rights," though occasionally misinterpreted, is now a popular shibboleth. A practical understanding of these rights on the part of the Japanese was greatly furthered by the prolonged visit early in the Occupation of Roger N. Baldwin, then director of the American Civil Liberties Union. With marked success he channeled the interest of the Japanese intellectuals, and particularly of practicing lawyers, into the work of the Japanese Civil Liberties Union, which under his inspiration came to have notable influence.

There continue to be, of course, many elements in Japanese society that have no interest or sympathy with these civil rights. Some law enforcement officers, long accustomed to high-handed methods, either tried to continue surreptitiously with their old ways or else became so overcautious as to be ineffective. But thanks to the vigilance of the portion of the public whose interest has been awakened, spurred by the efforts of the Civil Liberties Union, the various bar associations, the press, and other enlightened groups, flagrant violations of civil rights seldom escape attention. Although active concern is undoubtedly still confined to a minority aided by the now unequivocal constitutional provisions, this minority can generally succeed in bringing enough clamorous public pressure to bear so that abuses by officials have become comparatively rare.

Among the personal liberties now conspicuously respected, the most notable is the right of free speech. During the Occupation, there were inevitably subtle restraints as well as the outright censorship imposed by the American military authorities. But since the end of the Occupation, freedom of speech has been exercised almost with abandon. Noting the social pressures toward conformity of thought and attitudes in the United States, many Japanese visitors insist that there is now much greater freedom of thought and of speech in Japan than in America. This observation may be a questionable one, inasmuch as the freedom in these regards in Japan stems far less from principle than from a temporary set of circumstances. It is the reaction to an unpleasant past, the discrediting of old beliefs, the abandonment of outworn standards, the breakdown of traditional controls, and the resulting confusion and disagreements about the future that are primarily responsible for the vigorous and even violent interplay of ideas now prevalent in Japan, rather than any positive devotion to the principle of free speech. But it is a fact that one encounters more diverse opinions expressed with less restraint in Japan today than in other parts of the world where public opinion is more stabilized. Once this present practice of free expression in Japan becomes established as a permanent habit independent of the social circumstances of the moment—and becomes more self-disciplined and maturely reflective as well—true freedom of speech essential to democracy will have prevailed. In the meantime, the present phenomenon represents a highly promising, if a somewhat trying, preparatory stage.

The protection of democratic rights and liberties was further strengthened by the introduction into the constitution of the characteristically American doctrine of judicial review. From a theoretical point of view it poses some problems, for by conferring on the courts the power to rule on the constitutionality of "any law, order, regulation or official act," it tends to establish the supremacy of the judiciary. It may be logical for the American form of government with its separation of powers, but it is somewhat difficult to reconcile with the principle of parliamentary supremacy which is stipulated for Japan in the constitutional provision that the Diet is "the highest organ of state power." In the British prototype of parliamentary government judicial review significantly does not exist, and the highest judicial power in the land is vested in the House of Lords. But judicial review is not altogether incompatible with parliamentary government, as its recent spread at least in limited form into several European parliamentary governments indicates. Although the Japanese courts, lacking a tradition of judicial review, still tend to be somewhat timid in exercising this power, their growing experience points to the possibility of its increasing importance. While it is by no means essential to democracy, as the example of Great Britain and other democratic parliamentary nations shows, judicial review nevertheless constitutes a useful safeguard for democracy in helping to uphold the sanctity of the constitution against arbitrary executive action or against demagogic legislative abuse.

The internal reform of the judiciary, instituted by the Occupation, also strengthened the democratic role of the courts. The

Japanese judicial system had been closely modeled after that of France, but incorporated some traditional Japanese legal concepts along with the materials adapted from the Code Napoléon. The reforms instituted by the Occupation made only minor changes in the structure of the courts, leaving them with much the form of the original French model. But with respect to underlying doctrines and practices, the Occupation introduced considerable modifications so that to the older Franco-Japanese synthesis there were now added some notable Anglo-American elements.

Thus, except for some changes in nomenclature, the court system continues to be much the same as before, consisting of 570 Summary Courts (formerly Local Courts), which are courts of first instance for petty cases; 49 District Courts, which are courts of first instance for important cases and are also the lowest of the appellate courts; 8 High Courts (formerly Courts of Appeal), which are the principal appellate courts; and the Supreme Court. As in the past, each of these courts, except the Summary Court presided over by a single judge, has a collegiate bench, with three judges sitting on each case in the District Court, three to five in the High Court, and five in each of the three sections of the Supreme Court except in cases involving interpretation of the constitution, which require all fifteen justices to sit together as a single court. Except for members of the Supreme Court, who are appointed by the Cabinet for life, subject to a referendum every ten years, all the judges are appointed for renewable ten-year terms on nomination by the Supreme Court on the basis of competitive examinations and previous record. Although the nominating role of the Supreme Court is new, this method of selection through examination and experience does not differ very greatly in effect from the method previously in use. In addition, there are special courts with more informal procedures and more flexibly selected personnel, like the Juvenile Courts and the Courts of Domestic Relations, whose numbers have now been increased but whose beginnings go back to the pre-Occupation period.

More important was the separation of the courts from the administrative jurisdiction of the Ministry of Justice. The Supreme Court has now been vested with the responsibility for supervising the inferior courts and of drawing up the rules of procedure for all courts. The integrity of the Japanese judiciary had always been quite high; whatever questions there might have been concerning the conduct of the judges had stemmed from their generally narrow and inflexible outlook rather than from any subservience to executive control. But all possibility of questionable ties with the political branches of the government has now been removed by the establishment of the full independence of the judiciary as a constitutional principle.

Even more significant have been the changes in the operating procedures of the courts. These formerly had conformed quite closely to the French practice, in which the presiding judge steers the conduct of the trial through his questioning of both parties. Inasmuch as both the judges and the prosecutors were members of the same judicial service, even without intentional collusion the judges tended to have more understanding of the prosecution's side of the case than the defendant's. This tendency was aggravated by the practice of admitting as evidence materials secured by the judge in preliminary hearings closed to the public and attended by the prosecutor but not by the defendant's counsel. The new procedures abolish such preliminary hearings and, in other ways as well, place the prosecution and the defense on exactly equal terms. Furthermore, although the judges continue to take an active role in the questioning, counsel for both sides now participates to a great extent in the shaping of the proceedings through examination and cross-examination of witnesses.

One change which Americans generally seem to regard as of dubious merit has been the abolition of the jury system. The experiment which was started in the 1920's of permitting the defendant, under most conditions, to choose whether or not to be tried by jury has been dropped. Most defendants who had faith in their own case preferred to trust the judgment of a bench of three to five trained judges than the judgment of twelve laymen picked at random. If a defendant asked for a jury trial, it was almost like confessing that his case had so little merit that he preferred to gamble on swaying inexperienced amateurs than to try to convince professional judges. Even in England and France the shortcomings of the jury system under modern conditions have led to limitations in the role of juries which Americans have not accepted for themselves. For the Japanese, with no historical traditions of the jury system save for the limited experiment of the 1920's, its abandonment was a matter of no great interest or significance.

Another change was the abolition of the Court of Administrative Litigation, which was technically an agency of the administrative rather than of the judicial branch of the government. Now, in accordance with Anglo-Saxon practice, disputes between different agencies of the government or between the government and private individuals are handled in the ordinary courts so that the government in its litigations stands before the law in exactly the same status as private citizens. The experience of many Continental European countries where governmental litigations are handled in special administrative courts shows that in practice the private citizen does not suffer from this arrangement and in fact may benefit greatly from the simpler and more expeditious procedure which this arrangement makes possible. The adoption of the Anglo-Saxon practice has, however, removed any suspicions which might be raised over the theoretical special privilege the government might enjoy through the exercise of essentially judicial functions by an administrative agency.

A political change upon which the Occupation apparently placed much hope for the strengthening of democracy was the extension of local autonomy. In principle Japan continues to be a unitary state in which all governmental authority resides in the national government, and local governmental units exercise only such powers as have specifically been delegated to them by the national government. But through new constitutional and statutory provisions, considerable changes have been instituted in practice. The Ministry of Home Affairs, which used to exercise jurisdiction over local government, was abolished and most of its functions dispersed among the local governmental units in a move to give them greater autonomy. The residual functions of the former Home Ministry have been placed under the much less important Local Autonomy Board.

Governors of prefectures as well as subordinate prefectural officials are no longer members of the national civil service assigned to their posts by the Home Ministry. Instead, the prefectural governors are now elected locally, while the lesser administrative officers belong to independent prefectural civil services. The popularly elected prefectural assemblies can no longer be overridden by the governors, who are instead responsible to the assemblies. The range of functions delegated to prefectural governments has been greatly expanded. Less change has been necessary in the case of municipalities—comprising city, town, and village governments—for they had always enjoyed somewhat more autonomy than prefectures; but here also the former indirect election of mayors and other executive officials by the popularly elected municipal assemblies has been replaced by direct election of these officers by popular vote. Referendum, initiative, and recall have also been provided for at both the municipal and prefectural levels.

These changes were based on the popular American theory, advocated by the Occupation officials, that the federal system of government is more desirable than centralized government, and that where federalism does not exist there should at least be as much local autonomy as possible, on the assumption that democracy thrives best at the grass-roots level. In a small country like Japan where regional diversity is not as great as in larger countries, however, federalism may not be at all desirable. It is true that too strong a centralized government carries the danger of national regimentation and totalitarian controls, but it is also true that a unitary system of government does not preclude the possibility of democracy. The prewar system of local government in Japan was, like the judicial system, almost identical with that of France, and France was hardly the archetype of political regimentation and discipline. On the other hand imperial Germany and Communist Russia, as well as the United States, are examples of the federal form of government.

Thus the Occupation's great concern with extending local autonomy in Japan was not altogether relevant to the goal of democratization. In fact, in contrast to American experience, under Japanese conditions centralized government more often than not provides greater opportunity for democratic practices than does local autonomy. Smaller communities are apt to be more backward and less accessible to the progressive influences that play upon the more modernized urban centers. Closer personal contacts in the smaller communities tend to enable a few personages of importance to bind their followers in a web of traditional social obligations, while in the larger cities the greater impersonality and anonymity of social relations permit a greater emancipation of individual will and behavior. Historically, the countryside has been the stronghold of conservatism, while the cities have been the centers for the dissemination of liberalism and progressivism. Under a system of centralized government, the more capable and active population of the metropolitan centers tended to exert more than their proportionate share of influence on the shaping of national policy, which the more backward areas were then forced to follow to their own edification. Under a system of local autonomy, however, although a few metropolitan centers might become more democratic than ever, the rest of the country would be perfectly free to continue with their old ways. By lessening national pressure for progress, local autonomy has enabled boss rule to become more unrestrained in many communities.

Probably the most serious problem of local governments, however, has been their financial weakness. In the past, because of the greater range and importance of its functions, the national government pre-empted the most productive sources of tax revenues. Now, in view of the expanded functions of local governments, some revision has been made in the tax structure; but the revision has not been sufficient, with the result that local governments are constantly bedeviled by operating deficits. This situation has been accentuated by the fact that in addition to their proper local functions the prefectural governments have been saddled with the local enforcement of many national measures. The latter responsibility is not an altogether unmitigated disadvantage to the prefectural governments, for it gives them greater authority than would be the case were the various ministries of the national government to maintain their own operating offices in each region. But it adds to the financial difficulties of the prefectural governments, forcing them to depend on substantial subventions and grants-in-aid from the national government. These enable the national government to exert an indirect influence over prefectural governments, a fact which tends to counterbalance the autonomy which the latter had gained.

Moreover, because the old system did not provide opportunity for strong local leadership to develop, many individuals who had formerly held appointments from the national government to prefectural posts found it easy in the beginning to win election to similar posts under the new system. It was feared that these men would perpetuate the undue influence of the national government. This fear proved to be unwarranted, however, for even former bureaucrats began to act like typical local politicians as they learned soon enough that they had to cater to popular local opinion in order to be re-elected. They soon became indistinguishable from the new purely local leadership which quickly emerged under the new conditions.

Another problem of prefectural government lies in the number and smallness of these units. Even when prefectures used to be essentially not much more than administrative subdivisions of the national government, they suffered from the fact that their territories seldom comprised a natural geographic or economic unit. In fact their boundaries had originally been intentionally drawn to break up the solidarity of the feudal states of the earlier regime. The prefectures not only were thus purely artificial units, but the development of modern transportation and communications had quickly rendered them too small for the most efficient operation. Their consolidation and reorganization had long been discussed. During the war the prefectures had actually been grouped into nine large regional administrative units, but these had been abolished immediately after the surrender because they had been too closely geared to plans for last-ditch military defense against invasion. But the fact remains that for a country the size of Japan about nine or a dozen regional units would be far more logical than the forty-six prefectures that now exist.[1] The autonomy and the

[1] Exceptions to the prefectural pattern are the metropolitan district of Tokyo, which does not lie within any prefecture but has a legal status comparable to that of a prefecture rather than a municipality; and the large island of Hokkaido in the north, which has a governmental organization resembling that of a prefecture but embracing the entire island, which comprises a natural geographic and economic region.

expansion of prefectural functions now make it more desirable than ever that the prefectures be strengthened. At the same time, increased popular participation in prefectural government affairs is creating in the public something of a vested interest in the structure as it now stands. Although the average Japanese feels toward his prefecture nothing like the pride and loyalty the average American feels toward his state, nevertheless the sense of personal identification with the existing prefectures which comes from growing democratic participation in their affairs makes it all the more politically impracticable to attempt the drastic consolidation and restructuring which logically are so needed.

On balance it can probably be said that local autonomy is proving to be more of a success than otherwise. It did not result automatically in the invigoration of a grass-roots democracy as the Occupation had apparently hoped for, and in some respects it even served to hamper the process of democratization. On the other hand, despite some serious defects and abuses, local autonomy has increased the opportunities for popular participation in government, and there can be little doubt that its long-range effects will be to bring responsibility for good government closer home to the people. A growing general appreciation of the long-run implications of local autonomy is indicated by the fact that while the conservatives are making strenuous efforts to restore some features of the old system—such as the national appointment of prefectural governors—popular support for local autonomy has already become so firmly established as to be generally successful in withstanding these assaults.

Closely related to the matter of local autonomy was the reform of the police system. Previously the police had been nationally organized under the control of the Ministry of Home Affairs, and prefectural governors had been responsible for the supervision of the police forces assigned to their jurisdiction, while smaller units had been detailed to each locality to work with the municipal authorities. The reform instituted by the Occupation abolished the national police organization and provided that each municipality with a population of more than five thousand must maintain its own independent police force, controlled by a public safety commission composed of lay citizens elected by popular vote. A small national rural police establishment was permitted to operate only in rural areas too thinly populated to maintain their own local police force. It was also charged with a few co-ordinating functions of a national character, and in time of grave emergency it might be assigned the responsibility for directing the combined operations of several co-operating police forces.

These changes, quite revolutionary for Japan, were based on the correct assumption that the old system of a national police divorced from popular local controls had been too easily used as an instrument of authoritarian oppression. Unfortunately, although the theory underlying the changes was sound enough, in practice the consequences left much to be desired. Many of the smaller towns found themselves financially unable to support an adequate police force. Decentralization also added to the burden of administrative paper work placed upon the police at the local level. Morale suffered from the fact that, except in the largest cities, the local police forces were too small to offer ambitious policemen much opportunity for advancement, whereas the national police organization had provided ample scope for an attractive career. With the opportunity for boss rule which the extension of local autonomy presented, the public safety commissions of some towns were soon packed with hirelings of special interests. In the minds of many people, it was a question whether a police tied to local racketeers was preferable to a police controlled from a distance by dictatorial but incorruptible bureaucrats.

Most serious of all, the reorganization of the police happened to come at the time when the Communists were engaging in a systematic campaign of riotous demonstrations. Operating under centralized control, the Communists timed and co-ordinated their nationwide activities with baffling flexibility, while the police, forced under the new system to arrange co-operation among many independent local forces through a cumbersome and unseasoned liaison machinery, were never able to take effective countermeasures in time. From the outset the police lost their own self-confidence as well as the confidence of the public. Even in the United States the public generally has more respect for the FBI or the state highway patrol than for the bumbling village constable. This attitude was magnified many times over under the conditions prevailing in postwar Japan. Because its aim was essentially sound, however, the experiment with police reform would undoubtedly have fared much better had the independent local police forces been confined perhaps to municipalities with populations of more than fifty thousand instead of five thousand, had the national rural police been somewhat more powerful, and had the new system enjoyed a chance to gain a little more experience before the Communists launched their offensive. As it was, the police reform became a conspicuous casualty of the "reverse course" of the post-Occupation era.

The new police reorganization measure passed by the Diet after a bitter struggle in 1954 has now replaced the independent municipal police forces with a prefectural police force in each prefecture, co-ordinated by the national police. The public safety commissions have lost their administrative control to appointed officials and are limited to an advisory capacity. These recent changes may be a disappointing retrogression, but the existence now of forty-nine separate police organizations under the jurisdiction of reasonably democratic self-governing units, instead of the one monolithic police organization under autocratic control that existed before the Occupation, would seem to indicate that there has been no really alarming return to anything like a police state. The fact that even these comparatively moderate revisions were resisted so bitterly and so nearly successfully makes it most unlikely that, barring an almost inconceivable contingency, there can ever be a complete return to the old system of a single nationally controlled police.

Not only with respect to the police but likewise with respect to practically all the reforms occasioned by the Occupation, it is most unlikely that a complete reversion to the past will ever be possible. General MacArthur stated that the Japanese people, once having tasted of even such democracy as the Occupation was able to impart during its brief duration, would never willingly go back to the past. This statement may have been a bit too categorical and optimistic. But, while some special interests find it unwelcome, democracy is attractive to most of the people who experience it, and the practice of democracy creates a body of supporters whose interests become bound up in its preservation. The reaction of the Japanese to the Occupation reforms, while hardly enthusiastic in every respect, has turned out to be sufficiently favorable to enable the essential features of the reforms to attain what appears to be permanent acceptance.

CHAPTER VII

The Location of
Political Power

In the process of Japan's democratization, no aspect is so important as the founding of political power on the will of the people. The purge, the bill of rights, the courts, and all the rest had vital contributions to make in providing favorable conditions, but the essence of political democracy lies in the exercise of ultimate power by the people. To this matter of ultimate power we must now turn our attention.

A significant indication of the undemocratic character of Japanese government in the past had been the relative weakness of the elected representatives of the people. The executive had always been more powerful than the legislative branch of the government. This was a situation to which the Occupation naturally gave great concern. In attempting to remedy the situation, instead of introducing the American system of checks and balances, it went so far as to sponsor the doctrine of legislative supremacy. This was one of the few occasions in which the Occupation recognized that the American model was not appropriate to the Japanese background and made allowance for the inclination which the Japanese parliamentary system had previously shown—particularly in the 1920's—to evolve in the direction of the British example.

Thus the Occupation-inspired new constitution declared the popularly elected Diet to be the "highest organ of state power." The multiple components of the executive like the

Privy Council and the Supreme Command, which had been particularly immune to popular control, were abolished so as to leave only the Cabinet; and the Cabinet was made completely responsible to the Diet. The Diet accordingly not only designates the prime minister from among its own members, but the majority of the other members of the Cabinet must also be selected from the Diet. Not only does the Diet have the power of the purse, but by voting non-confidence the Diet can force the Cabinet either to resign or to refer the issue to the general electorate by means of a dissolution of the House of Representatives, which immediately brings on a general election.

These drastic constitutional changes legally subordinating the Cabinet to the Diet, however, did not in practice automatically elevate the Diet to a position of undisputed supremacy. Although the Diet started immediately to make use of some of its new powers, it was not until very recently—several years after the Occupation was over—that it began to show signs of assuming fully all the powers it was meant to have. Its exercise of the actual powers commensurate with its constitutional authority was retarded by historical influences which took time to overcome.

One of these retarding forces was the Cabinet, which continued for some time, despite the new constitution, to be more important than the Diet. This situation should occasion no surprise, for even under the Meiji Constitution much of the superiority of the executive had rested less on constitutional provisions than on the inferior capabilities of the legislators which had prevented them from utilizing fully even such power as they might have constitutionally asserted. This handicap was one which the legislators were not able to outgrow overnight. Not only did the Cabinet profit from its traditional prestige, but the disparity in actual abilities also persisted. The Diet, containing many mediocre men and preoccupied with partisan politics, was often undignified and uninspiring. The Cabinet, although itself not nonpartisan, was a select body whose responsibilities forced it to consider broader national interests. Moreover, while postwar Cabinets generally included fewer men of bureaucratic background than prewar Cabinets, the Cabinet still commanded the services of the civil service bureaucracy. The technical competence of this bureaucracy enabled the Cabinet to continue to hold an advantage over the Diet despite the change in their constitutional relationship, although this advantage is now beginning to disappear.

On the other hand, the Cabinet should not be thought of solely in contradistinction to the Diet. Unlike the American government, in parliamentary governments like the Japanese there is—to use the British expression—a fusion of powers instead of a separation of powers. The Cabinet, composed mostly of members of the Diet and responsible to the Diet, is in a sense the executive committee of the Diet. It therefore has, in addition to its purely executive functions, the legislative function of initiating and preparing the legislative program of the Diet. The fact that most legislative bills are government bills originating in the Cabinet and sponsored by the Cabinet does not constitute a subversion of the Diet's function but merely accords with the way parliamentary governments are meant to function. Nevertheless, the Cabinet's legitimate function of steering these bills through the Diet did have the perhaps undesirable incidental effect of perpetuating a pattern of Cabinet leadership in the Diet. This leadership pattern was strengthened by the fact that Cabinet members were almost invariably important party leaders to start with. Although the initial authority of the Cabinet stems from the Diet, the Diet may have been disposed until very recently to follow Cabinet leadership more than was really healthy.

The inclination of the Diet to relinquish initiative to the Cabinet, did not mean, however, that the Cabinet itself was essentially strong or that the prime minister exercised great power. The powers of the Cabinet and the prime minister tended to be unstable, leaving the real power in government to be manifested through less institutionalized channels. This situation turned out to be potentially conducive to the eventual assertion by the Diet of its rightful legal powers. The inadequacy of the Cabinet and the prime minister requires some explanation.

It is true that the prime minister enjoys quite impressive formal powers. He alone among the members of the Cabinet is formally designated by the Diet. He not only appoints the other members of the Cabinet, but he has the legal power to remove them as he sees fit. He countersigns all laws and all Cabinet orders signed by other members of the Cabinet. But in practice his authority is nothing like that of the American President or even of the British Prime Minister. This weakness of Japanese prime ministers was hidden for a while by the almost arbitrary personal rule exercised by Prime Minister Shigeru Yoshida during what was for Japan his unprecedentedly long tenure of office from 1948 to 1954. Yoshida was a person of unusual personal qualities who also profited from extraordinary circumstances. During most of his term of office his party commanded an absolute majority in the Diet, which was unusual, and he came at a time when the removal of the veteran leaders of the party by the purge enabled him to pack the party's political machine with his personal protégés. He was also able to maneuver so as to utilize the power of the Occupation to his advantage. It is significant that, despite these circumstances, widespread resentment against his "one-man rule" resulted eventually in the defection of his outraged associates and finally in his downfall.

Except for Yoshida, none of the postwar prime ministers has been able to exercise strong leadership, notwithstanding the strong constitutional authority of the office. The existence until 1955 of four major parties of roughly comparable strength, except during a part of Yoshida's term of office, meant that the tenure of most prime ministers was precarious. Inasmuch as a single party in such a multiparty system was seldom likely to have an absolute majority in the Diet, the designation of a prime minister almost always depended on the arrangement of complicated deals by which the plurality party secured the temporary support or acquiescence of one or more of the rival parties. A prime minister chosen under such conditions, owing his position to a precarious temporary working arrangement with diverse groups, was in no position to make unchallenged use of his full legal powers. The emergence of a two-party system in 1955 has not fundamentally changed this situation, for both of the two present parties were formed by mergers, and as mergers they still retain many of the unstable characteristics of coalitions. The factions within each party must therefore continue to be handled pretty much as separate parties, with the result that the precariousness of the prime minister's position remains.

Such absence of strong individual leadership had been characteristic of the Japanese political scene for many years even before the war. Although Japanese history is replete with examples of able and aggressive individuals forging to the top —indeed Japanese society is characterized by great recognition accorded to individual achievement despite the apparently rigid formal social organization—for some reason such individualism had no been evident in politics for some time. Following the death of powerful *genro* like Ito and Yamagata, such rival groups that openly began to clash, like the militarists, the party politicians, big business, the bureaucrats, and the others —despite temporary superiority of one or another—were perhaps too nearly evenly matched to permit the emergence of anything other than balance-of-power politics. In the postwar period, another balance of power, this time among the political parties, succeeded it. Whatever the reason, the politics of balance of power, rather than the politics of individual leadership, have been the dynamics of the Japanese political process for many years.

In such a political system, there is a welter of rival groups instead of a monolithic power structure. Within each group a rigidly hierarchical boss-henchman (*oyabun-kobun*) relationship may prevail, but these groups themselves interact as free agents in a competitive struggle to climb above one another. In order to improve their relative positions, groups seek to bind one another in complex alignments and contractual obligations ramifying in various directions so that they form an overlapping and interlocking web. The man who fares best in this kind of system is one who can subtly take advantage of the constantly shifting balance of power among these interacting groups to maneuver his own group to the top. This process places a premium on the wily bargainer and the nimble opportunist, rather than on the dominating leader.[1]

---

[1] Thus Tojo was not a personal dictator like Hitler or Mussolini, but was more the representative of the military clique that had maneuvered itself temporarily to the top. Even during the war Japan, while authoritarian, was not totalitarian, for Japanese society with its interacting groups could hardly be wholly regimented or disciplined under a single leadership (see chap. iii).

The Cabinet is the focal point where the interaction among the rival groups in the political competition comes to a head. The prime minister is likely to be the representative of the group that has at the moment maneuvered itself into position atop a precarious balance of power. He has probably selected his Cabinet members from among several groups with an eye to maintaining, this balance. Rather than take imperious action which might upset it, he is much more likely to try to preserve it by continuing to mollify and cajole the various groups that support him. He needs collective approval and group co-operation in order to survive, whatever may be his legal authority. He is therefore apt to be the kind of person upon whom many groups can compromise, rather than an individual with forceful leadership qualities. All postwar prime ministers other than Yoshida, and indeed most of the prewar ones, have had this characteristic in common.

If the prime minister was so weak, his Cabinet so unstable, and the Diet even more ineffective, who then wielded the power? Part of the answer was to be found in the bureaucracy, which was another of the forces that retarded the rise of the Diet to full effectiveness. Ostensibly the bureaucracy is recruited and constituted on a democratic basis, and it supposedly serves merely as an instrument of the Cabinet. Whenever the Cabinet happened to be relatively strong, or whenever the Cabinet was controlled by a strong superior power like the *genro* or the militarists, the bureaucracy indeed performed its proper function as an instrument. But whenever there was no effective superior power to wield it as an instrument, the bureaucracy always tended to usurp for itself the role of controlling policy on its own initiative. In the postwar period, because of the weakness of most of the Cabinets and the inexperience of the Diet, the bureaucracy continued this traditional tendency to assume effective power by default, a tendency which the Occupation reforms were not able to change and which in fact the Occupation even accentuated.

The tradition of bureaucratic power goes as far back as the seventh century, when the Japanese adopted the justly admired Chinese model of the civil service system. The historic prestige of the bureaucracy was greatly enhanced in the nineteenth century, when the rapid modernization of Japan on the Western model was made possible largely by direction from above applied through the instrumentality of the bureaucracy. In a sense, therefore, modern Japan was the handiwork of the bureaucracy, a fact which strengthened the bureaucrats' consciousness of their own power. Furthermore, as the operational arm of the executive, the bureaucrats could regard themselves as agents of the sovereign Emperor and therefore superior to legislators, who were mere representatives of the subject populace.

But more significantly, the power and prestige of the bureaucracy rested on its actual abilities. Because of the rewards it offered, government service has traditionally attracted a large share of the best brains of the nation. Entrance into the bureaucracy, except for the lowest category of clerical jobs, was by means of highly competitive civil service examinations. Approximately three-fourths of all who succeeded in passing were graduates of the Law School of Tokyo Imperial University. This university was specifically designed primarily to produce government officials; its faculty and its facilities were outstandingly the best of any university in the nation; and its reputation attracted the most ambitious and most capable students from all over the country selected through mercilessly competitive entrance examinations. It is not strange that the products of this competition mill were conspicuously successful in going on to win a disproportionate share of the competitive civil service posts.

In the early Meiji period, most of the bureaucrats were former samurai, for they were the only ones who then had the educational qualifications. But as education became more general, the bureaucracy, open to all on the basis of merit alone, drew increasingly from all classes until today the sons of farmers outnumber those of any other origin. It was the surest road to power and position for the relatively unprivileged young man of ambition and ability. If he had the plenitude of brains and the modicum of means necessary to be admitted to Tokyo Imperial University, which was not an expensive school, his abilities alone generally determined how high he could go. A promising young official, even of undistinguished family background, usually had little difficulty in marrying the daughter of some well-placed parents who could give him wealth and social connections. While the bureaucrat's pay was comparatively modest, many official positions carried attractive perquisites, and he was sure of a comfortable pension when he retired. If he chose to retire early, or if he reached an impasse in his official career, he could usually utilize his government connections to find a good position in some private business company.

With such advantages, the morale of the bureaucrats was high. Conscious of their own prowess, they were arrogant and headstrong. Whatever their family backgrounds, they were welded together by their common educational preparation, their common career experiences, and their common pride in having achieved recognized status so that they comprised a highly exclusive, tightly knit, self-conscious, and self-assertive fraternity. It was only natural for members of such an elite group to feel that they had a right to special privileges. As highly select professionals, they felt they knew best how to govern the nation. While ostensibly serving whatever Cabinet happened to be in office at the time, they were constantly concerned chiefly with preserving their own monopolistic control over the mechanics of governmental power. With this control they could often even manipulate the formulation of policy as well, for weak Cabinets naturally leaned heavily on them, not only for technical services, but for general advice as well. Whenever opportunity permitted, therefore, the bureaucrats were more than willing to take advantage of their influence over the Cabinet on the bland assumption that their own interests coincided with the interests of the nation at large. The bureaucracy thus came to constitute an independent political force largely responsible only to itself and concerned primarily with preserving the status quo which assured it of such power.

For all its indisputable abilities, the bureaucracy had the faults one might naturally expect to find in such a group. Although individually highly intelligent, in their official capacities the bureaucrats were often singularly unperceptive and devoid of common sense in matters outside their established routine. Their intense but narrow legal training and their sense of their own importance inclined them to place great value on elaborate regulations and procedures with which they over-awed the lay public. Japanese bureaucracy was among the world's worst for red tape, and while it could sometimes be very efficient, it was more often maddeningly cumbersome. It presented a strong united front against all other groups, but within itself it was torn by jealousies. "Empire-building" and resultant jurisdictional rivalries, common to all bureaucracies, were particularly rampant in Japan.

Although initial appointment was based on competitive examinations, subsequent advancement depended as much on seniority and on favorable service ratings turned in by one's superiors as on objectively measured merit. Hence, to get ahead a junior needed to cultivate the patronage of some superior; the superior on his part welcomed the support of capable juniors. Each important official in every ministry there-fore found himself at the head of a string of protégés who had hitched their wagons to his star and whom he pulled along whenever opportunity afforded. Every office in consequence was ridden by intra-office intrigue and politicking among rival cliques of senior officials and their protégés. In such a situation most officials found it safer to put in time merely shuffling paper than to show originality and initiative with the attendant risk of possible miscarriage which rival cliques might exploit. All these faults, however, were not sufficient to prevent the bureaucracy from being the most capable and most effectively organized sector of the Japanese government.

The Occupation was not able to change these traditional characteristics of the bureaucracy to any significant extent. It is true that the civil service examinations were modified to break the near monopoly of Tokyo University graduates and to facili-tate the entrance of those with more heterogeneous prepara-tion. Changes in job classifications and new practical tests at various levels as prerequisites for promotion were designed to overcome the traditional weakness for legalism and time-serving. A National Personnel Authority was established as a new independent executive agency to administer the civil service scientifically and to take away the exclusive control over personnel matters from the politics-ridden individual ministries. The general atmosphere of the postwar period also helped to curb somewhat the privileged position of the bureaucracy. Lip service, at least, came to be paid to the new concept of the public servant as opposed to the old concept of the agent of the Emperor. In the fluid and uncertain economic and social conditions of the postwar period, the income from government employment—both financial and psychic—was no longer as rewarding as it used to be. The public, which had always hated the bureaucrats, regarded them now with less fear and more open contempt than before. The bureaucrats have therefore lost some of their brashness and have adopted a somewhat defensive attitude.

Yet despite these not inconsiderable changes, the bureaucracy remains the aspect of the Japanese government that has altered the least from prewar days. Many of the same individuals still remain in the government service. The same types of young men continue to enter the civil service for the same motives. Both the Occupation authorities and the postwar Japanese government found the bureaucrats indispensable in keeping the machinery of government functioning smoothly through the difficult period of adjustment. The very complexity of postwar administration and reforms helped to expand the powers of the bureaucrats, for only they had the technical competence to carry out the reforms which the Occupation initiated. The bureaucracy thus largely maintained its traditional position of importance in the Japanese government. Only very recently have there become discernible some signs of significant impending changes, as will be noted presently.[2]

The historical momentum of the Cabinet and the bureaucracy were not the only forces that hampered the growth of the Diet's powers. In an even more fundamental way, the Occupation itself exerted a retarding effect on the development of responsible popular government. For all the efforts made by the Occupation to encourage democratic government, it was read-

[2] Some of the foregoing material relating to the historical background of the Diet, the Cabinet, and the bureaucracy has been previously presented in a different context in the chapter "The Formulation and Recent Character of Japanese Foreign Policy," contributed by the present author to Philip W. Buck and Martin W. Travis, Jr. (eds.), *Control of Foreign Relations in Modern Nations* (New York: W. W. Norton & Co., 1957).

ily apparent to the Japanese that they had no real control over their own affairs. In the very nature of things, under the Occupation the ultimate power had to rest with the Occupation authorities. Whatever the pretense, SCAP made the decisions; the Cabinet then received instructions from SCAP and transmitted them to the proper operating agencies, whereupon the professional bureaucrats proceeded to put them into effect. Except within very restricted limits, the elected representatives of the people could only approve what they had no power to change. Through varying degrees of reluctance in voting their approval, they might register some measure of protest, but this power was no more than that which the Diet had always had. The responsibility of the people was thus largely make-believe.

The first postwar general election came in 1946, not from any Japanese decision, but from the decision of General MacArthur to have an election at that time. The conservative administration thus placed in office came to its end in 1947, again not from any Japanese decision, but from General MacArthur's decision to call for another election. The Socialist-Democratic government which next succeeded to office had a short life, because it was an unnatural coalition which could not unite on a strong program and because SCAP forced it to impose unpopular restraints on labor which caused it to lose an important portion of its supporters. Thus its fortunes were determined as much by SCAP as by any internal factor. When the Yoshida Cabinet embarked in 1948 on its long and successful term, it was tremendously aided by a notable economic recovery which was the direct result of a change in SCAP policy. Although ironically the Yoshida government resisted many of the key features of the Occupation's new economic program, it profited from the results. Here also the attitude of the Japanese government had less practical effect than the actions of SCAP. Under these circumstances it was inevitable that Japanese politics should tend to be concerned, not with substantive issues which were almost all beyond control, but merely with personalities and with the spoils of office which alone had reality. The relative popularity of the Communists, particularly in the election of 1949, was due in considerable part to the fact that they represented an overt protest against this situation, whereas the

other parties acquiesced in it. Once the Occupation was ended
—although other factors were also involved—the Communist
voting strength melted away.

Despite these negative effects, the efforts of the Occupation
to promote the development of democratic political processes
were by no means altogether futile. While relatively meager
results were apparent during the Occupation itself, the Occupation reforms created new basic conditions which in the long
run seem likely to lead to a significant measure of popular
political control. In the relatively short time that has elapsed
since the end of the Occupation, a new pattern of political
power has begun to emerge. Although post-Occupation events
do not lie strictly within the scope of the present study, this
new development, coming as a delayed consequence of the
Occupation's efforts, needs to be noted. Its outlines are still
quite fluid and imprecise, but they seem to indicate that the
political parties are now beginning to overshadow both the
Cabinet and the bureaucracy. While the Diet itself remains
relatively unimportant as yet, this rise in importance of the
political parties stems basically from the new constitutional
powers of the Diet. Logically, therefore, the shift of effective
power to the political parties would seem to be a transitional
step presaging an eventual further shift of effective power to
the Diet itself. Although this new pattern does not conform to
any familiar Western pattern, its democratic implications seem
to be beyond much doubt.

Specifically, the Diet itself as yet does little to formulate
policy. Diet proceedings continue to be considerably influenced
by the old practice of the political parties which imposed such
tight discipline over the actions of their members in the Diet
that no member of the Diet could deviate from the party line
once that line was formally adopted by his party executive or
in his party caucus.[3] If he was a member of the Government
party, he was committed to supporting the Cabinet policy; if

[3] The only alternative to absolute conformity was to bolt from the party,
which is one of the major reasons why Japanese politicians until recently
used to bolt so frequently to form splinter groups or to go over to a rival
party. The formation of a two-party system has now made such mobility
much more impracticable. New developments are now also providing more
practical alternatives short of bolting.

he was a member of the Opposition party, he was committed to attacking the Cabinet policy. There was little room for flexibility of action which would permit the hammering-out and shaping of policy in the Diet. The Diet merely furnished the arena where the opposing parties publicly confronted each other for a showdown on the positions they had previously determined for themselves within their own respective councils.

This meant that the real hammering-out of the substance of policy was carried on not in the Diet but within the councils of the parties. Here is where the clash and adjustment of individual and factional views took place. Before the formation of the two-party system, the Government party—often lacking an absolute majority in the Diet—had to appeal for the support of some other party. This process involved direct bargaining between parties which often resulted in important modifications of the Cabinet's program before the Cabinet felt confident enough to present it to the Diet for formal consideration. Since the emergence of the two-party system, a very similar process takes place within the parties, for the dominant faction of a party must bargain for the support of rival factions before the party can agree on a legislative program. In this process, a good deal of trimming and reshaping is often required before a unified party program emerges. Thus, while the individual Diet member may have little room to maneuver once the great issues are joined on the floor or even in the committees of the Diet, he does have considerable opportunity to make his influence felt during the earlier exploratory stages of the process of policy formation within the party. He may be acting more in the capacity of a party member than in his official capacity as a member of the Diet, but he does have opportunity to share in the making of decisions. While membership in the Diet helps to enhance one's standing in the party, it is thus the party rather than the Diet that affords the politician the channel through which to exercise his abilities.

The Cabinet usually still has enough strength to push its legislative program to successful vote in the Diet, but the legislative program is seldom any longer of its own making. Almost always constituted to represent a balance of power among the various factions of the Government party, the

Cabinet seldom has a mind of its own; it merely reflects the decisions that emerge from the bargaining among the intra-party factions. Thus it is the party, rather than the Cabinet or the Diet, that tends to develop as the center of effective power.

In the face of this growing importance of the political parties, even the bureaucracy is beginning to show some signs of catering to the parties. It is no longer enough for the bureaucrats to influence the Cabinet, for the Cabinet can do nothing without support from the various factions of the Government party. Many bureaucrats are therefore beginning to bypass the Cabinet and to cultivate direct relations with important party politicians. In getting official approval for their pet projects, ministries now find that the favors of influential party politicians are often of more practical value than representation by a persuasive minister in the Cabinet. Party politicians on their side welcome a private pipeline from the bureaucracy which provides them with the advantage of the same inside knowledge about government operations that heretofore used to be available only to members of the Cabinet.

This enhancement of the strength of party politicians from aid offered by the bureaucrats not only strengthens the power of the political parties but tends eventually to facilitate the shift of power from the parties to the Diet itself. Once becoming accustomed to using inside knowledge provided by the bureaucrats to advance himself in the factional bargaining within the party, a party politician finds it an easy transition to use the same knowledge to extend his bargaining into the committee meetings of the Diet, should the bargaining within party councils turn out to be disappointing to him. Heretofore, lacking the ability to fend for himself, he had to defer to party discipline or else bolt the party if it moved contrary to his desires. He could get little help from the professional investigative staffs of Diet committees, for, undermanned and relatively inexperienced, they were no match for the bureaucracy, whose superior resources were then available only to the Cabinet. Now, armed with data supplied to him by friends within the bureaucracy, he can dare to express his dissatisfaction with party decisions by effectively badgering the Cabinet and the party leadership in discussions in the Diet. In view of this increasing effectiveness of the legislators, a systematic working partnership between certain sections of the bureaucracy and various standing committees of the Diet appears to be forming which may become as potent as the earlier intimate relations between the Cabinet and the bureaucracy. Such a development might well mean the end of the Diet's deference to Cabinet leadership.

This tendency of bureaucrats to form close relationships with individual politicians or with various political groups also presages the dissipation of the influence of the bureaucracy as a unified independent political force. Whereas formerly, in order to exert its power, the bureaucracy would concentrate its efforts on influencing the Cabinet, now the bureaucrats currying the favor of various political factions find themselves working with groups opposed to one another and sometimes opposed to the Cabinet. The result is a fragmentation of the bureaucracy's influence. This tendency has been accentuated by the fact that many of the younger officials, strongly affected by the social ferment of the postwar period, have broken out of the mold of the traditional bureaucrat. In their rebellion against the conservatism of their seniors in the ministries in which they work, these younger bureaucrats show a marked willingness to co-operate with Socialist politicians. Thus the Opposition party for the first time has the help of allies within the government, a fact which vastly strengthens the ability of the Socialist tacticians to maneuver effectively in the Diet. If the Socialists should ever gain the majority in the Diet, knowing that the senior bureaucrats would be unsympathetic toward them, they would probably seek to make the fullest use of the Diet's constitutional authority to force the ministries to comply with the Diet's program. The decision-making power in the government would thus come to rest almost exclusively with the Socialist majority in the Diet, and the influence of the bureaucracy as a distinctive entity would cease to be a factor in the process of policy formation.

This emergence of the political parties to pre-eminence over the Cabinet and the bureaucracy, while reminiscent of the situ-

ation of the 1920's when the parties somewhat similarly enjoyed great prominence,[4] nevertheless differs from it in significant respects. In the earlier era, both of the two major parties
were pretty much under the control of big business so that the
distinctions between them were quite unsubstantial, while the
proletarian parties which did differ were too weak to count for
much. The vital issues, therefore, were not those that were
fought out among the parties. The vital issues were, rather,
those that were fought out in extraconstitutional areas where
political parties constituted only one of the adversaries, sometimes contending alone against the Cabinet, the *genro,* the
Privy Council, the bureaucracy, and the military, and sometimes in combination with one or more of them against the
others. Today, in contrast, great as is the influence of the business interests, no political party is wholly under the control of
big business. Business needs help from political parties at least
as much as the parties need help from business; in fact, the
Socialists have become a major party largely in opposition to
business. Most importantly, with the Diet tending toward supremacy over the Cabinet and the bureaucracy, all the vital
issues in government center on the activities of the parties
whose members comprise the Diet. The importance of the
parties, therefore, is far more absolute than it was in the 1920's.

The essential reason for the importance of the political
parties today can be attributed to the fact that they are becoming the instrumentality for manipulating the exercise of the
supreme governmental authority which the constitution vests
in the Diet. The Diet in the 1920's had no such unequivocal
constitutional authority to provide the political parties with a
legal base for their power. In other words, the power of the
political parties today stems from the authority of the increasingly powerful Diet, for to the degree the parties can place
their own members in the Diet, they can channel this authority
through their hands. Likewise, the relative strengths of the
various factions within the parties depend largely on the number of Diet seats the respective factions can manage to capture. Thus in the final analysis political power has come to depend on the votes of the electorate.

[4] See chap. iii.

At the same time, while their power is based on the votes of the electorate, the political parties do not necessarily directly reflect the interests of the general public. The parties are sufficiently independent and self-willed entities to be capable of bending or modifying the popular will as they transmute that will into practical effect in the acts of the Diet. The political parties also have well-organized machines which may unduly influence the voters, who, being often politically immature and inexperienced, are prone to make unwise choices. Politicians may consequently find it more rewarding to concentrate on easily understood personalities rather than on difficult issues; and when personal relations become more important than issues, opportunity arises for subordinating the public interest to private advantage. The classical medium of such political use of personal influence for special advantage, familiar in any country, is patronage—the control of a political machine by the granting of favors by the boss to his henchmen in return for their unquestioning support. The persistence in Japanese society of the feudalistic *oyabun-kobun* system based on the concept of *on* and *giri*—a system of patron-protégé relationship involving a strict code of balancing obligations and favors—sometimes served to accentuate political patronage. It is true that very often the *oyabun-kobun* system constituted a machinery of great responsiveness which provided a channel of intimate personal communication between local groups and top governmental personages which assured a hearing to the interests of the little men at the local level and redounded to the general welfare of the whole community. The same machinery might, on the other hand, be used in some cases to tighten the grip of a political machine, in which event the political machine enjoyed an institutionalized sanction more powerful than anything familiar in Western countries. Accordingly, advancement for the politician often depended less on satisfying the general mass of voters than on cultivating the proper relations of *quid pro quo* with other politicians who could be of help and with specific groups of voters who could be of support. The voters also, particularly in the smaller communities where personal contacts were more intimate, committed their votes in accord with their continuing personal relations with local political bosses rather than in accord with their individual views concerning issues. "Log-rolling" among politicians and bloc-voting of organized groups herded by ward-heelers are not unknown in other countries, but in Japan they were often intensified by vestiges of feudalistic social ties.

To a considerable extent this traditional pattern of personal loyalties in politics still persists, but it seems to be clear that this pattern is beginning to break down. The causes are complex, involving mostly factors essentially non-political in nature which will be touched upon later in other connections. But they also include strictly political factors that are obvious enough.

For one thing, the purge eliminated many of the old political leaders and severed the ties which had held their followers to them. Moreover, the politicians who were purged included many of the biggest bosses, while those who escaped the purge were generally the more progressive individuals who were less involved in traditional practices. The new generation of politicians which has emerged since the purge has had neither the inclination nor sufficient time as yet to develop personal connections as widely as the veterans whom they replaced. Also, in the many reorganizations and splits and mergers which characterized the political parties during the very fluid immediate post-surrender years, many old lines of personal relationships were quite thoroughly scrambled and thereby weakened. Postwar conditions, furthermore, greatly strengthened the Socialist party, whose members represented much the same elements as the antitraditional proletarian parties of the 1920's. Although even they were not free from the traditional pattern of personal loyalties, in comparison with the conservatives they were much more concerned with issues, doctrines, ideologies, and principles than with personalities or spoils. In other words the political spectrum has shifted definitely to the left: the prewar conservatives have been dropped off; those who would have been considered liberal and progressive in the prewar era now occupy the extreme right; the prewar left now occupies a position of respectable prominence near the center; and the left now consists of those who formerly would not have been legally tolerated. In such a new political orientation, the practices of the past naturally tend to fade.

Finally, issues are becoming too important for the politicians and the voters to neglect. As long as the ultimate power of decision on great issues lay beyond their reach in the hands of oligarchs, bureaucrats, militarists, or SCAP, it was only natural for the politicians and the voters to be more concerned with matters of personalities and spoils of office over which they did have some control. But now, not only do they possess decisive power over issues of great importance, but in the momentous era of profound changes in which postwar Japan finds itself these issues obviously impinge closely on the life of each individual so that there can be no escape. So, while old habits die hard, there is nevertheless increasing pressure for issues to assert themselves over personalities.

In terms of practical politics, this means that the party leaders at the national level can no longer draw political sustenance through a chain of henchmen extending down to the voting precinct. If votes are to be cast on the basis of issues, the leaders cannot simply put up their most faithful protégés as local candidates and count on the power of the machine to get them elected. The candidates must be selected on the basis of their local vote-attracting appeal. Local popularity rather than faithfulness to the machine becomes more valued under these conditions. Successful candidates, aware that their own voter appeal is more important than the patronage of their boss, are tempted to assert their independence, and the whole structure of the political machine tends to break down.

Recognizing that personal political machines are thus beginning to break down, the party leaders are trying to replace them in part by recruiting popular support for local chapters of national parties. The hope is not only that such territorial units would provide a more stable base for the party than the crumbling local ramifications of personal machines but that they would also help to eliminate destructive factional competition among what remains of rival personal machines of the same party in each locality. But these local chapters fostered by the party's national organization are proving to be altogether too artificial to have much vitality. What seems to be emerging in place of the old personal machines is not these local extensions of the national party organization but autonomous groups of successful local politicians who owe their power to their own vote-getting ability and not to patronage from a boss or to sponsorship by the national party organization. Because of their tendency toward independence, such men are often very unwelcome to the party leadership at the national level, but the party needs the votes they can bring in. Hence the party reluctantly extends them its formal blessings, and within the party these men then begin to exert an influence on party councils almost directly proportional to the number of votes they can muster in a general election. Incidentally, the extension of autonomy to local governmental units has helped these men, for election to local office provides them with a springboard to launch themselves into national politics.

Thus the pattern of the political process within the parties is undergoing significant transformation. Power within the party is no longer monopolized by the great bosses whose machines ramify from the capital through their henchmen hierarchically down to the precinct and who struggle for advantage over other bosses through subtle bargaining and maneuvering. This pattern is being disrupted by the intrusion of the free-wheeling individual politician whose local popularity enables him in a sense to blackmail his way into the party organization while retaining considerable freedom of movement. This development within the party is of a piece with the earlier noted tendency of individual members of the Diet to extend their maneuvering from the councils of their party into the Diet itself. These developments indicate that the behavior of the Japanese politician is breaking out of the traditional mold and is moving in the direction of the more flexible individualistic behavior of the American politician.

This direction of development may be indicated in the reactions of the special interest groups. While unsophisticated interest groups have always staged public demonstrations or directed petitions to the Cabinet or to the Diet, these methods

failed to get at the real center of power. The more knowledgeable pressure groups have always recognized more clearly
where their efforts would have the most telling effects. Thus in
the past their efforts were directed at tying up key individuals
in the government and in the political parties in a web of personal obligations to them. More recently, recognizing the growing importance of the parties as such rather than individual
bosses, the special interests have been striving to gain more
direct control of the party organization. Thus, business groups
have been contributing heavily to the campaign funds of the
conservative parties so that these parties will espouse the policies which the business community favors. Labor unions have
been directing their members to vote for the Socialist party so
that this party and organized labor represent simply different
facets of the same movement. Now, however, with the rise of
the power of relatively independent individuals within the
parties, it is logical to suppose that pressure groups will resort
to the kind of lobbying tactics familiar in the United States,
namely, efforts aimed not so much at getting direct control of
a political machine or a political party as at influencing the
voting of individual members of the legislature.

These recent developments should not, of course, be accorded greater significance than they deserve. After all, they are not
much more than hints of a trend rather than accomplished
facts; in large part the older practices still remain. Furthermore, even individualized behavior by politicians who owe
their power to the votes of the people does not necessarily insure desirable democratic practices. The now supposedly democratic Diet continues, for instance, to engage frequently in
disgraceful brawls. The fact that these usually do not represent
ordinary uncontrolled disorder but constitute a sophisticated
delaying tactic, a form of filibuster designed to circumvent
cloture, does not make them any less undesirable as a parliamentary practice. Minorities often still fail to understand why
"mere numbers" should entitle the majority always to have its
way. Their belief that greater fairness lies in a compromise
which embodies in proportional degree the interests of both
the majority and the minority—while perhaps no less reason-

able than the Western convention of attaching almost mystic value to the formula of half-the-total-plus-one—nevertheless indicates unfamiliarity with democratic processes. These and other examples show that Japan still has far to go before satisfactory democratic politics can be considered an accomplished fact. But insofar as the votes of the electorate have come to constitute the ultimate source of power of the political parties and of their members who wield the dominant effective power in government, politics in Japan is now essentially democratic in nature. To the degree that this development has occurred, the Occupation's aim of putting ultimate power in the hands of the people has proved successful.

CHAPTER VIII

Economic Reforms

Little attention was apparently paid to the factor of economics at the beginning of the Occupation. All that the Allies were interested in, initially, was that Japan should never again possess the economic potential to wage aggressive war. Accordingly, although no Morgenthau had proposed a plan for the pastoralization of Japan, the original Allied policy had called not only for heavy reparations but also for drastic restrictions on Japanese industrial activity. If these measures resulted in economic hardship for the Japanese, it was of no concern to the Allies. They felt it to be no more than just retribution that the Japanese should be made to suffer for their past sins. In fact, many Allied spokesmen openly hinted that it might be a good thing if economic desperation were to goad the Japanese into a revolutionary upheaval.

Even during the war, however, there had been some voices raised in the Allied countries against such a merely negative policy of punishment and prevention.[1] Their argument was based on practical rather than humanitarian grounds. It was held that such a restrictive policy would require a large occupation force to police the conquered country for so long a period as to be prohibitive in cost. Such a policy would also keep the conquered country so weak economically that it would have to be supported indefinitely by the victors. The permanent pauperization of countries like Germany and Japan,

[1] See Edward H. Carr, *The Conditions of Peace* (New York: Macmillan Co., 1942), for a cogent wartime presentation of this point of view.

whose large and capable populations normally play such a central role in the economy of their respective regions, would throw the economy of the whole world into dangerous imbalance. If for no other reason than sheer self-interest, the Allies would need to protect themselves by associating and integrating the interests of Germany and Japan as quickly as possible with their own, while encouraging the German and Japanese economies to recover to the maximum extent possible.

While the general Allied public found such ideas at first emotionally difficult to accept, the Occupation authorities in Japan very quickly discovered that the logic of reality permitted them no other choice. The Occupation therefore led the way for the general acceptance of these ideas and found itself increasingly involved in the rehabilitation and reordering of Japan's economy. Unprepared for this task, the Occupation's efforts in this field were far from distinguished and favorable results were slow to appear. But the Occupation painfully learned its economics on the job, and in the end the results turned out to be creditable enough. From the vantage point of hindsight, it can be seen that developments in the field of economics had such a vital bearing on the process of democratization that the future of democracy in Japan may really depend largely on how successfully the Occupation achieved its final economic objectives.

At the outset, however, in accordance with the original plans the Occupation forces dismantled all plants that had been engaged in military production, closed up all factories that had been producing goods which contributed to the war effort, and impounded industrial equipment which might be suitable for reparations. Japanese industrial production was to be confined virtually to consumer goods necessary for the minimum level of daily living of the people. Accordingly, preliminary studies of the permanent limits that might be imposed upon Japanese industry were apparently undertaken by SCAP.

These activities, however, were soon seen to be utterly unrealistic. At the time of the surrender Japan was so prostrate economically that there was very little left to prohibit or to restrict. The extent to which the nation had been bled white in the war was almost beyond description. Almost all the cities, including most of the factories, had been leveled to the ground by the bombings. The factories that had escaped destruction were immobilized by the organizational dislocations that followed the sudden end of the war. The stock of raw materials was practically gone; fuel of all kinds was gone; and industrial production was virtually at a standstill. What production there was amounted to about 10 per cent of the normal prewar level —not of the high wartime level—and even this meager production was confined largely to such makeshift efforts as turning discarded steel helmets into pots and pans, carving wood scraps into clogs, and making wood pulp into ersatz cloth that became like soggy old newspaper in the rain.

The shops were bare not only of practically all manufactured goods but of food as well. Chemical fertilizer plants had been converted to making explosives; farm land had been neglected by the diversion of manpower into the armed forces and the war industries; and now to cap it all came a prolonged spell of unusually bad weather. The result was to reduce harvests to abnormally low levels. Wartime destruction of boats, shortage of motor fuel, and shortage of materials for nets also curtailed fishing. Official rations dropped to 1,050 calories per person a day—about one-third the requirement for normal physical well-being and about one-fifth the amount furnished to each American soldier daily. Even these paltry rations were often as much as two weeks late in being delivered, and when they came they sometimes consisted of such unpalatable substitutes as acorn meal or the residue from the extraction of soybean oil. To eke out the inadequate rations, housewives sometimes even foraged for edible weeds, following identification charts printed in the newspapers; city people swarmed through the country-side trying to exchange their family heirlooms for a few vegetables from the farmers.

To add to the shortage of all commodities, the Occupation commandeered buildings by the thousands to billet its personnel and to house its offices, and required that they be remodeled and re-equipped according to American standards. Reimbursement for these Occupation procurements were borne by the Japanese government, which resulted in considerable money being put into circulation. Furthermore, the end of the war caused the government to pay off the demobilized soldiers, to end the virtually compulsory sale of war bonds, and to discontinue the practice of forcing people to deposit a large part of their earnings in frozen savings accounts, all of which suddenly put additional loose money into circulation at a time when there were no goods available which could be bought with this money. The situation was ripe for the start of runaway inflation.

People whose energies were absorbed in struggling to keep barely alive amid the wreckage of war devastation were in no condition to appreciate the democratic reforms envisaged by the Occupation. Even in America with its democratic traditions, as the depression years of the early 1930's had demonstrated, people in want value social security more than theoretical concepts of political freedom. For a people like the Japanese who had no established democratic habits, it is understandable that some minimum level of physical well-being had to be assured before they would take interest in anything but the problem of mere physical existence. Quickly recognizing this situation, the Occupation authorities began directing toward America the idea that "you cannot teach democracy to a hungry people." At the same time, even without waiting for the American public to become enlightened, General MacArthur called for emergency shipments of food and medicine into Japan on the grounds that they were required to safeguard the health and security of the American military forces which might otherwise be endangered by contact with the surrounding diseased and hungry Japanese populace.

But great confusion prevailed as to just how much imported food was needed. The minimum Japanese estimate was that two million tons of grain would be necessary the first year if a million people were not to starve to death; other estimates reached almost twice this amount. Some SCAP officials angrily rejected these figures as deliberate exaggerations, while others gave them credence. Former President Herbert Hoover, on a quick trip of inspection, tended to substantiate the Japanese estimates. While one high SCAP official kept insisting from the statistics in his office that not a single Japanese died of starvation at any time during the Occupation, American correspondents—not to speak of thousands of Japanese—testified to seeing many people simply keel over and drop in the streets from hunger. Fortunately, both the highest and the lowest estimates of the need were eventually proved to be wrong. Thus, although the Occupation did not start bringing in food until the spring of 1946 and then only about eight hundred thousand tons during the ensuing year, this amount—while not sufficient to prevent considerable suffering—was sufficient to avert mass starvation.

The Occupation officials were irritated, however, by what they considered lack of proper appreciation on the part of the Japanese. While formal delegations of notables effusively thanked the Occupation authorities in every locality amid much speech-making and picture-taking, the common people complained. Owing to hasty distribution arrangements, people in some areas received nothing but rancid butter for several days as their sole rations; people in other areas received nothing but sugar. But the greatest complaints arose over the cracked corn that constituted a large part of the imported food. Japanese complaints were peremptorily shut off by Occupation officials who lectured at great length that beggars can't be choosers and that corn bread and corn muffins were delicacies in America.

What the American officials ensconced in their offices apparently could not comprehend was that the people who received the rations did not consider themselves beggars, for they were paying for these rations as they received them even though full accounting by the Japanese government to the United States was being deferred. Furthermore, cracked corn had to be ground into corn meal, but the people had no milling facilities; corn meal could not be made into bread or muffins without some wheat flour to serve as binder, but the people had no wheat flour; some leavening and shortening were necessary, which were not available; the people had no ovens because Japanese cooking does not make use of ovens, and even if they had ovens they did not have enough fuel for baking. To add insult to injury, the Occupation authorities brought over a group of home economics experts from the United States to educate the Japanese on the palatability of corn bread, but they could do no more than infuriate the Japanese by giving wide publicity to recipes that called for adding to the corn meal generous quantities of eggs and milk and butter, little of which was available in Japan at that time. So the Japanese simply parboiled the cracked corn and chewed on it three times a day for week after week and continued to grumble.

This was the sort of failure in perception and communication which plagued many of the Occupation's earlier activities but which fortunately was largely corrected in due time. Meanwhile, despite the dissatisfactions it caused, the cracked corn did prevent mass starvation and enabled the Occupation to turn soon to more important business.

SCAP's insistence on the desirability of a more constructive economic policy for the Occupation caused the United States government to dispatch a succession of experts on fact-finding missions to reappraise the situation. It is impossible here to describe the various missions and their findings, significant as they were. It need only be noted that the initial recommendations for heavy reparations and severe limitations on Japanese industry were successively moderated until in the end the various experts agreed, in the words of one of them, that the problem was "not to keep Japan down but to hold her up." Accordingly, the official United States policy eventually called for the cessation of reparations altogether and the encouragement of unlimited revival of Japanese economy. The argument used with most telling effect on the American public was that Japan would continue to be a burden on the American taxpayer unless her economy were restored; but no doubt equally important in the minds of the responsible authorities were the bearing of economic recovery on the Occupation's objective of democratization and the considerations of the Cold War.

Even after the Occupation formally embarked on the policy of encouraging the revival of Japanese economy, however, for a long time recovery continued to be discouragingly slow. So meager were the results that many Americans accused the Japanese of deliberately sabotaging the Occupation's efforts, although it is difficult to see why the Japanese would do anything that would hurt themselves more than the Occupation. Actually, the rebuilding of a national economy after such a holocaust as Japan had undergone involved much more complex problems than was generally realized.

The seeming apathy and lethargy of the Japanese, so different from their traditional habit of diligence, were not intentional but were due to profound shock. The defeat and the collapse of their old familiar world left them numb and dazed and deprived of any sense of direction or purpose; it took time for them to emerge from their bewilderment. Despite the benefits of imported food, the cumulative effects of wartime privations and the continuing difficulties in living conditions sapped the strength of the Japanese so that most of them felt constantly exhausted physically as well as spiritually. A more tangible factor was the uncertainty regarding the Occupation's intentions. No factory owner could be expected to expend much money or effort to rehabilitate his enterprise so long as he could not be sure that his equipment would not be confiscated for reparations or that his factory would not be closed up under some limitation imposed upon production or that his company would not be liquidated in some scheme for economic deconcentration.

The very measures the Occupation took in its efforts to stabilize the Japanese economy often had the effect of merely paralyzing it. For instance, in order to check the incipient inflation, the Occupation caused the Japanese government to impose rigid price ceilings on all commodities, to drain off excess money by imposing a heavy capital levy on assets, and to cause all income above a very modest level to be impounded in frozen savings accounts—measures which were in effect a revival of the wartime practices. They undoubtedly prevented the inflation from getting completely out of hand, but the cost of living nevertheless continued to rise by about 10 per cent each month for about two years. Under the prevailing conditions, such a rise was natural, but it was enough to cause havoc with plans for economic recovery. Factory owners found, for instance, that while their operating costs rose in keeping with the rise in the general cost of living, the price at which they could sell their products remained frozen by law. Therefore, as time went on, the more they produced and sold, the more money they lost. The only way they could avoid losing money was to stop producing or to sell on the black market at above the official ceiling prices—or, better yet, to sell what raw materials they had at black-market prices without going to the expense of fabricating them into usable goods. Thus, although the Occupation turned back to the Japanese the military supplies confiscated from the Japanese armed forces, instead of being converted to productive use much of this material leaked into the black market to be used for speculative manipulation.

It was this situation which led to the disagreement between Finance Minister Tanzan Ishibashi and the Occupation officials which, as noted earlier, is alleged to have been the real reason for his purge.[2] The only remedy the Occupation could propose was more rigid controls. Ishibashi, as a classical economist, scorned government controls as the sterile refuge of bureaucratic bunglers. He advocated instead the abolition of controls and price ceilings, or at least the tacit tolerance of certain types of black-market transactions. Such a policy would admittedly accelerate inflation for a while, but by affording producers an opportunity to make profits it would offer incentive to production. The resulting increased production would eventually restore the balance between supply and demand, and the inflation would automatically come to an end. This, he argued, was the only way in which permanent economic recovery could come about.

Unwilling to gamble on such a course, the Occupation continued with measures which only very slowly brought about modest improvements. It was not until the United States decided upon massive pump-priming, which did not begin to take much noticeable effect until after 1949, that recovery really got under way. The efforts of the Occupation to aid economic recovery, however, very early caused important modifications in many of the Occupation's original projects relating to changes in the Japanese economy.

One of the first casualties of the new economic orientation of SCAP was the original reparations program, as already noted. As a matter which vitally concerned many Allied nations, the problem of reparations was discussed at length by the Far Eastern Commission. Pending decision by this inter-

[2] See chap. vi.

Allied body, SCAP tentatively designated 1,110 industrial plants as subject to removal for reparations and, on authorization of the United States government, actually started to distribute a small number of these plants as interim instalments to several claimant countries.

As their reappraisal of the general Japanese economic situation progressed, however, the Americans became increasingly unhappy over the whole matter of reparations. SCAP and the United States government, while acknowledging Japan's moral obligation to pay reparations, became convinced that the burden of reparations would jeopardize Japanese economic recovery. At the same time, although essential to Japan for her own recovery, the plants earmarked for reparations were in such poor condition as to be not worth the bother of dismantling and transporting to other countries. Heavy industries especially could not be moved from their original sites without inordinate loss of efficiency. Moreover, many of the nations most clamorous in their demands for Japanese industrial equipment did not have the capability of operating such equipment. Some of the nations most insistent in their claims failed to take even the interim instalments when SCAP got them ready for shipment, and some of the equipment which was taken lay unused after reaching the recipient country.

Meanwhile the claims filed by the various nations totaled more than the entire existing economic assets of Japan, and the Far Eastern Commission seemed to be unable to reach any agreement on how these claims could be cut down to practicable proportions. The Americans feared that in order to prevent the collapse of Japan's economy the United States would have to send into Japan as much in economic aid as was taken out in reparations, so in effect it would be the United States rather than Japan that would ultimately be paying for the reparations. Hence, utilizing the authority which it possessed to issue "urgent unilateral interim directives," the United States government in the spring of 1949 overrode the Far Eastern Commission and declared the entire reparations program to be at an end. Many of the Asian nations that had suffered from Japanese invasion remained gravely dissatisfied, but this arbitrary American action closed the reparations issue for at least the duration of the Occupation.[3] Whatever the American motives, the American action with respect to reparations was one which won the warm appreciation of the Japanese.

The most controversial of the Occupation's economic measures were probably those that related to its program of economic deconcentration, or "zaibatsu-busting" program. As is generally well known, an unduly great proportion of Japan's modern industrial and commercial enterprises had been under the control of about a dozen gigantic financier families commonly known as the "zaibatsu," or the "money clique," an appellation which has connotations similar to "Wall Street" in America. In accordance with its aim of advancing the economic democratization of Japan, the Occupation sought to break the power of the zaibatsu. The somewhat erratic course of this program is easy enough to trace. The motives, effectiveness, wisdom, and effect on the Japanese of this program, on the other hand, are difficult to evaluate and are subject to differing interpretations.

Although the Japanese were effectively prevented from learning about it at the time, apparently a group of experts headed by Professor Corwin Edwards of Northwestern University, a former economic adviser on antitrust matters to the Attorney General of the United States, very quietly made a study of the zaibatsu problem at the outset of the Occupation. This mission seems to have made a very thorough analysis of the structure of the zaibatsu organization, tracing its highly intricate ramifications through thousands of interlocking corporations, and also to have outlined the steps which should be taken to tear down this structure. From the narrow technical point of view, this report was apparently a masterly piece of work. When it was made the basis for SCAP's anti-zaibatsu program, however, it was found to be a political booby trap.

The early phases of the Occupation's anti-zaibatsu program encountered relatively little opposition. The key holding companies at the apex of the zaibatsu's elaborate corporate struc-

[3] After the signing of the peace treaty in 1951, Japan found it necessary to negotiate separate reparations agreements with several Asian states before they would ratify the treaty or resume normal commercial relations.

tures were required to dispose of their stocks to the general public on the open market. The actual sales of the shares were handled by the Holding Company Liquidation Commission, a Japanese government agency created for this purpose under the very close direction of SCAP. The sales went very slowly for a considerable time because of the chaotic and unstable condition of Japan's economy in the early post-surrender period, but inasmuch as the Liquidation Commission held the stocks until they were all eventually sold the zaibatsu were deprived of control from the very outset. The second major phase of the anti-zaibatsu program consisted of the adoption by the Japanese government, under strong SCAP pressure, of an Anti-Monopoly Law. In brief, incorporating many of the features of American antitrust legislation like the Sherman Act and the Clayton Act, this law prohibited trusts, cartels, interlocking corporate controls, agreements "in restraint of trade," and other arrangements tending toward monopolies, and created a Fair Trade Commission to police business against practices that threatened free and open competition. While Japanese businessmen were not particularly enthusiastic over either the dissolution of the holding companies or the stringent restrictions on their customary business practices, they raised no serious objections; and these aspects of the anti-zaibatsu program were carried out with considerable vigor and success.

The story was altogether different with respect to the Law for the Elimination of Excessive Concentrations of Economic Power, commonly known as the Deconcentration Law, which became the crux of the complicated controversy over the "zaibatsu-busting" program. The purport of this measure was submitted by the United States government to the Far Eastern Commission for its approval, where under the designation "FEC-230" it was eventually to gain much notoriety. Without waiting for the Far Eastern Commission's decision, however, SCAP pressured the Japanese Diet into passing the Deconcentration Law in December, 1947, a SCAP representative refusing to budge from the Diet building until a very reluctant Diet had finally been made to pass the bill in a prolonged and tumultuous session that lasted far into the night. This law conferred upon the Holding Company Liquidation Commission, operating under SCAP direction, the authority to order the dissolution or reorganization of any corporation. Presumably the corporations to be so dissolved or reorganized were those whose size or structure was such as to give them the character of monopolies, but the law itself set up no standards or criteria. The Holding Company Liquidation Commission was given blanket authority to be the sole judge of what should be done—which in effect meant that SCAP could arbitrarily break up any company it saw fit.

Information leaking out of SCAP, and reported by American correspondents, was to the effect that about 1,200 companies had already been tentatively designated for dissolution. SCAP gave no official explanation to the Japanese, however, as to its reasons, criteria, or intended method of procedure. In fact, the American military censors clamped down on any discussion of the Deconcentration Law in the Japanese press, permitting only the reproduction of the very unrevealing SCAP press releases on the subject.[4] This air of conspiracy in SCAP convinced most Japanese that the deconcentration program was intended to punish Japanese business for having given economic sustenance to the military during the war or else that it was intended to cripple Japanese business so that it could never again compete with American business. Of course, the chief motive of the people in SCAP was their belief that the zaibatsu constituted an evil influence in Japanese society whose power had to be broken before Japan could become democratized. But this idea was never clearly explained to the Japanese. The curtain of mystery erected by the American censorship and the conspiratorial atmosphere at SCAP headquarters not only pre-

[4] The present writer was once invited to call on the chief of the Anti-Trust and Cartels Division of SCAP, who proceeded to take up most of the meeting denouncing Japanese businessmen for attempting to influence him with gifts and obsequious attention. About the Deconcentration Law itself he revealed virtually nothing, except to insist that it must be a good law because it was opposed by both the reactionaries and the Communists—neglecting to mention that it was opposed by the middle-of-the-road elements as well. In reply to a specific question, he stated that he saw no reason why the Japanese should not be allowed to discuss anything that concerned them so vitally as the Deconcentration Law. But the present writer's editorial the next day paraphrasing this statement was promptly suppressed by the censors.

vented the Japanese from openly expressing their opinions about the deconcentration plan but even more effectively prevented them from learning what SCAP really had in mind. It was only natural, therefore, that the Japanese suspected the worst.[5]

Undoubtedly this inept performance on the part of the SCAP officials stemmed from the fact that they had hypnotized themselves into undue nervousness over the vaunted resourcefulness of the zaibatsu. Fearing that the zaibatsu, with their legendary power and ingenuity, would devise ways to thwart SCAP's efforts if details of the deconcentration plan became too widely known, these officials apparently hoped to strike as suddenly and as silently as possible. But a sweeping reordering of a nation's economic and social system cannot be executed like a commando raid under cover of a communications blackout, and the attempt to use such assault tactics only aroused suspicion. The Occupation was able to carry out drastic reforms in other fields of activity which also encountered the opposition of strong vested interests—such as the purge and the reform of local government and the police system—but in these cases the Occupation enlisted the support of Japanese groups whose interests conflicted with the traditional vested interests. It is true that the zaibatsu were capable of putting up a more subtle and tenacious resistance than the other vested interests, and it is true that Japanese groups likely to associate themselves with the SCAP program in this field—particularly in the extreme and arbitrary form taken in the Deconcentration Law —must have seemed pretty scarce, but people who deplored the power of the zaibatsu were not altogether lacking in Japan.

[5] It was with great excitement that some Japanese officials came across an article which gave them their first rational explanation of the reasoning behind SCAP's deconcentration program (Eleanor M. Hadley, "Trust Busting in Japan," *Harvard Business Review*, July 4, 1948). Capably written by a woman official in SCAP who had something of a reputation for brains, beauty, and personality, it convinced the Japanese officials who knew her that SCAP did not harbor some hidden ulterior motive for persecuting Japanese business. But American publications were not freely accessible in Japan at that time, and one copy of the *Harvard Business Review* passed around among a few English-reading Japanese officials could not reverse the impression which SCAP's antitrust officers had already created among the Japanese public.

If these people had been cultivated by SCAP, instead of having been treated with suspicion and sometimes actually rebuffed, the purpose of the deconcentration program, if not the Deconcentration Law itself, might have won some useful support. As it was, SCAP by its own attitude made it inevitable that the deconcentration program would gain virtually no friends among the Japanese.

It was the Americans at home rather than the Japanese, however, who finally swung the ax on the deconcentration program. Late in 1947, American newspapers and magazines, which had been paying little attention to the progress of the program in Japan, suddenly discovered "FEC-230" pending in the Far Eastern Commission and turned their spotlight on it. The reaction was startling. Under Secretary of the Army Kenneth C. Royall was reported by the press to have "hit the ceiling." Apparently through lack of co-ordination within the United States government he had hitherto been unaware of how seriously economic deconcentration might jeopardize the economic recovery in which he was particularly interested. American business groups protested that such "atomization" of Japanese economy as embodied in the deconcentration plan would permanently prevent Japan's economic recovery and that the United States as a result would never be able to do business profitably with Japan again. Senator William F. Knowland was reported to have denounced the deconcentration plan as "socialistic," which was a bit difficult to understand. To break up Japanese business into too many highly competitive little units —which was what the American businessmen were objecting to as "atomization"—might indeed be unsound but it was hardly socialistic. More to the point were the cries raised in some quarters that New Dealers who had infiltrated into the SCAP organization were trying to use Japan as a guinea pig for economic experiments which were far more radical than anything that would be tolerated in the United States and that in so doing they were exercising unwarranted arbitrary power. Whatever the arguments, in response to this outcry within the United States, the United States government stopped pushing "FEC-230" in the Far Eastern Commission and eventually formally withdrew the proposal.

By this time, however, SCAP had already pressured the Japanese government into adopting the Deconcentration Law. General MacArthur's underlings had apparently sold him a bill of goods whose implications he had not fully understood and which had now been repudiated by the United States government. He could not very well tell the Japanese that it had all been a mistake, so the Deconcentration Law was allowed to stand and the Holding Company Liquidation Commission started to move against the 1,200 corporations originally slated for dissolution or reorganization. But General MacArthur now invited five prominent businessmen from the United States to comprise a Deconcentration Review Board which was to appraise the actions of the Holding Company Liquidation Commission. This Deconcentration Review Board quickly found one reason or another to whittle down the number of corporations to be dissolved from 1,200 to 325, then to 30, then to 19, and finally when 9 corporations had been dissolved it announced that the deconcentration program had been satisfactorily completed. The SCAP official who a few months earlier had been berating the Japanese for their lack of enthusiasm for the Deconcentration Law now gave the Japanese press the tortured explanation that there had been no change in the American policy, that there was no disagreement between SCAP and Washington, that there was no inconsistency between the actions of the Holding Company Liquidation Commission and the Deconcentration Review Board, but that the Japanese had been enforcing their fair trade laws so vigorously and so effectively that the aim of economic democratization had now already been achieved without need for further recourse to the Deconcentration Law.

Although the Deconcentration Law thus ended in a fiasco, the anti-zaibatsu program as a whole was not altogether a failure. The official explanation contained a small grain of truth in that other measures were indeed proving successful in curbing the power of the zaibatsu to some extent. Without recourse to the Deconcentration Law, 83 zaibatsu holding companies had been broken up and some 5,000 companies were forced to go through financial reorganization. These measures no doubt fell far short of what the authors of the Deconcentration Law had intended, but the effects were not altogether negligible. When for instance the two great zaibatsu trading companies, the Mitsui and the Mitsubishi, were broken up into some 240 separate companies, the change was far from negligible. Although ten years later most of these companies reunited to form a structure closely resembling the old organization, this outcome cannot be blamed on the lack of severity of the Occupation's anti-zaibatsu measures. The Deconcentration Law could not have been any more effective. If the zaibatsu in recent years have managed to regain a good part of their pre-Occupation power, it is not because the Deconcentration Law was watered down; it is because the whole philosophy of the Occupation's deconcentration program failed to take adequately into account the basic historic factors underlying the zaibatsu's position and missed the mark by attacking merely the external manifestations.

The intended objective of the Occupation's anti-zaibatsu program was sound enough. When about a dozen colossal financial houses controlled about 80 per cent of the nation's industrial, commercial, and financial enterprises, of course there was an unhealthy situation. Such excessive concentration of economic power was obviously a serious hindrance to political and social democracy which the Occupation was quite justified in attempting to remove. But the means which the Occupation took, and even more the manner and spirit in which these means were carried out, and the explanations which were given by the proponents of this program when it failed to come up to expectations indicate some of the flaws in the thinking of the SCAP planners.

The disappointed proponents of the "zaibatsu-busting" policy tend to blame the conservativism of the American businessmen, who supposedly regarded the zaibatsu sympathetically as their own counterparts, and to blame also the shift in American policy from desirable reforms to the building-up of Japan as an instrument in the Cold War. Even more, they tend to blame the Japanese for failing to understand the evils of the zaibatsu. They hold that the Japanese do not have the intellectual or philosophical background to appreciate the competitive approach, that they are more congenial to subordinating themselves to a collective hierarchical organization than to asserting their individual capabilities, that they fail to see that such monopolistic corporate enterprises hide waste and inefficiency and are conducive to practices like price-fixing at home and dumping abroad—practices which may bring small advantages temporarily but which result in greater disadvantages in the long run.

Although the proponents of the anti-zaibatsu policy are undoubtedly sincere in their claim that the breakup of the zaibatsu would have been to the benefit of the Japanese, it is difficult to escape the suspicion that much of the intensity of feeling against the zaibatsu on the part of many Americans stems from their unconscious tendency to regard the zaibatsu as a feudalistic institution that not only engaged in unfair competition against Western business but also worked hand in glove with the militarists in an unholy alliance to conquer the world. Undoubtedly this conception of the zaibatsu is influenced by the old American stereotype—more recently adopted by the Communists—of portraying "Wall Street" as the instigator of "imperialism." Whatever the evils of the zaibatsu, however, in the Japanese historical and social context they did not conform to the Western stereotype.

In the first place, the power of the zaibatsu was not the result of planned collusion between the government and a privileged group; it was the spontaneous and inevitable outcome of historical circumstances. When in the middle of the nineteenth century Japan was pulled out of her hermit existence by the coming of Commodore Perry, her pressing concern was how to survive in the dangerous world of power politics in which she suddenly found herself. Her leaders thought the solution lay in making her over into a modern nation-state strong enough to play the international game on equal terms with the Western nations. This necessitated, among other things, the development of modern industry. But the development of industry requires capital, and a nation engaged largely in subsistence farming has no opportunity to accumulate savings which can be channeled into industrial investment. In the absence of an investing public, there are only two possible ways to secure industrial capital. One is to invite foreign capital, which carries the risk of foreign economic domination. Aware of the fate of other Asian countries that had fallen under Western imperialistic control, the Japanese leaders were determined not to run this risk. The only other possibility is for the government itself to build the industrial enterprises, channeling its tax revenues into investment. This was the course which the Japanese leaders took. Most of the modern industries of the early Meiji period were thus started as state enterprises.

But while modern Communist nations are committed to state ownership and control as a desirable end in itself, and while many of the Asian nations that have become independent in recent times are willing to accept a large measure of state planning or even state socialism as a means to industrialize rapidly, the Japanese leaders of the early Meiji period had no inclination toward such policies. If anything, they were attracted toward the classical economic concept of the value of capitalistic free enterprise, which seemed to them to be the key to the power of the leading Western industrial nations of that period. Hence the establishment of industrial enterprises by the government was regarded by the Japanese as an unavoidable temporary expedient and not as a permanent policy. In fact, practically all the actions of the Japanese leaders during that period represented trial-and-error responses to immediate contingencies rather than conformity to any preconceived plan.

Viewing state ownership as nothing more than a temporary expedient, the government sought to transfer these new enterprises into private hands as quickly as possible. Thus, in the 1880's, the government sold most of its industrial plants to private interests, often at very low prices because in a still predominantly agricultural society there were not many prospective buyers who had the necessary means. The only ones who could afford to purchase these enterprises were families like the Mitsui, who had made a fortune in the domestic trade in staples during the Tokugawa period, or the Iwasaki, the founders of the Mitsubishi combine who were among the very few former aristocrats with acumen enough to adjust themselves quickly to business. Having got in on the ground floor, so to speak, of the new industrial development which was destined to experience phenomenal expansion, they were in a position to make a killing as their enterprises boomed. Instead of dissipating their profits in high living, in conformity with native habits of thrift they plowed their earnings back into further investments until they parlayed their initial investments into gigantic economic empires. Using their banks and holding companies as their instruments of control, they operated mines, factories, shipping companies, insurance companies, trading companies, and countless other business activities ramifying into almost every field and having dealings with almost every part of the world. This result was not the product of a conscious plan, for such a development could not have been foreseen. It was the spontaneous consequence of the few people who had capital seizing the main chance in a period of a rapidly expanding economy.

However unhealthy such a concentration of economic power might be in the long run, in the formative period of the modern Japanese nation these zaibatsu performed an indispensable service. Japan could not have become a modern industrial and commercial power without their capitalistic dynamism. The only alternatives to them would have been either foreign imperialistic domination or a bureaucratic economy stultified by the rigidities of statism.

It is incorrect to think of the zaibatsu as a feudalistic familial institution which reached out from the past to hold Japan back. The zaibatsu were a modern phenomenon which came into existence in response to the need for rapid modernization. They were a new group recruited from widely disparate origins. Families like the Mitsui represented the new mercantile element whose rising power in the Tokugawa period undermined the feudal structure, while the Iwasaki represented those among the former aristocrats who most eagerly abandoned their traditional privileges to seek a different role in the new society.[6] Although vestiges of feudal habits influenced zaibatsu practices—as they influenced the practices of all elements of Japanese society—and although the zaibatsu in their publicity material even deliberately tried to surround themselves with feudalistic claptrap in an attempt to disguise their

[6] See chap. iii.

brashly parvenu character, the zaibatsu were essentially among the least feudalistic elements in Japanese society.

Although the original families held most of the stock and remained nominal owners, the zaibatsu organizations soon lost their family character. They became a great complex of impersonal corporations held together by all the intricate devices of modern corporate financing, manned by hundreds of thousands of employees selected solely for their abilities, and managed by executives who rose through competition from among the thousands of bright young university graduates who sought a career in these organizations. So completely were these corporations dominated by a professional managerial class that the original zaibatsu families eventually became practically divorced from the business except periodically to clip the coupons of their bonds. The best-known member of the Mitsui family today has spent most of his life running a fashionable little private school with progressive tendencies and more recently has been devoting all his energies to the M.R.A., the Buchmanite moral rearmament movement, while his son has at times flirted in dilettante fashion with Communist activities. The zaibatsu were hardly a feudalistic family institution in the sense that most Westerners imagine.

As for the unfair competitive practices which their size and combination of enterprises under centralized management supposedly enabled the zaibatsu to engage in, it is true that purchases of raw materials in bulk and the handling of all phases of distribution and marketing through a single system of related organizations conferred the advantage of greatly enhanced bargaining power. But it is doubtful whether without such a bargaining advantage an inexperienced newcomer like Japan could have broken into world trade at all in competition with the older established Western trading nations. Even so, for all their wide ramifications into various fields of business activities, the zaibatsu remained inferior in size and resources and thus in bargaining power to many of the great corporate enterprises of America.

Furthermore, the Japanese companies most guilty of the evils to which Western competitors objected—like dumping, pirating of designs, shoddy quality, and exploitation of "sweatshop" labor—were not the zaibatsu concerns but were the smaller marginal operators. Operating on the proverbial shoe-string, desperately competing with one another in a jungle struggle for survival, eager to keep their factories running even if it meant shaving profits to the disappearing point, these smaller independent companies were—and are—easy prey for the buyers from fly-by-night American cut-rate stores who set the cheapest possible specifications and beat down the prices by getting one Japanese manufacturer to bid against another. Although the zaibatsu also utilized such marginal operators under subcontracts to some extent, in the main the zaibatsu concerns, not in need of constantly bailing themselves out of chronic emergencies by desperate measures, could afford to build soundly for the long haul. They tended to promote name brands, to maintain quality standards, to make good on their guarantees, and to win acceptance for their products through good will rather than on the price factor alone. It is no wonder that Americans who had practical experience with Japanese business, in contrast to bureaucratic or ivory-tower reformers to whom sheer size seemed somehow evil, were alarmed at the Deconcentration Law, which seemed to threaten to reduce all Japanese enterprises to the level of the cut-throat sweatshops.

Neither were the zaibatsu the evil genius behind the militarists' program of imperialistic expansion, as is so commonly believed in the West. In fact, the zaibatsu and the military adventurers represented diametrically opposed philosophies regarding the destiny of the nation. The zaibatsu's ideal of national policy was best exemplified by the so-called Shidehara Policy, named after Baron Kijuro Shidehara, the Minister for Foreign Affairs through most of the 1920's who was related by marriage to the Iwasaki family. Its keynote of "live and let live, prosper and let prosper" was based on the premise that Japan had to trade in order to live, that trade could flourish only if it was mutually profitable to both parties, that customers' good will had to be cultivated through conciliation, co-operation, and friendship. The zaibatsu were thus strongly opposed to military adventurism, for as businessmen they believed that not only would taxes for armaments eat up the profits they were most interested in, but military activities would destroy profitable trade by antagonizing prospective foreign customers and by arousing resistance in areas that could furnish raw materials to Japan. Acting on the sound business maxim that "the customer is always right," zaibatsu executives roamed the world exuding cosmopolitan good fellowship in the best Chamber of Commerce–Rotary Club manner.

In sharp contrast, the ultranationalistic and xenophobic militarists felt that trade based on the good will of other nations was too uncertain, that in order to be secure, Japan should gain control of essential market areas and sources of raw materials at any cost and even by military force if necessary, and that the zaibatsu and other business interests were traitors who were willing to court dangerous risks to the national security for the sake of their selfish capitalistic profits. The zaibatsu leaders as much as the liberal political leaders were therefore the targets of the assassination plots of the military extremists who sought by terrorism to bring on a national-socialist dictatorship. When the militarists finally set up their empire in the puppet state of Manchukuo, it is significant that they projected an industrial development from which the zaibatsu were rigidly excluded, in which private profit was taboo, and where all enterprises were to be state-controlled. The conflict between the militarists and big business cannot be dismissed as mere internecine rivalry between factions of the same ruling class; the conflict represented a basic incompatibility between opposing national policies.

To the superficial observer, the picture is blurred somewhat by the fact that there were some important industrial groups, like the Kuhara and the Aikawa interests, which were closely associated with the military. These were the neo-zaibatsu who came into prominence in the 1930's by catering to the military in the field of munitions and heavy industry related to military preparations. They were quite distinct from the long-established zaibatsu who had as great a stake in foreign trade—in such commodities as textiles and sundries—as in domestic production. The neo-zaibatsu, for all their spectacular rise as they were pulled along by the ascending star of the militarists, never approached regular zaibatsu like the Mitsui and the Mitsubishi in the size and scope of their activities.

The picture is further blurred by the fact that, in the late 1930's when it finally became obvious that the military could no longer be stopped from seizing dominant political power, the zaibatsu reluctantly ceased their open opposition to the military and came to terms with them. Even though militaristic imperialism was damaging to their established business, instead of holding out and thus risking complete ruin the zaibatsu decided to cut their losses and salvage what they could by doing business with the military. On their side the military, having discovered that their own talents were sadly inadequate to operate a system of state socialism, became willing to moderate their economic program sufficiently to deal the zaibatsu in on some profits in exchange for technological and managerial help. Thus, by the time the war came along, the resources of the zaibatsu were fully mobilized in the national war effort.

This wary working arrangement between the mutually suspicious military and zaibatsu, entered into after the military had already irrevocably committed Japan to a course of aggressive expansionism, cannot in any way be construed as evidence that the zaibatsu were fascistic collaborators of the military in instigating the war. As in any modern nation with an integrated economy, the zaibatsu in wartime could no more escape being utilized in the Japanese war effort than American industry could avoid being converted into an instrument of the American war effort. As it was, despite the seeming capitulation of the zaibatsu to the military, a continuing tug-of-war between the two carried on just below the surface of the wartime unity was the chief feature of domestic politics during the war years. The military, in their striving toward a totalitarian state, sought to place the entire economy of the nation under bureaucratic controls. The zaibatsu, while hardly the advocates of pure laissez faire in the manner of their nineteenth-century English counterparts, were nevertheless contemptuous of the economic competence of militarists and bureaucrats and sought for business and industry the greatest possible independence from government control. By 1944, as the military extremists were discredited by their inability to maintain the necessary productive levels in industry or to continue to win

military victories, the more moderate elements which reflected
the point of view of the zaibatsu regained some of the power
they had previously enjoyed before the rise of the militarists.
It was these moderate elements that eventually steered the nation toward ending the war, a war which would never have
occurred in the first place had they been constantly in power.

In the light of these historic traits, it should be understandable that most Japanese were puzzled by the tendency of many
Americans to attribute war guilt as well as many basic evils of
Japanese society to the zaibatsu. Many Japanese deplored the
great concentration of economic power in the zaibatsu organizations and would have welcomed a social evolution which
would gradually diffuse economic resources more widely, but
the only Japanese who shared with the Americans any emotional animus toward the zaibatsu were the now discredited
fascist-militarists who hated the zaibatsu for having long been
the chief obstacle to their dreams of a totalitarian state. While
many Japanese hoped that Japanese economy would reach the
stage of development wherein the zaibatsu would become
superfluous, few of them believed that a sudden wholesale
smashing of the zaibatsu system would result in anything but
irreparable damage to the national economy.

Most Japanese assume that the growth in concentration and
size of economic enterprises is an inevitable world-wide
modern phenomenon and, like most Europeans, tend to regard
American efforts at "trust-busting" as a luxury possible only in
a country that can afford to be wasteful. The Japanese, like
most Europeans, would accept economic concentration as inevitable and would seek to obviate its evils by means other
than dissolution. The means that would appeal to most Japanese, save for the business entrepreneurs themselves, would
probably be nationalization or "socialization." Both the Socialists and the Communists favored keeping the zaibatsu structure fairly intact, for such larger concentrations would be
easier to nationalize eventually than a myriad of smaller enterprises. But if extreme deconcentration as originally envisaged
by SCAP was ill-conceived, on its part nationalization would
raise other problems equally serious in nature. There is no
assurance that public collectivism would prove to be much

more democratic than the private collectivism of the zaibatsu, while the bureaucracy necessary to run such a nationalized economy would almost inevitably be more cumbersome and less efficient than the zaibatsu's profit-motivated managerial class. Furthermore, at least some aspects of this nationalization were likely to resemble much too closely for comfort the old military-fascists' dream of a totalitarian state.

The extremes of "atomization" and nationalization need not, however, constitute the only possible alternatives to the excesses of capitalism. The course which SCAP finally settled for, namely, to police the zaibatsu without actually destroying them altogether, points the way by which slower but sounder improvement might be brought about. To be sure, the Anti-Monopoly Law, upon which SCAP fell back, was not adequate for the purpose. Even in a country with a strong antitrust tradition like the United States, the policing of a free competitive economy has proved difficult and not wholly effective; it is inconceivable that similar measures would prove more effective in a country like Japan where conditions were even more unfavorable. But even the inadequate Anti-Monopoly Law had some notable salutary effects. Intensification and elaboration of measures of this type in the direction of somewhat more governmental regulation and participation than were actually undertaken might well have proved sufficient to curb the chief evils of big capitalism without going to the extent of effecting a revolutionary disruption of the existing social order. It is unfortunate that SCAP did not pursue this possibility more than it did and that it did not educate the Japanese during the Occupation to continue in a similar direction. As it was, the Japanese, conditioned by the unpalatable manner in which the Deconcentration Law had been presented to them, carried over their distaste by association to the Anti-Monopoly Law also. Thus, instead of continuing and developing this promising line of attack, the Japanese partly emasculated the Anti-Monopoly Law as soon as the Occupation was ended. Here again, as in so many other aspects of the Occupation's program, more might actually have been accomplished if less had been attempted in the first place.

The result has been the partial resurrection of the zaibatsu in recent years, much to the alarm of some foreign observers. But significant differences from the past should not be overlooked. Although many of the zaibatsu corporations that had been broken up into smaller units during the early stages of the Occupation have now regrouped and reunited, they are not yet so large and strong as they once were. It may be doubted whether they ever will be, for it was the weaker units which pushed for reunification, while the stronger units, finding that they could stand successfully as independent companies, have understandably been reluctant to reunite with weaker components which they would have to help carry. A reconstituted combine lacking some of the strongest of its former components can hardly hope to be as strong as the original. Another difference from the past is the fact that, while in outward form the combines might be reconstructed, internally they are likely to be more democratic. The forced sale by the Holding Company Liquidation Commission of shares formerly owned by the original zaibatsu families has caused the dispersion of ownership among a large group of smaller investors. While organizationally and operationally the combines might continue to hold together because of obvious business advantages, the situation can hardly be identical to that which prevailed under far more restricted ownership. If growing general prosperity should enable an increasing proportion of the general Japanese public to continue to buy shares, in the manner of some well-known corporation shares in America that are very widely held, the result will be an unconscious trend toward a form of voluntary "socialization" under private auspices.

Probably the most effective of the forces working for change in the character of the zaibatsu system are not those that were directly connected with any of SCAP's reforms of a specifically economic character. More potent are the various countervailing forces of a more general character which the Occupation set loose in Japanese society against the traditional vested interests of every kind. For instance, the formidable labor union movement and the Socialist party, which now control more than a third of the seats in the Diet, constitute the kind of opposition and restraint which the zaibatsu organization cannot dare ignore. Against such active and militant countervailing forces operating in the now comparatively free social and political milieu, the zaibatsu can no longer exercise a monopoly of power such as they enjoyed in the 1920's or the military enjoyed in the late 1930's and early 1940's. A balance of competing forces, making for at least greater political circumspection and greater social reasonableness if not greater moral responsibility, has come to characterize the Japanese scene. What can this be but a promising basis for democracy? Despite the apparently dismal outcome of its deconcentration program, the Occupation may have created a better basis for economic democracy in Japan than it realized.

CHAPTER IX

Labor, Agriculture, and
Economic Recovery

Another socioeconomic reform with political implications even more controversial than the "zaibatsu-busting" program was the Occupation's program with respect to organized labor. Whereas the controversy over the zaibatsu is primarily an academic one which arouses more interest abroad than within Japan, the controversy over labor continues to rend Japan internally in a bitter political and economic conflict.

It was natural for the Occupation to concern itself intensely from the outset with the problem of labor, for labor constituted a large segment of the Japanese population that had been oppressed and exploited in the past. A liberated working class was envisaged as constituting the backbone of the kind of democratic society which the Occupation hoped to foster. Consequently, at the very beginning of the Occupation, SCAP ordered the removal of the wartime regulations by which labor had been restricted, controlled, and regimented. The way was thus opened for the resurrection of the labor union movement.

The response of the workers caught SCAP completely by surprise. Instead of shaping up into a protégé which SCAP could nurture and guide, Japanese labor quickly took off on a self-propelled movement whose speed and direction allowed SCAP no chance of control. By 1949, out of the total national industrial working force of about 15,000,000, there were some 7,000,000 members enrolled in more than 35,000 unions grouped

160

largely in two great rival federations. Despite a dip in membership to about 5,500,000 between 1949 and 1951, the unions again soon passed the 6,000,000 mark and have remained above that level ever since. Thus, with an organization ratio exceeding the United States ratio of 35 per cent and approaching the British ratio of 45 per cent, the labor union movement in Japan is now the fourth or fifth largest in the free world.

This spectacular postwar development is all the more remarkable because union membership in Japan had never reached half a million at any time before the war. Despite rapid industrialization since World War I, about 40 per cent of the nation's working population is still in agriculture; even now the industrial workers are for the most part relatively fresh from the farm, and many of them until recently continued to regard their factory employment as merely temporary. This was especially true of the large numbers of women workers who took short-term employment in the important textile industry. Another large proportion of the labor force is employed in very small shops where the workers feel themselves to be virtually members of their employer's household. Among such workers as these, there was naturally little consciousness of their distinctive class interests to cause them to espouse labor union activities. The comparatively few who pioneered in organized efforts to fight for labor found that there was always a large reservoir of fresh manpower in the countryside ready to flow into industry to dilute whatever gains might be won, for, exploited as the industrial workers generally were, they were still better off than the workers on the overcrowded farms. Add to these basic conditions the fact that the union leaders had not yet had time to gain much experience, that they had had very limited financial resources, and that antagonistic employers and an unsympathetic government had harassed them at every turn. It is no wonder that, despite a brave show of promising developments in the 1920's, organized labor had been frustrated and eventually almost wiped out when wartime mobilization placed all labor under government control.

But something must have happened since its prewar days of impotence to cause Japanese labor to break out with explosive dynamism once the Occupation removed its wartime shackles.

The contagious atmosphere of reform and the general willingness to fall in with the Occupation's desires which pervaded all
of Japanese society in the first post-surrender months undoubtedly had great influence, but labor was unique in the
vigor of its response. Union activity met a need which Japanese
labor had begun to feel with great intensity by this time. Possibly the wartime shift in emphasis from textiles to heavy machines and chemicals had tipped the balance of power in labor
from the country-girl mill operative to the skilled and experienced workman who was more conscious of his permanent role
in society and was anxious to improve on it. Possibly the workers had been building up resentment at having been driven
during the war to excessive exertions ultimately to no useful
purpose, while at the same time their obvious indispensability
for war production had given them a new sense of their own
power. They might have felt that the opportune occasion had
come at last to redress their grievances. A most compelling incentive to do something now, also lay in the postwar inflation
which was making their wages meaningless. At the same time,
their employers were confused and paralyzed by the economic
consequences of the defeat; the government, which had traditionally sided with their employers against them, was now help-
less before SCAP. Socialist and Communist politicians, even if
for special reasons of their own, contributed invaluable organ-
izing talent where labor's own abilities were inadequate. This
combination of circumstances resulted in the phenomenal
burst of union activity which has continued ever since. Although changing circumstances have subsequently caused this
activity to fluctuate in effectiveness, there has been little letup
in intensity of effort, indicating that labor unions are now here
to stay as a dynamic force in Japanese life.

For a while the unions profited directly from SCAP's labor
program, while SCAP on its side—though perfectly able to impose its will in any case—undoubtedly found the union activities a useful club to wave over the Japanese government in
getting it to adopt progressive labor legislation. Among the
basic labor legislation thus passed was the Trade Union Law
of 1945, based closely on the United States National Labor Relations Act of 1935 (Wagner Act), which safeguarded the

right of labor to organize, to engage in collective bargaining, and to strike, and which provided for labor relations boards at both the national and prefectural levels to mediate in labor disputes. Another basic piece of legislation was the Labor Relations Adjustment Law of 1946 which specified the procedures for the grievance machinery provided to labor. The most progressive of the labor laws sponsored by the Occupation was the Labor Standards Law of 1947, which set the minimum standards for working hours, vacations, safety and sanitation safeguards, sick leaves, accident compensation, restrictions on women and child labor, and other matters concerning the workers' welfare. The standards so set were quite comparable to the highest anywhere in the world and so far above anything which had prevailed in Japan in the past that their sudden enforcement was considered by many to be impracticable, especially in the precarious condition of Japan's economy at the time. But in highly unionized industries where infractions could be reported by the unions this law was strictly enforced, although in small shops where the unorganized workers raised no protest the law tended to be largely ignored.

This paternalistic Occupation sponsorship of union interests soon came to an end, however, when the union movement began to seem to SCAP an ugly duckling with strange and disagreeable ways. Part of these strange and disagreeable ways were the relatively innocent excesses understandably committed by inexperienced union leaders in their first flush of unaccustomed power, such as demanding that the lunch hour be counted in the eight-hour working day, that union meetings be permitted on company time and on company premises, that the unions be allowed to use the companies' office facilities to carry on union business, and the like.

But excesses with more dangerous implications arose out of the tremendous wave of industrial disputes that swept over the nation as soon as the unions began to feel their power. The workers had good reason to take desperate action, for the steadily mounting inflation made it difficult for them to live on their wages. But in the shattered state of the nation's economy in the early post-surrender period, the employers were in as desperate straits as the employees and usually simply could not meet the workers' demands. Strikes therefore produced no results except to arouse the resentment of the inconvenienced general public. The unions then resorted to ingenious and original methods to give point to their grievances. In one instance, striking employees of an interurban railway came back to operate the trains for the convenience of the passengers but refused to collect any fares. In numerous cases the employees shut out the owners and proceeded to operate the enterprise themselves, taking out what they considered fair wages for themselves, which often seemed to work well for a while but which almost inevitably meant eating into invested capital. Most alarming of all, the unions resorted to large-scale political action, backing up their political demands with mass demonstrations that threatened to get out of hand.

These labor tactics, strange to American experience, baffled SCAP officials. Continued labor turmoil endangered the economic recovery which SCAP increasingly desired. Preaching to the Japanese that good American unions eschewed political demonstrations and confined themselves to orderly collective bargaining made no impression. From an ugly duckling the Japanese unions appeared to SCAP more and more like a Frankenstein monster. Eventually SCAP decided to curb the power of the unions.

The first Occupation crackdown on labor came when General MacArthur invoked the threat of military force to compel the calling-off of a general railway strike just as it was about to start on February 1, 1947. From then on with increasing frequency, as overly energetic strikers and labor demonstrators clashed with the Japanese police, American military police in jeeps and occasionally even American combat troops with tanks maneuvered conspicuously into supporting positions behind the Japanese police to exercise an overawing effect. In 1948 when General MacArthur personally ordered Prime Minister Hitoshi Ashida to impose severe restrictions on the union activities of employees in government-owned enterprises, the respected chief of SCAP's Labor Division, who had had a distinguished career in the American trade union movement, resigned in protest. Through the lesser men who succeeded him, SCAP pressured the Japanese government into revising in 1949

the Trade Union Law of 1945 to follow more closely the example of the restrictive provisions of the Taft-Hartley Act rather
than the liberal provisions of the Wagner Act, into removing
union leaders from positions of influence as a condition for
receiving large-scale American aid, and into conducting in
1950 an extensive purge which sent Communist-affiliated labor
leaders into hiding. The result, combined with generally improving economic conditions which deprived labor of some of
its incentive to aggressiveness, was a blow to the union movement from which it has never fully recovered.

The initial reaction of the Japanese workers to the new
SCAP policy was one of amazed disbelief; then bitter disillusionment hardened into distrust and resentment of the Occupation and the United States. The workers felt that the Occupation, for all its talk about economic democracy and the interests of the little man, had betrayed them. They became convinced that the United States was an incorrigibly capitalistic
nation which was willing, in the name of economic recovery, to
sacrifice the workers in favor of the big vested interests. Of
course the Communists lost no time in making use of this impression to present themselves as the only true friends of the
workingman. The impression of the hopelessly reactionary inclination of the United States became so widespread among
the workers that the moderate leaders who were willing to
co-operate with the Americans were discredited, throwing the
Japanese labor movement more than ever in the direction of
radicalism. The impression made so strongly at this time has
persisted so that Japanese labor generally—and the Socialist
party, which is closely connected with organized labor—remains cool and distrustful toward the United States to this
day. This loss of understanding between the Americans and
the Japanese Socialists is particularly unfortunate, not only because the Socialists are steadily growing in strength so that very
likely they will some day assume the dominant political power,
but also because the Socialists—despite some characteristics
strange to American notions—are essentially more firmly committed to democratic principles and aims than the superficially
more seemingly pro-American groups on which the United
States lavishes its favors. The United States may have thus

forfeited contact with the group which in the long run might have turned out to be her most worthwhile friend.

But lest SCAP be criticized unfairly for its seemingly inept and reactionary labor policy, it should be recognized that SCAP was confronted with a terrible dilemma. The military men in SCAP may have been more heavy-handed than seemed justifiable to civilian labor experts like the one who departed from SCAP in protest, but it is difficult to imagine what real choice SCAP had in the matter. There could be no real gains for labor unless the general economy of the nation was restored, but labor was obstructing this necessary economic revival by its excessive demands. It is understandable that labor, having so often received scant consideration in the past, should be in no mood to be conciliatory now, but there was real danger in its impatience and its inclination to resort to extreme action such as was being urged by Communist leaders who falsely promised quick results. Unfortunate as were the consequences of SCAP's attempt at suppressing these labor activities, the consequences might have been even more unfortunate had these activities not been checked.

It might be argued that SCAP, while suppressing the unavoidable minimum of labor's excesses, could have simultaneously taken more positive measures to help labor attain its more legitimate demands. Instead, aside from its measures of suppression, SCAP merely lectured to the workers in quite abstract terms or else tried to use Communist tactics in reverse by infiltrating the union organizations with "Democratization Leagues," which were essentially SCAP-sponsored anti-Communist "cells." It might be argued that SCAP should have realized that, given the unstable condition of Japanese economy at that time and the relatively large proportion of workers in government-owned enterprises, American-style collective bargaining could not benefit the workers as effectively as European-style political action by labor organizations and that therefore SCAP should have aided and guided labor's political activities instead of trying to discourage them. It might be argued that SCAP should not have liberated the Japanese workers so completely and so suddenly through such advanced labor legislation, only to have to crack down on them later, but should have granted concessions to labor much more gradually and as labor proved its capacity to make responsible use of them. But while it is easy enough to raise such arguments with the benefit of hindsight, it is doubtful whether anyone, confronted with the unpredictable explosiveness of the Japanese labor situation in the immediate post-surrender period, could at that time have improvised a really successful policy. It is not surprising that SCAP encountered in its relations with labor one of its most unhappy experiences.

SCAP's shortcomings, however, were by no means the principal reason for the unfortunate turn the Japanese labor movement has taken. The basic reasons lay of course in the circumstances inherent in the Japanese background. Probably the most troublesome of the characteristics of the Japanese labor movement—at least from the American point of view—was its strongly political character which contrasted sharply with the predominantly economic character of American union activities. This political orientation of Japanese labor is not only natural because of the large number of workers in the extensive government-owned enterprises which are sensitive to political pressures, but also because the Japanese labor movement in the past had been hurt by political restrictions imposed by a government dominated by big business or by the military-fascists. It therefore seemed reasonable to the Japanese workers to assume that their most effective weapon was to be found in acquiring general political power.

Logical as was this preoccupation with politics, however, it had serious disadvantages. All too often the unions dissipated their energies in political struggles at the national level which had only slight relevance to the immediate interests of the rank and file of the workers. The great concern of the union leaders with national politics also caused the labor movement to be split by diverse political ideologies. Communist and Socialist politicians rushed into union organization activities to align the unions with their respective parties. Although the unions undoubtedly would have divided into competing groups in any event over differences in tactics, the prominent influence of conflicting political ideologies stemming from party affiliation intensified the split within the labor movement. Thus, although

Communist influence has now dwindled until it has no more than nuisance value, the sharp differences between the left-wing Socialists and the right-wing Socialists continue to split the labor movement to this day. This schism is reflected in the persistence in one form or another—despite numerous splinterings and mergers and realignments—of a radically inclined federation of unions and a moderately inclined federation constantly quarreling with each other,[1] while a group of independents wavers uneasily between. Such a schism, frozen into an almost permanent condition, is hardly an element of strength for the labor movement.

Another schism, although less overt, also serves to weaken the Japanese labor movement. This schism stems from the fact that a marked bifurcation exists in Japanese industry between a group of large corporate enterprises—mostly zaibatsu-affiliated—on the one hand, and a very large number of very small factories—mostly individually owned—which are not much more than household shops, on the other. The former were quickly almost completely unionized, for their large concentrations of workers made organization easy. The latter have resisted unionization, for the workers in the smaller units are not only physically and geographically more difficult to organize but traditional attitudes persist in these smaller shops where personal ties between employer and employee are generally intimate. The unionized portion of labor, rather homogeneous in its characteristics and interests, tends to become more sharply differentiated than ever from the non-unionized workers as the unions succeed in their activities. For instance, the average wage of the unionized worker is now almost double the average wage of the non-unionized worker.

This widening gap between the two sectors of labor, reflecting the basic dichotomy in Japanese industry, makes it more difficult than ever for the unions to shape their activities so as to spread into the unorganized shops, for the natural temptation of the unions is to conserve the advantageous position of

[1] Originally *Sanbetsu* (Congress of Industrial Unions) and *Sodomei* (General Federation of Labor Unions), respectively, about equally matched; today *Sohyo* (General Council of Trade Unions) with about 3,000,000 members, and *Zenro* (All-Japan Trade Union Congress) with about 700,000 members, indicating the steady decline of the right wing.

their members rather than to venture into new and difficult fields. Even with respect to employees of the same company, the unions tend to confine their activities to protecting the advantageous position already won by their present members and are reluctant to extend their protection to the newer or lower-ranking or temporary employees whose inclusion might undermine the level already attained. The result is that the Japanese labor union movement has already just about reached the limit of its phenomenal growth. Expansion from now on is likely to be slow and difficult; but as long as organized labor does not succeed in absorbing the present unorganized workers, Japanese labor will not be able to enjoy the benefits of solidarity.

Another weakness of the Japanese labor movement lies in the preponderant organization of unions on an enterprise basis. This is a strictly postwar phenomenon, for the earlier Japanese unions were organized on an industry-wide, craft, or regional basis. The reasons for the shift to an enterprise basis in the postwar period are too complex to be analyzed here, save merely to note that the shift was due in part to the success of the union movement, which won for the organized worker the status of a privileged member of the company "family." Such an advantageous status was regarded as a new vested interest worth protecting; hence the workers became predominantly concerned with their relations with their own particular company. Thus conceiving of their own interests more in terms of specific relations with one particular company than in terms of the relations of labor as a whole to industry as a whole, they inclined toward the enterprise basis in the organization of their unions. This did not mean that the unions were company unions, for they were not company-controlled and in fact usually fought the companies bitterly. But they did feel that the most practical gains they could make would be with respect to their relative position within their respective enterprises.

Such a circumscribing of their activity and interest is in a way an element of stability, for it provides the unions with a basis of reality and practicality; but it also tends toward a fragmentation of effort which weakens the union movement as a whole. There is hence an inconsistency and an ambivalence in the Japanese labor movement. While national federations of unions strive to nurture common political interests and also to co-ordinate extensive "labor offensives" periodically, these generalized appeals cannot fully overcome the diversified pull of the local interests rooted in specific intra-enterprise issues. The result is that a considerable gap persists between the quixotic political inclination of the national labor leaders and the myopic preoccupations of the local rank and file.

Notwithstanding all these and other faults, however, the Japanese labor movement must be regarded in its over-all effects as one of the most significant forces for democracy set in motion by the Occupation. While the lot of the Japanese workers is still much inferior to that of the workers in most Western countries, the unions have succeeded in winning for the Japanese workers a much larger share of the national income and a better general social treatment than ever before in history. While the demands of the workers have aroused the bitter opposition of many employers so that in a sense a clear-cut class conflict has come to characterize contemporary Japanese society, in many ways the interests of the working class have been generally recognized and even the employers have learned increasingly to make reasonable adjustments. In particular, the growing strength of the Socialist party means that the workers now have a political instrument which assures that the elements that have traditionally enjoyed power and privilege will not go unchallenged but must conduct themselves with increasing circumspection. While the workers might often be rash and crude and unwise, in their union activities they are steadly acquiring invaluable experience in methods of organized activity for their own welfare; in other words they are gaining training in citizenship and public affairs. While the specific tactics employed by labor might often appear undesirable or even dangerous, in the long run the capability which the workingman has acquired to fight for his own interests against the traditional forces of special privilege that used to exploit him can be nothing other than an asset in the democratization of Japan.

In contrast to its experience with labor, the Occupation

found its reforms on behalf of the farmers to be much more successful. At the time of the abolition of feudalism in the early 1870's, the peasants had been given outright title to the lands they cultivated. Thus, as freeholders, the Japanese farmers in modern times had suffered from no legal or political disabilities, but economic conditions had generally worked to their disadvantage. Too many people in too small a country caused many of the farms to be too small to be profitable. The government's policy of encouraging modern industry caused agriculture to be taxed much more heavily than industry. Unable to make ends meet, many farmers fell into debt, eventually lost their lands to their creditors, and were reduced to tenancy.

By the time of the surrender, although about half of all the farmers still owned some land, only about 30 per cent owned enough or more than enough for their sustenance, while the other 70 per cent were either fully tenants or at least had to rent some land to supplement what they owned. In point of acreage, almost half of all agricultural land was cultivated by tenants. This did not mean the growth of a class of great landlords, for, although about two thousand individuals owned as much as one hundred acres, most landlords owned no more than ten acres, which were enough—in a country where the average farm was about two and a half acres—to enable them to rent out a considerable portion of their holdings rather than to cultivate them all themselves. Furthermore, ownership of land was not particularly profitable. Even though rentals in kind commonly went as high as 50 per cent of the main crop of rice—subsidiary crops being kept wholly by the tenant—high taxes and the high price of land due to the pressure of population caused returns on investment in land to be generally considerably smaller than returns on other forms of investment. Thus the landlord was often not much better off than the tenant. Nevertheless, between the landlord and the tenant there was usually sufficient disparity in wealth, social prestige, and political influence to put the tenant pretty much at the mercy of the landlord. There could not be much political or social democracy in a community where the economic dependence of the tenants upon the landlords caused the former to defer to the will of the latter in practically all public matters.

As a part of its program of democratization, the Occupation therefore pressured the Japanese government to work out a reform of the land system. The Japanese themselves had earlier attempted to tackle this problem on several occasions, but with only meager results because of the political power of the land-lords. The first plan submitted by the Japanese government did not go much beyond these earlier efforts and was rejected by SCAP as inadequate. Thereupon, although the Russian repre-sentative on the Allied Council for Japan urged a sweeping confiscation of land from the owners and a redistribution to the tenants without compensation, the Australian member made some constructive suggestions which were taken up by SCAP in one of the rare instances when the Allied Council was able to make its influence felt. These suggestions were then in-corporated in the Farm Land Reform Law, which the Japanese Diet passed in October, 1946.

Under the terms of this law absentee landlordism was wholly prohibited, but a landlord might keep up to two and a half acres in the community in which he lived. An actual cultivator was allowed to own as much as seven and a half acres for his own use and an additional two and a half acres to be rented out. With some allowances for climatic reasons in the extreme north, all land in excess of these limits, as well as absentee-owned land, was to be bought up by the government, which in turn was to sell it on easy terms to former tenants. The desig-nation and appraisal of the land to be transferred as well as the actual transfer itself were handled by the people in each com-munity through approximately 13,000 locally elected land com-missions, each consisting of five tenant farmers, two owner-cultivators, and three landlords. These local commissions in turn chose prefectural land commissions to co-ordinate activi-ties prefecturally, while national supervision was provided by a Central Agricultural Land Commission under the chairman-ship of the Minister of Agriculture and Forestry and composed of eight tenant farmers, eight landlords, two representatives of farm organizations, and five non-affiliated agricultural experts.

Although preliminary preparations went so slowly as to in-vite some skepticism in the beginning, once the program got under way it was completed with speed and efficiency. Between the time the basis of compensation was determined and the time the transfers actually took place, however, the rapidly mounting inflation which characterized Japan's economy in those years caused the predetermined land prices to become utterly unrealistic. Thus the land was bought up by the government in some cases at a price per acre about equivalent to the black-market price for one carton of cigarettes and was then sold to the former tenants at a correspondingly low price payable in instalments spread over a thirty-year period at 3.2 per cent interest. The transfers, moreover, took place mostly at a time when the severe shortage of food enabled the farmers temporarily to make fabulous profits by diverting portions of their produce into the black market. Under these conditions there was no peasant however poor who could not easily afford to buy as much land as could be made available. Thus, although the principle of due compensation was maintained in theory, the actual effect was hardly distinguishable from the outright confiscation advocated by the Russians and vigorously denounced as immoral by SCAP. The landlords were hard hit by this obvious inequity, some individuals among them suffering dire personal tragedy; but as a class they were able to weather the blow without too much hardship. From the point of view of the former tenants, the land reform was an undreamed-of windfall.

Whatever the unfairness to many individuals, from the social point of view the benefits of the land reform were profound. About 5,000,000 acres were transferred. About 2,000,000 tenants, or about 75 per cent of the total, have become owners. Only 12 per cent of all arable land remains under tenancy, and payments of rentals in kind has been replaced by cash rentals at low rates set by law. Although in the rural communities the traditional social hierarchy still persists in large measure, as compared with the past the change in status of the former tenants to that of landowner has caused individual distinctions in wealth, social prestige, and influence in the community to become very much blurred. While old patterns of social behavior die hard, the former tenant, now freed from economic dependence on the landlord, tends increasingly to manifest his own will as a free individual. Most important of all, the peasants of Japan have been transformed in their own right into little capitalists who have a tangible stake in the existing regime. While this situation has from one point of view unfortunately tended to strengthen the natural conservatism of the peasants, it has from another point of view fortunately made them completely immune to the blandishments of the Communists. When it is seen to what extent the desperation of the landless peasantry of so many Asian countries feed the fires of revolutionary unrest in those countries, the stability and social health which the successful land reform has given to rural Japan stand in significant contrast.

The land reform, however, has obviously done nothing to cure the basic economic problem of the Japanese farmer, which is rooted in the fact that there simply is not enough land available for all the people in the country. The land reform has removed the source of social discontent by removing the inequity in holdings, but in a sense it has merely equalized the economic misery. The postwar revision of the Civil Code, which abolishes primogeniture and entitles all the children to inherit an equal share of their father's property, increases fragmentation of agricultural holdings and thus produces further misery. It is not surprising that, regardless of the provisions of the new law, economic necessity generally causes the younger children to choose to forego their inheritance in favor of the eldest son and to go elsewhere to seek employment so that the family farm can be passed down intact as in the past. Either Japanese agriculture must become much more productive than it is now, so that more and more people can be supported on smaller and smaller farms, or Japanese industry must expand rapidly enough to absorb all the younger children for whom enough land cannot be found or there must be a smaller total number of Japanese. Otherwise the beneficial effects of the land reform will again become nullified after a few decades as were the effects of the earlier land reform at the time of the abolition of feudalism.

A solution to the problem through significant increase in agricultural productivity must be ruled out as practically impossible. The productivity of Japanese agriculture is already outstandingly the highest in the world, owing largely to the approximately 80 per cent increase in the yield per acre of rice achieved over the past sixty years. Although much of this increase was an absolute gain brought about by improved scientific methods, too much of it was due simply to heavy application of expensive fertilizers and of more labor so that the profit to the individual farmer remained low. Although crop yields are even now constantly being increased through incessant scientific experimentation, the possible limit for any phenomenal increase seems to have been already reached. Apart from the unforeseeable discovery of some totally new revolutionary agricultural technique, increased productivity holds out little hope for the economic plight of the Japanese farmer. Most of the busy work now being done by and for the Japanese farmers therefore consists of mere palliatives. Better credit facilities have been established so that the farmers will not have to give up their land in times of temporary financial stress. Agricultural co-operatives, which have long been widespread in Japan, have now been made more democratic in their control so that in their many important activities—including bulk purchases of farmers' supplies and joint marketing of produce—they work in the interests of the majority rather than of the bigger operators. The increased political and civic consciousness which has been stimulated by the various Occupation-sponsored reforms, especially among the younger people, has resulted in a burst of self-help activities of various kinds for community improvement in many agricultural villages. These are all to the good, but they cannot get to the heart of the problem.

The most fundamental solution would be, of course, the stoppage of the natural increase of population. Until recently this solution had hardly ever been regarded as possible in view of the formidable birthrate which characterized modern Japan for about eighty years and which resulted in almost tripling the population during that time. But within the last few years there has taken place a spectacular drop in the birthrate; in contrast to the rate of 36.2 per 1,000 of population in the peak year of 1920 it had dropped by 1957 to only 17.2, considerably undercutting the current United States rate of more than 24. Apparently population movement in Japan has followed by

about half a century the familiar pattern of population movement in western Europe, where the shift from a preponderantly agricultural economy to a preponderantly industrial economy was accompanied by a rapid population increase until in
time new social forces brought about a leveling-off of the
population. In the case of Japan the usual social factors, such
as delay in age of marriage, rise in level of education, rise in
standard of living, increase in family planning, and the like,
have been supplemented by the government's recent policy of
leniency with respect to wholesale legalized abortions, which,
for all its undesirable aspects, is unquestionably effective. At
this rate the population problem of Japan, which has long been
a frightening specter, seems at last to be well on the way toward being reduced to manageable proportions within a relatively short time.

But the stoppage of population growth, while fundamental,
will not by itself immediately and automatically solve Japan's
economic problems. Some years must elapse before the population in Japan reaches equilibrium. By then a few more millions will have been born who will somehow have to be taken
care of; indeed there are several million children already born
for whom places must somehow be found in the nation's existing economy. The limit in agriculture has just about been
reached. The era when profitable empires could be carved out
by force is over, as has already been painfully impressed upon
the Japanese. They are not likely to forget this lesson soon, as
their present intense revulsion against their wartime experience
indicates. Even if their present pacifistic mood should eventually pass away, in the postwar world dominated by the United
States and the Soviet Union the realities of power relationships
make it impossible for a secondary nation like Japan to embark
again on an independent program of conquest. Emigration also
offers no solution. Even in the unlikely event that countries
could be found which would not object to large-scale Japanese
immigration, the impossibility of providing sufficient transportation and the impossibility of finding enough capital to get the
immigrants economically established in their new homes would
limit the physical resettlement of Japanese overseas to an in-
significant trickle.

The only practicable means of providing for the livelihood of the Japanese people for some years to come, therefore, is to be found in the expansion of industry. Thus, as has already been noted earlier, after some indecision the United States finally adopted the policy of encouraging the industrial rehabilitation of Japan. Discovering that exhortation was not enough, the United States eventually resorted to the pumping-in of substantial amounts of economic aid, which totaled somewhat more than two billion dollars by the time the Occupation was ended in 1952. A small part of this aid was in self-liquidating short-term loans; most of it was in the form of grants of food, raw materials, equipment, support for the retraining of Japanese technicians, and the like, which were in principle to be repaid by the Japanese eventually but under terms to be negotiated later, by which it was assumed that final settlement would be made for considerably less than the actual cost to the United States. This aid was rather late in coming and did not reach a sizable amount until 1947, rose to a peak of $535 million in 1949, dropped to half that amount the next year, and then quickly tapered to an end. Although some new grants have been made subsequently, almost all in support of rearmament, by the end of the Occupation the economic-aid program was practically finished and Japan had begun to make at least some small payments in return.

Although economic aid to Japan to the extent of more than two billion dollars seems large, it was a much smaller amount than the economic aid granted by the United States to any of the major nations of western Europe in the postwar period and also a much smaller amount on a per capita basis than the American aid granted to many of the smaller nations of Asia. That this comparatively modest amount should have resulted in such a rapid economic recovery in Japan that the aid could be so quickly discontinued is noteworthy. The reasons for the effectiveness of this pump-priming deserve to be recognized.

One of the reasons was that through the Occupation the United States could impose firm control in Japan over the uses to which the economic aid was put, in contrast to the deference which the United States had to show toward fully independent nations even when they might not always be making the best possible use of American aid. In Japan the United States was able to couple the grant of economic aid with the requirement that the Japanese adhere to a life of strict austerity, that the American aid be channeled almost entirely into basic productive investment and not into consumption, and that the Japanese tax themselves heavily to expand their investments far beyond the American-aided projects. These requirements were spelled out in a nine-point program laid down by Joseph M. Dodge, the tough-minded Detroit banker and later Director of the Budget of the United States, who was sent out to assist General MacArthur in economic matters. Although the "Dodge Plan" was in some respects unduly rigid and lacking in imagination, it provided basically just the sort of drastic discipline needed to put Japan's economy firmly on its feet. The Japanese politicians understandably found it expedient publicly to protest against such a severe measure, but privately they recognized its essential soundness and were quite willing to have it imposed upon them so long as it was SCAP and not themselves who had to bear the onus for imposing it. When it eventually brought about the return of prosperity and the relaxation of austerity, these same politicians ironically were able to turn it to their own credit.

Some of the credit for Japan's successful economic recovery, however, must legitimately be attributed to the Japanese themselves. Unlike the underdeveloped countries of the world where economic improvement must laboriously be built from the ground up, Japan possessed a background of indigenous industrial development which provided a ready-made foundation on which the postwar rehabilitation could be based. Japan had an abundance—in some respects even a glut—of competent and experienced scientists, engineers, technicians, administrators, and business entrepreneurs capable of carrying on by themselves with the minimum of American help, once the American decision to extend economic support had created an encouraging atmosphere. The traditional national traits of energy, diligence, and ambition—temporarily paralyzed by the shock of defeat—readily revived when hope was rekindled by American aid. Although some graft and boondoggling were inevitable, these evils were kept to an almost negligible minimum, and thus American aid was made to yield close to the maximum possible benefits.

Japan's economic recovery was aided also by some fortuitous circumstances of great importance. The time of American aid coincided with a period of unprecedented bumper crops after a stretch of several lean years. Also, although Japan's obligation to contribute to the costs of the Occupation consumed about one-third of her national budget during the first few years, eventually the diminishing Occupation costs and the increasing official disbursements in Japan by the Occupation for supplies and services as well as the private spending of Occupation personnel provided the Japanese economy with a very substantial net profit. This profit reached gigantic scale during the war in Korea when Japanese companies received fat contracts to manufacture supplies and equipment for the United States armed forces, to repair war-damaged American ships, tanks, jeeps, and aircraft, and to provide shipping and other services, while the use of Japan as a staging area and as a rest and recreation area by the United Nations forces brought additional income from the spending of the hundreds of thousands of foreign troops who passed through Japan.

The result of the combination of all these factors was the spectacular return of prosperity to Japan, comparable only to the developments in West Germany. In contrast to the material want, the physical shabbiness, and the spiritual despair which had plagued Japan for about the first three years of the Occupation, by the end of the Occupation impressive new buildings were transforming the landscape, shops were overflowing with goods of every kind, streets were jammed with new cars, and smartly dressed people were working and playing in an almost carnival atmosphere of buoyancy and vitality. Even after the end of the fighting in Korea and the end of the Occupation had sharply reduced American spending in Japan, the continuing bumper harvests and an export boom enabled Japan to maintain a level of material well-being that matched the most prosperous years of the prewar era.

Yet, for all the impressive economic gains made by Japan under American patronage, the basic economy of the nation remains highly precarious. There is no need to labor facts so generally known. More than ninety million people are crowded into a country about the size of the state of Montana, and about 85 per cent of the area is too mountainous for agriculture. The mountains provide attractive scenery but—unlike Montana—provide astonishingly little in the way of mineral or other natural resources. In normal years about 20 per cent of the food and about 80 per cent of the raw materials and fuel necessary to sustain the present population must be sought abroad. To pay for these essential imports, Japan must sell her manufactures abroad. A mere balance of exports to imports at the present level will not suffice, for Japanese commerce and industry must be constantly expanded to absorb the few more millions who will come on the labor market before the population finally reaches stabilization. Japan must also earn enough to repay a good portion of the American economic aid, to pay reparations to various Asian countries, to carry out the rearmament which is unavoidable under present world conditions, and to provide for the social welfare and higher living standards which the Japanese people are increasingly demanding.

This necessary industrial expansion depends essentially on expansion of exports. Yet, even now, Japan is not able to sell abroad as much as she buys. The United States, with whom Japan has the most extensive trade relations, has for some time bought only about half as much from Japan as Japan has been buying from the United States, and only within the past two or three years has this imbalance been somewhat moderated. Tariffs, quotas, and public resistance in the United States against Japanese goods make it unlikely that Japanese sales to America can be quickly increased to the extent necessary to meet Japan's requirements. Some Western nations maintain even more discriminatory barriers against Japanese trade. Theoretically, the best prospects for Japanese trade seem to lie in South and Southeast Asia, but the residue of wartime animosities, European and Communist Chinese competition, political instability in some of the countries of this area, and low purchasing power due to the generally underdeveloped state of this area's economy, all operate to hamper Japan's attempts to expand her trade in this direction. In this situation the Japanese are sorely tempted to try to increase substantially their trade with Communist China, even though responsible Japanese leaders are well aware of the risks that attend dealing with the Communists. So far Japan has seemingly managed to fare very well, but a national economy based in considerable part on such ephemeral supports as American aid and the Korean war boom does not offer much assurance for the future. Particularly, when it is estimated that, in order to support her people, Japan's exports must reach the equivalent of five billion dollars annually by 1965, or double the amount of the 1955 exports, there can be little room for optimism.

The matter of Japan's economic viability in the future has a direct bearing on the objectives of the Occupation. To say that any nation must be kept economically healthy in order to prevent it from succumbing to communism is of course an oversimplification. But if in the early days of the Occupation General MacArthur was correct in assuming that "you cannot teach democracy to a hungry people," it continues to be correct to assume that democracy cannot be maintained without a certain minimum basis of continued economic well-being. Granted that political and social democracy are not directly conditional on any particular level of economic development, it is nevertheless true that the most successful democratic societies occur where the material amenities of life are reasonably abundant and equitably distributed. Of course the factors of tradition and ideology are not to be minimized, but it is probably not an accident that the most virile democracies are found in the relatively prosperous industrialized countries of western Europe and North America which have preponderantly middle-class populations. Where economic conditions cause most of the people to belong to a depressed proletariat or peasantry rather than to a prosperous middle class, the people apparently tend to have less confidence in what they might achieve through their own democratic efforts and are more likely to pin their hopes on the demagogic promises of charismatic leaders of the extreme left or the extreme right.

By this reasoning, Japan is at present in a relatively fortunate position. No other non-Western nation approaches as closely as does Japan the social configurations of the middle-class industrialized nations of western Europe and North

America. The economic developments of the past century have created in Japanese society a relatively large middle-class and petit bourgeois element. The resurgent labor movement and the successful land reform of the Occupation period have moved the social and economic status of even the Japanese proletariat and peasantry somewhat in the direction of the position of the middle class. The present prosperous condition of the economy of Japan, linked more closely than ever with the capitalistic free-enterprise economy of the West, also tends to inhibit any temptation to flirt with totalitarian economic systems. The economic conditions for the time being are thus favorable for the development of democracy. But if the present level of Japan's economic well-being cannot be maintained, if the present substantial middle class is depressed to the status of a dissatisfied inferior class, there is no assurance that the moderate democratic methods of self-improvement will not be abandoned in favor of extremist panaceas of one kind or another.

But the economic future of Japan does not lie in the hands of the Japanese alone. It depends on such factors as the willingness of other peoples to buy Japanese goods, the ability of the nations of the world to devise a global economic system which will accord reciprocal benefits to all peoples—in other words, the practical recognition of the economic interdependence of all mankind. Whether the Occupation's objective of democratizing Japan has been successful or not in the long run may thus be determined less by what the Occupation did to and for the Japanese, or by how the Japanese reacted to the Occupation's efforts, than by what the whole world can eventually achieve in the way of constructing an integrated international economy.

CHAPTER X

The New Basic Education

The Occupation might impose sweeping changes in the political, economic, or social organization of Japan, but the permanent acceptance of these changes depended ultimately on how successfully the Japanese were educated to appreciate them. The role of education was in this respect fundamental to the whole Occupation program.

The general assumption, among Japanese as well as among foreigners, is that the prewar system of education in Japan had been a notorious instrument for propagating a reactionary and ultranationalistic point of view and that a revolutionary reform of the educational system was necessary before democracy could make much headway. In the main this assumption is correct, but in many particulars the prewar educational system was not without some merit. The Occupation's efforts in the field of education, therefore, cannot be properly evaluated except against the background of Japan's earlier system.

Japan's modern system of education, organized soon after the establishment of the Meiji government, had been specifically designed to further the great aim of this regime, which was to transform Japan as quickly as possible from a conglomeration of petty feudal states into a unified, modern nation-state. Both the strengths and the weaknesses of the system stemmed from its being directly harnessed to this national objective.

The importance attached by the Meiji regime to education as a means of attaining its great objective had the fortunate effect of spurring the rapid spread of popular education. This official policy was aided by the general public's respect for education derived from the Confucian tradition and by the new faith in education as the key to the secrets of the power of the West which the Japanese wanted to emulate. Even in the premodern period Japan had already possessed some basis for mass education in the *terakoya*, or parish schools maintained by the Buddhist temples, which had reached the sections of the population neglected by the aristocratic schools. With the establishment of a modern public school system, the government in 1872 made attendance in the elementary schools compulsory for all children. At that early date universal, compulsory education for both sexes of all classes was something of an innovation even among the advanced nations of the West. Although this compulsory schooling did not exceed six years with an additional two years of required part-time attendance, it was enough to provide everyone in the nation with at least an elementary education, while facilities for secondary and higher education were steadily expanded in an effort to catch up with the ever insatiable popular demand. At least in extent, if not in quality, Japanese education thus came to rank fairly close to the top among the nations of the world. Widespread literacy in itself is, of course, no guarantee of democratic conduct. But, on the other hand, the operation of a modern democratic government is hardly possible among an illiterate people. From this point of view the Japanese educational system had served the nation well in producing a populace which enjoyed virtually universal literacy.

The Japanese educational system had other indirectly democratizing, or at least liberalizing, effects. A uniform compulsory education imparted without serious discrimination to children of all classes could not help exerting some democratizing influence. It also helped to break down the sectionalism which was at the root of the feudalism whose lingering influence the regime was so determined to eliminate. Furthermore, however different in point of view and interpretation, at least the content of the subjects taught in the Japanese schools—save for a few unique courses like "ethics"—was practically indistinguishable from that of schools in Western countries. The modern

Japanese therefore came to take for granted at least some of the cultural heritage of the West as a part of his own cultural heritage. This common fund of knowledge thus shared with the rest of the world made the Japanese, despite strong nationalistic bias, a member of the modern world community in a sense not true of less eclectic and more traditional non-Western peoples.

At the same time, the advanced state of educational development in Japan after the early Meiji period made it unnecessary for the Japanese to go abroad to study, although a year or two abroad on a sort of grand tour of observation after being established in one's career was highly prized. Thus, unlike many Asian nations, Japan never developed a highly Westernized elite class predominantly educated abroad and so culturally alienated from the rest of the population as to result in an undemocratic chasm between the leaders and the masses. The leaders of Japan were products of the same educational system as the masses, which enabled the two to remain in comparative rapport with each other. Also, although the general educational level was not high enough to assure that the people would not be misled by the leaders, the widespread literacy provided a large reading public which made possible a reasonably informed public opinion.

Some grave faults, on the other hand, characterized the Japanese educational system and made it unsuitable as an instrument of democracy. Basically, the purpose of the education was not to provide for the fullest unfolding of the individual's personality, except incidentally, but to produce useful servants of the state and of society. To assure that there would be no dissipation of effort in directions that did not contribute directly to the objectives of the state, educational activity was strictly prescribed and controlled by the central authorities. The subordination of the individual to social and political ends resulted in a regimentation which tended to force all individuals into a standardized mold and thereby blunted initiative and originality. While distinctive and vibrant personalities were not rare among the Japanese, they managed to emerge in spite of the educational system and not because of it. This was not, of course, peculiar to the Japanese; any people who are driven too hard to attain some fixed goal are likely to lose their sense of proportion and become inflexible in outlook, as witnessed by the reshaping of the national character of peoples under contemporary Communist dictatorships. But there was something tragically wrong with a system which so repressed the individuality of the children that by the time they emerged from the schools most of them were conditioned—despite whatever vague personal dissatisfactions they might retain—to subordinate their own desires to their obligations to society as conceived by the state.

The Japanese educational system was also highly utilitarian in character. One would not guess it from the ivory-tower outlook of most Japanese intellectuals, but the system itself emphasized technology and the sciences which had practical application, while by comparison it neglected the social sciences which were likely to stimulate too critical an attitude toward the ends of the state. There was also a serious neglect of women's education, reflecting the inferior status accorded women in traditional Japanese society. While coeducation prevailed through the elementary grades and again to a very limited degree in the universities, generally the separate schools for girls at the other levels maintained standards inferior to those of the schools for boys. Thus, although in organization, pedagogical methods, and even in content the Japanese system was modern—at least in the nineteenth-century if not the twentieth-century sense—and essentially Western in character, it was slanted to the aims of an authoritarian and paternalistic government and pervaded by the value system of a society which differed very greatly from the individualistic, democratic societies of the West.

Among Japanese educators themselves there had long been many who were gravely dissatisfied with the official educational system. The widespread disillusionment with almost all aspects of the past which swept over the Japanese people after their defeat in war assured that there would be popular support for educational reforms of some sort. But there was no consensus as to just what changes there should be. In this situation, it was natural that the initiative for proposals for educational reforms would come entirely from SCAP. Although some of SCAP's proposals seemed highly inappropriate to many Japanese, they themselves were in no position to propose anything better.

At the outset of the Occupation, as a stopgap measure, SCAP ordered not only the elimination of military training and supposedly martial sports like fencing and wrestling but also the suspension of all courses in geography, history, and particularly "ethics," which were considered to have served most importantly for the indoctrination of authoritarian and ultra-nationalistic ideas. Pending the writing of new textbooks, objectionable passages were ordered deleted from the existing textbooks; this was effected in some cases by having the pupils themselves simply draw a line through the offending passages. And of course all the teachers were screened through the purge. A more thorough reshaping of the educational system awaited the coming of a highly touted educational mission sent from the United States in March, 1946, to advise SCAP.

This United States Education Mission was composed of twenty-seven prominent American educators under the chairmanship of Dr. George D. Stoddard, who became president of the University of Illinois soon after his return from Japan. It spent a little more than three weeks in Japan. Approximately two weeks were spent in studying the Japanese educational system, primarily through briefings from SCAP officials and through conferences with Japanese educators. The remainder of the mission's stay in Japan was taken up in writing its report. This report then became the master plan for SCAP's program for the reform of the Japanese educational system.

The report in essence recommended the complete recasting of the Japanese educational system in the image of the American system. Such an outcome was to have been expected. Obviously the Japanese system needed reform, but the Japanese were not agreed on what specific changes should be made and Japanese educators who did have definite ideas were not sure how politic it would be for them to insist on their ideas in the face of the views of SCAP and the American experts. The members of the United States Education Mission, although highly competent, were not in Japan long enough to appreciate fully the subtleties of the unique problems inherent in the local situation. They were forced to get much of their information about Japan from the education officers of SCAP, who were military officers hurriedly picked up from the various units under MacArthur's command and assigned to educational duties because they had taught school at some time or other in civilian life. As former teachers in uniform, with only brief experience in Japan, their point of view fitted in nicely with the predispositions of the United States Education Mission, which, while including several eminent independent scholars, was heavily weighted with school administrators and professional educationists who were closely committed to the system prevailing in America. In fact, so similar were the points of view of the SCAP officers and of the visiting experts that the report of the United States Education Mission seems in large part to have been merely an indorsement of the proposed recommendations that had been prepared in advance by these obscure SCAP officers.

The report of the United States Education Mission was, however, eminently reasonable in tone and its specific recommendations were mostly quite sound in principle. The difficulties which eventually arose stemmed largely from the peculiarities of the abnormal postwar Japanese environment and from the overenthusiastic and somewhat precipitous manner in which the SCAP officers proceeded to apply the recommendations. In theory the Japanese were merely invited to consider these recommendations and to adopt as many of them as they might choose. In actuality the SCAP officers drew up highly detailed projects for putting these recommendations into effect and then pressured the Japanese into carrying them out.

One of the major recommendations of the United States Education Mission called for the decentralization of the Japanese educational system and the dispersal of its control among autonomous, popularly elected local bodies. The uniform textbooks, the rigid curriculums, the identical method of instruction, all prescribed throughout the nation by the Ministry of Education in the past were certainly not conducive to the free spirit necessary for an education for democracy. Ironically, in its efforts to carry out reforms SCAP's Civil Information and Education Section—commonly known as CI&E—merely intensified the centralized bureaucratic controls over the Japanese educational system, for CI&E prescribed all the reform measures, imposed them upon the Ministry of Education, and charged the Ministry with seeing to it that they were carried out throughout the nation. Eventually popularly elected boards of education were constituted in each prefecture and in most of the municipalities, with power to appoint local school superintendents, to authorize the hiring of teachers, to pass on what textbooks should be adopted, and to exercise general responsibility over the school system in their respective districts. The Ministry of Education was thus deprived of most of its administrative powers and was reduced to giving merely technical advice to the now supposedly autonomous local school systems. But as long as there remained any of its recommendations that had not yet been fully carried out, CI&E continued in effect to exercise strong direction from above, regardless of the changed administrative structure of the Japanese educational system.

Control from the top, to which they were accustomed, in itself did not bother the Japanese educators as much as the fact that many of them had little confidence in SCAP's educational personnel. The chief of CI&E was a marine corps reserve lieutenant colonel who in civilian life had been a small-town high-school principal. The members of his staff, at first wholly military but later predominantly civilian, were mostly people of about the same level of background and experience. The education officers of the district military government teams, whose duties were to supervise the educational activities of local governments, were generally young men of even less background and experience. Their incomparable idealism and intense dedication to their work should have served as an inspiring example, but many Japanese educators and particularly the university professors were conscious only of their own wider experience or greater erudition and tended to be supercilious toward these American educational officers and their ideas.

Where the popularly elected local boards of education assumed increasing responsibility, the results were often far from those anticipated by the Americans. As in the case of local governments, autonomy under popularly elected officials often meant that effective control was taken out of the hands of bureaucratic but competent professionals working in the comparatively enlightened atmosphere of the metropolitan capital and put in the hands of venal and reactionary petty political bosses of the backward local communities. Where the teachers in self-defense successfully entered local politics, the result was to make the local boards of education mere puppets of highly organized teachers' lobbies. Even where the general lay public itself was sufficiently emancipated to repudiate the local political bosses, many of the people were so confused by the flood of new educational problems that now arose that they often preferred to intrust their decisions to the teachers than to take an independent stand for themselves. Although undoubtedly preferable to control by ignorant political bosses, such assumption of control by a professional group who comprised a directly interested party was not what the Americans had envisaged.

Another basic recommendation of the United States Education Mission called for the reorganization of the system of schools. The Japanese educational system had been egalitarian in the sense that the system was uniform throughout the whole country and that the schools were legally open to all without discrimination. This did not mean, however, that all received exactly the same kind of education, because economic reasons and stiff competitive entrance examinations at all but the elementary level caused distinct differentiation in the kinds of schools selected by the students. There was complete equality and uniformity through the compulsory elementary school of six years. But beyond this point a choice had to be made among three distinct types of schools: (1) part-time continuation classes which were compulsory for two years for those who immediately went to work; (2) the commercial and the technical middle schools of five years, which were essentially terminal trade schools for those who did not expect to go further; and (3) the academic middle schools of five years, which prepared for higher education. Finally at the level of higher education, there were still further choices, as will be described later. Inasmuch as only those who qualified for the best choice at each step could receive the kind of education which prepared for leadership at the highest level, there was terrific competition to get into the elite group, with attendant unwholesome strains on both the children and their parents.

The United States Education Mission recommended that in the place of this multiple system of schools, there should be a single educational ladder consisting of the six-year elementary school, the three-year junior high school, the three-year senior high school, and finally the institutions of higher learning. The American experts and SCAP also called for coeducation at every level and for the extension of compulsory schooling through the junior high school instead of only through the elementary school.

Theoretically, the reasons advanced by the American authorities were good. They argued that it was undemocratic to segregate the children in different kinds of schools on the basis of how long they could continue in school as determined by their intellectual aptitude or by the financial condition of their parents. They argued that a system which, at the end of only six years of common schooling, sorted out the young children into different educational channels so that in effect they were predestined at such a tender age to different stations in life could not be reconciled with democratic ends. They held that legitimate variations in needs and aptitudes could be provided for by different electives within the same school wherein all types of students were democratically mingled together.

In practice the reform produced results similar to those found in the United States: the vocational courses are no longer practical enough to be of much use; the academic courses tend to be watered down by the presence of too many disinterested or incapable students; and electives offer the temptation to too many pupils to choose the easiest possible course. There may now be democratic equality, but an equality of unsatisfactory education for all. In response to real need, many of the postwar generalized senior high schools are therefore now showing a tendency to revert to the differentiation between academic and vocational schools. At the same time, there is a sufficient core of common subject matter so that it is not impossible for a pupil, with proper effort, to transfer from one kind of school to the other, as indeed he could even under the old system.

As for the division of secondary education into the separate junior and senior high schools, one of the reasons the American authorities gave was that the old five-year middle schools mixed pre-adolescent children and adolescent youngsters in the same school, which was pedagogically unwise, especially with coeducation. The Japanese felt, on the other hand, that the less sophisticated Japanese children brought up in a different social milieu offered no problems at the middle-school level like those presented by the socially precocious American children of similar age. Changing social customs and standards in Japan make it appear, however, that the American position may in the long run prove to have been the wiser one.

The other reason given by the Americans for the establishment of separate junior and senior high schools in place of the five-year middle school was that compulsory education should be extended to at least nine years and that the cutoff point should coincide with graduation from a school rather than occur in the middle of a school's course. The Japanese had no quarrel with this argument, but they were greatly disturbed over the financial problem involved in the building of the new facilities necessary in order to divide the middle school into two separate schools. During the war many of the school buildings had been destroyed, the remaining ones had fallen into disrepair, and there now existed a serious shortage of building materials. The need to erect new school buildings also came at just the time when the great expansion of local governmental functions with the postwar extension of local autonomy suddenly threw heavy new financial burdens on the local communities. The Japanese could not understand why the extension of the six-year elementary schools into compulsory eight-year schools, as had been projected earlier but suspended during the war, would not serve almost as well as the establishment of entirely new junior high schools; and it would cost very much less.

But CI&E insisted that there must be no compromise in the school reorganization. Ironically, just about the time the Japanese reluctantly got an extensive school building program under way, ESS, or the Economic and Scientific Section of SCAP, imposed the "Dodge Plan" for drastic austerity, under which expenditure for anything other than productive investment was rigidly curtailed.[1] ESS accordingly ruled that deficit financing for the building of schools was not permissible. The Japanese authorities were thus caught between CI&E's pressure for the building of schools and ESS' denial of the means by which the school-building program could be financed. Apparently there was a conflict of policy within SCAP between these two staff sections which was never resolved, for when the Japanese authorities asked how the opposing directives could be reconciled they were curtly told that SCAP was not operating the Japanese government, that SCAP intended merely to point out desirable general policies, and that it was up to the Japanese to figure out for themselves how to implement these policies. To escape this intolerable squeeze, several mayors, municipal councilmen, and school superintendents resigned. The building program was stalled. But while classes were temporarily scheduled in shifts in abandoned military barracks, temples, and sometimes even in the open air, the building program was eventually pushed to completion through strenuous and unorthodox methods of financing, often involving substantial "voluntary" contributions from the parents of the school children. The educational results in the long run may possibly have been worth the effort, but this episode strained the relations between the local Japanese officials and SCAP for some time.

SCAP educational experts also undertook to sponsor thorough revision of the curriculums of the Japanese schools. Particularly, geography, history, and "ethics," the teaching of which had been suspended, were replaced by a new curriculum in social studies designed to teach good citizenship. Whereas traditional values emphasizing obligations to the existing social and political system had been inculcated in the old courses in "ethics," the new curriculum was to provide no conscious indoctrination of any kind; democracy was to be fostered by carrying out "projects" in civic education. The study of all sub-

[1] See chap. ix.

jects as subjects was minimized, and emphasis placed on a "core curriculum" around which various subjects were brought to bear in integrated study projects which would provide balanced comprehension of all phenomena.

In time satisfactory new textbooks appeared embodying this point of view. Some of these new textbooks were apparently remarkably good. Now that the Ministry of Education had no control over the textbooks, however, in some instances minor scandals occurred as a few publishers used questionable tactics to get inferior books adopted by ignorant or corrupt local school boards. Eventually, although legal power to choose the textbooks remained with the local authorities, the situation was improved by the Ministry of Education's compiling lists of recommended textbooks from which the local school systems could safely make their selection.

SCAP also tackled the problem of reorienting the teachers to the new educational objectives and methods. This task was accomplished in large part through a series of conferences, institutes, and meetings of all sorts at which Japanese teachers were lectured to by visiting American educators. These visiting experts, brought to Japan on thirty-day or ninety-day tours and speaking through interpreters who themselves often needed better reorientation, could do little more than superficial work, but their contributions were undoubtedly stimulating, even if at times confusing.

A review of these reform measures shows that SCAP correctly diagnosed the defects of the old system of Japanese education and strenuously sought to remedy them by introducing the chief features of American education. The American effort was thus wholly commendable in purpose, but it might be questioned whether the American model was always the most desirable one for Japan. SCAP's actions contained some crudities and excesses—in method if not in substance—so that the immediate results were often chaotic. But by thoroughly shaking up the rigid old Japanese educational system SCAP forced the Japanese educators to engage in painful but badly needed soul-searching. In the long run the outcome will undoubtedly be the gradual emergence of a new system of education which will be eminently better than the old.

While the eventual consequences of SCAP's educational reform measures will probably turn out to be all for the good,
some less favorable observations must be made on the outcome
so far. Certainly CI&E was concerned far too much with the
external incidentals of education—administration, organization,
and the like—and not enough with the objectives, spirit, and
substance of education. The externals are, of course, much
easier to manipulate, and they show up much more impressive-
ly in the reports, replete with graphs, charts, and statistics so
dear to bureaucratic administrators whether military or educational, but they divert too much energy away from the essen-
tials. Even where CI&E was concerned with essential substantive matter, the results were understandably less apparent.
Americans usually did not know how to impart these substantive matters to the Japanese apart from the often irrelevant externals unique to American conditions. To do this task satisfactorily called for Americans who understood Japan almost as
well as they understood America, and obviously there were not
enough Americans with such qualifications. Conversely, to
adapt the essential substance of the American teachings to the
external forms suitable to unique Japanese conditions called
for Japanese adapters who understood America almost as well
as they understood Japan, and obviously there were not many
Japanese educators with such qualifications. Under the circumstances the outcome was perhaps as good as could have been
expected.

How inadequately many Japanese educators understood the
basic principles of American education is to be seen in the
often recurring plea of some of them for a comprehensive, authoritative pronouncement which would spell out the aims and
principles of the new education in much the same way that the
Imperial Rescript on Education of 1890 authoritatively spelled
out the aims and principles of the old education. It was not
only the traditionalists who sought to salvage some sense of
order and consistency through such a pronouncement, but
many who sincerely yearned after democracy felt baffled and
lost without a superior authority to which they could turn for
guidance. It is, however, to the credit of the majority of the
Japanese educators and of the general public that their vocif-

erous opposition has managed to defeat all official attempts to issue any such pronouncement. Not only do most of the people find the memory of an authoritative catechism distasteful, but enough of them apparently have come to know enough about democracy at least to suspect that democratic education is something which cannot be prescribed by external authority but must be constantly cultivated from within by its practitioners.

At the same time, while the rejection of the authoritarianism of the past is commendable, the disappearance of the old authority—before a new democratic self-discipline has had opportunity to develop—has created serious problems. This situation is to be seen most conspicuously, though by no means exclusively, among the so-called *après*, as the Japanese call their *après la guerre* generation. This Japanese counterpart of the "beat generation," brought up almost entirely in the years since the war, seems in many ways to be a breed altogether apart from the older Japanese whose lives reach back to the days before the war. However confused they might be, those who have some memory of the more stable prewar era, even while they now reject the ideals of that era, continue to strive for the reconstruction of some kind of a stable and consistent social order. To the *après*, on the other hand, the concept of a social order of any kind seems to be incomprehensible, and they exhibit an attitude which might be characterized as a sort of passive nihilism.

The reason for such an attitude is not hard to understand. In their early childhood, when they first became aware of their environment, the only world they saw was the world of authoritarian militarism. Then, while they were still impressionable little children, came the defeat and the surrender and the Occupation. The world they had barely known toppled over; their parents, their teachers, their heroes, and all the adult authority they had leaned upon and trusted were suddenly discredited. A flood of new propaganda for democracy filled the air, but they saw their elders confused, bewildered, and impotent. They were suddenly surrounded by incomprehensible flux and instability. Brought up in this insecure and disorderly era which they did not have the capacity to understand, they grew up distrustful and disrespectful of all adult authority. They did not know what it was to hope for a better world, because during all of their short lives they had never experienced anything better. Having faith in nothing, they aimed only at getting what transient pleasure they could for themselves by their own wits from day to day, without concern for others, who all seemed unreliable, and without concern for the apparently unpredictable future. Thus, many of this generation have become juvenile delinquents engaging in extreme self-indulgence without regard for the society which they despise. Many more of this generation conform outwardly to social conventions, perhaps even too easily and too glibly, having learned that clever manipulation and a charming manner can ease their path in the meaningless, shifting world in which they find themselves. But, however more attractive their manner and more genteel their methods, the latter share to some extent with the delinquents an amoral social irresponsibility which causes them to regard as only natural almost any unprincipled expediency for the sake of their own self-advantage. The *après* are an innocent but cynical generation.

Many Japanese educational theorists, agreeing with the line of thinking of some American critics of progressive education, contend that the system introduced into Japan by the Americans is largely responsible for aggravating this situation. They hold that American progressive education, in its emphasis on naturalism, emancipates the child from external bonds and provides for a "child-centered" education; and, in its emphasis on pragmatism, denies the validity of any fixed goal but calls for a fluid objective to be derived from the child's own experience through his interaction with his environment. They recognize that such an education serves a useful purpose in emancipating the child from dogmatic authority, but they nevertheless hold that this type of education has a basic inadequacy in that the child's range of experience is necessarily too limited to enable him to decide how he or his society should be improved. The child accepts his existing environment without question and merely learns to adjust himself to it. Education thus becomes simply the science of adjustment; it lacks a moral goal or a social program. The end product is the conformist, the "organization man" who has just enough low skills to get along smoothly with his fellows but not enough intellectual discipline or moral fervor to rebel effectively against, or to fight to remedy, the social injustices of this imperfect world.

This type of education, despite its inadequacies, might not be so bad for America, where, in ultimate consequence of the legacy of intellectual strivings and spiritual and social struggles handed down from such historical experiences as the Renaissance and Reformation, there already exists an essentially egalitarian middle-class society enjoying comparative well-being and absence of social inequities. But in a country like Japan which, for all the technological modernity it has recently achieved, is still so close to its feudal past as to be yet in the throes of a revolutionary intellectual, spiritual, and social struggle attendant on the process of modernization, comparatively great unenlightenment and social injustices remain to be remedied. Progressive education which induces the child to adjust himself complacently to whatever environment he encounters may be an improvement over the old education which compelled him forcibly to conform to a given environment; but it is not enough improvement to meet the demands of a society still crying for drastic change. Progressive education therefore appears to many Japanese to be lacking in a sense of dedicated purpose and in the ability to develop the tough self-discipline necessary to achieve such a purpose, leading them to question its value to Japan in her present situation.

Actually it is probably unfair to blame the new educational system for the shortcomings of the present generation of youngsters. As victims of the abnormal postwar period of sudden transition, this generation would probably show the same disturbing characteristics whatever the system of formal education. In time, as social conditions become increasingly more stabilized, the children trained in the new educational system will undoubtedly appear in a much more satisfactory light. In the meantime, there are widespread misgivings that the educational system is failing to do adequately the job which society expects of it.

In this situation the majority of Japanese educators are taking the sensible attitude of plugging away constantly at gradually modifying and improving the new educational system as they profit from increasing experience with it. Unfortunately, however, although they are definitely in the minority, there are just enough extremists to succeed in keeping educational circles in a constant turmoil. On the one side are some old administrators and school principals who, supported by the more conservative politicians, are distinctly unfriendly to the new system. While hardly any of them would go so far as to favor a return to the ideals of the past, they actively favor the reestablishment of some measure of superior external authority in education as represented by centralized direction, fixed goals, and prescribed indoctrination. So far they have succeeded to the extent of getting the popularly elected boards of education replaced by appointed boards, although the appointments are made by popularly elected chief executives of autonomous local political units with the approval of elected legislative bodies. On the other side are the more progressive teachers who are so fearful of how much further the reactionaries may go that they themselves go to the other extreme of engaging in unduly provocative and intemperate attacks on their opponents. So bitterly do the two extremes distrust each other that even perfectly reasonable and justifiable measures, if proposed by the one side, are automatically opposed by the other on the suspicion—unfortunately too often well founded—that these measures are being advanced merely as a cover for more objectionable ulterior ends. Thus the excesses of the one side merely serve to invite the excesses of the other.

This unfortunate situation is exemplified in the stormy role which the Japan Teachers' Union has been playing in recent years. A powerful organization whose membership includes the majority of the school teachers of the nation, its laudable general aims are not only to seek the improvement of the status and welfare of the teachers but also to promote an enlightened educational policy. But so apprehensive are its leaders over the opposition of the reactionaries to the new education that the organization has been stampeded into engaging in extremist actions in the opposite direction. This direction of activity has been facilitated by the economic plight of the teachers, which has caused them to allow their organization to become less a professional association concerned with education and more a labor union affiliated with the radical wing of organized labor in militant political action based on the idea of the class struggle. This orientation has provided opportunity for the organization to fall under the influence of leftist and even Communist-affiliated leaders who seek to steer it increasingly into disruptive political conflicts. The effect has been to goad the reactionary opponents of the new education into more unreasonable opposition than ever. Mutual intolerance has thus developed to the point that what normally would be routine differences of opinion over technical details of educational policy easily erupt into violent political controversy. Once the conflict is thus joined, rather than risk victory by the reactionaries, even the moderate members of the Teachers' Union often see no choice but to close ranks behind the radical leadership.

With the educational circles of Japan engaged in such turmoil, it can hardly be said that the new educational system has become a successful instrument for producing a democratic citizenry. But ferment indicates change, and while surface manifestations may be unattractive, below the surface the vast majority of the Japanese educators are engaged not in political conflict but in sober constructive tasks. At least the defective old system is gone, and, present confusion notwithstanding, the process of evolving a better new system is under way.

It may not yet be too common a sight, but one now does occasionally see school children on their civics "projects" swarming through the city hall in search of officials to interview or sprawling over the desks of a police station while pestering harassed police officers with embarrassingly frank questions. These children may not know as much arithmetic or as many names of ancient emperors as their parents did at their age, but they give the impression that they will eventually become more capable than their parents of understanding the responsibilities of democratic citizenship. They are still not quite as brash as American youngsters, but their comparatively uninhibited curiosity and their relative lack of fear of authority stand in wholesome contrast to the repression of the pupils under the old lock-step system of education. This much is an improvement. If this heart-warming sight is symbolic of what is to come, the present travail in Japan's educational system need be no cause for too much alarm.

CHAPTER XI

Higher Education and

Mass Education

The reform of the Japanese system of higher education entailed problems quite different from those at lower levels. CI&E apparently had less understanding of these problems than of the problems of basic education.

The old Japanese system of higher education confronted the students with a choice of directions and was therefore subject to much the same criticisms as already noted with respect to the differentiation in types of schools at the secondary level. One direction was represented by the *semmon-gakko,* literally "specialty school" but often translated as "college," and by roughly comparable institutions such as many of the normal schools. These institutions offered two- and three-year terminal courses. The other direction was represented by the *kōtō-gakko,* literally "higher school" but also often translated confusingly as "college," followed by the *daigaku,* or university proper. The *kōtō-gakko* offered two- or three-year courses in basic tool subjects and some liberal arts preparatory to the *daigaku,* which in turn offered three years of specialized or professional training for a total of five or six years of higher education.[1] This might

---

[1] In the case of private institutions the *kōtō-gakko* and the university proper were often combined in a single five- or six-year university, in which circumstance the former section was known as the *yoka* and the latter section the *honka.* In the case of public institutions the *kōtō-gakko* and the university proper were usually kept physically and administratively separate.

be followed by graduate studies. Thus there was a differentiation between the *semmon-gakko* and comparable institutions on the one hand, which were designed essentially to produce high-grade technicians of various kinds, and the *kōtō-gakko*–university sequence on the other, which was intended to produce leaders and thinkers of the most superior caliber.

In its report the United States Education Mission expressed many justified misgivings over the character of Japanese higher education. While it recognized that a respectable amount of general education was offered in the *kōtō-gakko,* the mission deplored the early and narrow specialization in the *semmon-gakko* which left no room for broad, humanistic studies. Even in the university proper, where specialization was appropriate, the mission felt that more broadening courses in widely related subjects would be desirable. However eminent the level of Japanese higher education from a technical point of view, it left very much to be desired from the point of view of developing a well-rounded, cultivated man. Hence the mission went on to offer much sound general advice bearing on the content and spirit of Japanese higher education. But in recognition of the complexity of the problems involved, and perhaps also because its own members could not agree among themselves, the mission did not make detailed recommendations for the reorganization of the system of higher education such as it made for the system of lower schools. Instead it merely called on the Japanese to devote their efforts to working out their own plans in line with the general direction it had pointed out.

But CI&E, apparently feeling constrained to bring about quick, tangible results, proceeded to take matters into its own hands. One of its first actions was to rule that all Japanese institutions of higher learning should be made over into four-year colleges or universities on the standard American pattern. Apparently the reasoning behind this move was that a year or two added to the old *semmon-gakko* would make possible the inclusion of the desired amount of general education and that in any case the existence of two kinds of higher education of differing levels was undemocratic. Whatever its intent, however, it was an injurious move bitterly opposed by the Japanese university people and having little to commend it save that it introduced a system familiar to the CI&E officers.

In order to escape extinction in the face of this decision by CI&E, all two- and three-year "colleges"—*semmon-gakko, kōtō-gakko*, normal schools, and all others indiscriminately—now naturally scrambled to transform themselves into four-year universities. Originally organized for altogether different functions, with inadequate facilities and inappropriate faculties for the purposes of a true university, these made-over institutions could not possibly hope to become universities in anything but name. The worst abuses were checked by a Chartering Committee, which passed on the accreditation of these institutions, but the criteria which could be used by such a body were necessarily quite mechanistic. Where the number of books in their library or the number of their faculty members possessing doctoral degrees fell short of the standards stipulated by the Chartering Committee, several institutions could pool their resources by "consolidating" into a single university. All too often such consolidations were consummated primarily on paper alone, as the campuses of the several component units were often miles apart—sometimes even in quite distant cities. At the same time, the true universities which used to have superior standards, whose students had previously been graduates of the *kōtō-gakko*, now found themselves pushed down by law to the same level as these erstwhile preparatory institutions.

The weaknesses of these new universities were compounded by CI&E's decree that in each prefecture there must be a university on the pattern of the state universities of America. The fact that Japanese prefectures were more comparable in most respects to counties than to American states was ignored. The result was that the new universities in the prefectures, added to the several existing national, municipal, and private universities and the many "colleges" that now reorganized themselves as universities, eventually brought the total number of universities in Japan to considerably more than two hundred. Considering that there are only twenty-nine universities in West Germany, twenty-seven in Italy, seventeen in France, and seventeen in Great Britain, and that no nation in the world except the United States has more universities than Japan, the impracticality of a small and poor country like Japan spreading its resources over so many universities is obvious. It is indeed remarkable that as many as perhaps ten or a dozen of the Japanese universities compare favorably with the great and famous universities of the world; it is not surprising that most of the two hundred others are quite inadequate as universities, while they might have been respectable technical institutes, junior colleges, or normal schools. The cause of higher education would have been served much better had Japan been allowed to concentrate her limited resources on improving the seventy or so universities she had before the war, which were already too many, instead of being forced to follow the Occupation's chimerical dream of a university education for the masses.

Not only was there thus a debasement of standards, but this enforced change flew in the face of the trend in American higher education itself. In the United States there is increasing emphasis on the junior colleges and the community colleges which can provide easy access to some measure of higher education at low cost to the many who for reasons of finance or aptitude find it inadvisable to go farther. At the same time, the universities are tightening their standards, strengthening the requirements in the "lower division" or "general education division" which must be completed before one can enter the advanced or professional divisions, thus steadily pushing the total time required for graduation in many lines of study beyond the traditional four years. In other words, in this respect Japan already had the kind of system toward which the American system is developing. The *semmon-gakko* were essentially junior colleges and community colleges; the *kōtō-gakko*–university sequence provided the sort of general education–professional-training sequence which the American universities are increasingly elaborating. But CI&E abolished all these and decreed the establishment of the generalized four-year institutions which are being overshadowed even in the country of their origin. True, some of the narrow and rigid attitudes in the Japanese institutions of higher learning badly needed correction, but such correction was not to be obtained through changing the organizational structure of the institutions.

Establishment of the four-year universities was also accompanied by the forced introduction of organized graduate schools on the American model. The old Japanese practice of the graduate student attaching himself as a personal disciple and assistant to some professor, being awarded the doctorate only after attaining professional recognition through his professor's sponsorship, was open to the abuses of personal favoritism and unduly long and onerous apprenticeship. The new system, which requires in addition to the thesis a series of prescribed courses and examinations for the doctorate as well as for the newly created master's degree, entails the kind of elaborate bookkeeping of "credits" which, although familiar enough in the highly institutionalized American system of graduate education, can hardly be regarded as compatible with the spirit of true advanced scholarship.

CI&E also tried to have the public universities placed under the control of lay boards of trustees as in the case of American universities. Undoubtedly the intention was to emancipate the universities from the bureaucratic control of the Ministry of Education. But what CI&E did not realize was that, while the Ministry of Education occasionally did intervene arbitrarily in university affairs, and particularly viciously in the reactionary period of the 1930's, the public universities—unlike the lower schools—had generally won for themselves a fair measure of autonomy so that the faculties were in many respects the supreme governing bodies, electing the president and the deans and generally running the university themselves somewhat in the European tradition of the self-governing guild of scholars. While no one in the last analysis enjoyed complete freedom of belief under the old regime, the universities did enjoy a large measure of freedom in managing their own internal affairs, and this measure of independence was jealously cherished by the university people. It should occasion no surprise, in view of even the typical American professor's attitude toward the businessmen and politicians who usually comprise the appointed trustees of American universities, that the Japanese professors reacted to CI&E's proposal with a sense of profound outrage.

So violently did the academicians oppose what appeared to them as an American scheme to defile the sanctity of the universities by imposing Philistine overlords upon them that the plan eventually had to be abandoned, but not until after it had aroused implacable distrust for CI&E.

Even while Japanese university circles were up in arms over the issue of boards of trustees, CI&E undertook to pressure the universities into getting rid of their professors who showed Communist inclinations. It is understandable that the prevalence of a theoretical, bookish radicalism among a large portion of Japanese scholars might well be regarded as a nuisance and even a danger by SCAP. But the method which CI&E used, of dispatching officials to the universities to admonish and preach to the faculties and the students, was too reminiscent of the way in which the Japanese militarists had tried to coerce the universities a few years earlier. At that time officers from another military headquarters had descended upon the universities to preach and to inveigh against these same radical professors. Both students and professors therefore now responded to the visitations of the SCAP representatives as a threat to academic freedom; the meetings at which the SCAP officials tried to speak were turned into pandemonium; and the objectionable professors who might through subtler means have been quietly discredited and rendered impotent were transfigured by CI&E's ineptitude into heroes and martyrs.

In its one example of flexibility in a major issue involving higher education, CI&E eventually modified its insistence on four-year institutions to authorize the establishment of junior colleges. This change, however, came about less in response to the pleas of the Japanese educators than as a by-product of a shift in CI&E personnel. The person who had been most adamant in insisting on a uniform pattern of four-year institutions completed her tour of duty with SCAP and went back to her position as dean of women in a western state college. The person who succeeded her as officer-in-charge of higher education was a former professor of education at another West Coast institution who undertook to campaign within CI&E on behalf of junior colleges. Despite the change, most Japanese university people continued to be disenchanted with CI&E, which should not be too hard to understand in view of the attitude common even in American faculty circles toward deans of women and professors of education. In any case the harm had already been done, for, once having strenuously transformed themselves into universities, even weak institutions were understandably reluctant to transform themselves back into junior colleges. About all that CI&E's belated authorization of junior colleges did was to encourage some two hundred high schools to transform themselves into junior colleges in yet another round of magnification of labels and debasement of standards.

CI&E thus aroused so much antagonism and scorn in Japanese university circles over matters of organization and administration that the more important matters concerning the contents and spirit of higher education were almost lost sight of. Only since the latter part of the Occupation have increasing non-official contacts between visiting American scholars and Japanese university people brought about some modification of the Japanese distrust of American higher education. In many specialties, particularly in the sciences and in technology where the Japanese themselves were relatively highly advanced, the Japanese scholars had the ability to recognize quickly the pre-eminence which American scholarship had wrested from Europe in recent years, and they were therefore eager to profit from close intellectual co-operation with the Americans. In other specialties there was considerable reluctance, which still persists, to recognize that the Americans had much of value to contribute. In a few instances some CI&E officials[2] rendered notable service in facilitating intellectual intercourse between Japanese and American scholars, but comparatively few of the CI&E people were themselves scholars capable of working effectively at the university level. Generally, therefore, except for efforts to keep technically abreast of the findings of American research and except for a modest increase in the amount of general education in their curriculums, the Japanese universities have shown little evidence of American influence apart from the changes in institutional form in-

[2] Notably those in the Public Opinion and Sociological Research Division, which operated virtually as an independent agency although placed within CI&E for administrative purposes.

sisted on by CI&E. In really important substantive matters concerning the basic nature of higher education, American influence has been negligible, and Japanese higher education continues to manifest most of its old faults with only slight abatement.

Thus, while in form the difference between the *semmon-gakko* and the *kōtō-gakko*–university sequence has been done away with through the transformation of all into uniform four-year institutions, democratic equality in higher education still does not exist. Despite nominal equality in standards, some of the older institutions—mostly those which used to be imperial universities—are actually incomparably better than the institutions recently elevated to universities. The better students therefore compete fiercely to get into the superior institutions, while the poorer students gravitate to the inferior ones, so that hierarchical divisions clearly persist in Japanese higher education. The faculties of the superior institutions, highly self-conscious of their prowess, tend to be exclusive and arrogant. The better universities thus generally recruit their professors almost solely from among their own graduates, a teacher usually being succeeded by his own immediate disciple. In some respects this exclusiveness serves to maintain standards, but in the long run it results in intellectual inbreeding with consequent cliquishness, factual jealousies, narrow outlook, loss of bold originality, and a restricted professional concern. The Japanese universities are thus still not very well designed to produce the liberal, humanistic, broad-minded, and intellectually independent individuals who are needed as leaders of a democratic society.

One aspect of Japanese higher education which has shown no improvement is to be seen in the Marxist bias of many Japanese intellectuals, reflected in the prevalence, already alluded to, of radicalism in Japanese university circles. From one point of view, this radicalism might be regarded as an encouraging phenomenon, for it indicates that Japanese intellectuals possess a social conscience which causes them to be deeply concerned with broader social problems beyond their academic specialties. The long persistence of a radical stream in Japanese university life, despite the fact that it was usually persecuted and driven underground by the authorities, also indicates that most intellectuals never willingly conformed to traditional authoritarianism even though they were powerless to do much about it in any practical way. It suggests that a potentiality exists for the emergence of a new non-authoritarian, non-traditional leadership from the universities, which is as it should be.

From another point of view, however, the fact that this potentiality for a possibly democratic leadership is as yet manifested by an inclination toward Marxism and radicalism is cause for disquiet if not alarm. It is understandable that, after long repression by the authorities, the freethinkers of the universities should now indulge in a fling of excess radicalism. After their past experience, it is understandable that they should regard all official authority with suspicion and be overly eager to challenge it. But the fact that the intellectuals should embrace Marxism and radicalism, instead of moderate democratic liberalism, as a vehicle for manifesting their opposition to the past is in part evidence of the ignorance and naïveté bred by the narrow professional influences in the Japanese universities which have prevented their people from acquiring the broad background necessary to comprehend adequately the complexities of the world at large. However brilliant these intellectuals may be in their own specialties, and however commendable their social impulses, their lack of practical experience with public affairs makes them easily captivated by a seemingly scientific system of thought like Marxism.

Part of this Marxist bias of Japanese intellectuals also stems from the compulsion which Japanese scholars have felt over the past several generations to catch up as quickly as possible with the West—a compulsion which has led them to seek a short cut, a pat formula, a key that would enable them to unlock the riddle of all Western historical phenomena. Marxism, with its comprehensive system purporting to explain almost everything, seemed to meet this need. The traditional Confucian background of the Japanese scholars also predisposes them toward Marxism, for Confucianism likewise is a comprehensive system of thought depending largely on deductive logic. In contrast to the impressiveness of such a dialectical system which seemingly has all the answers, the inductive method of American social science of patiently amassing empirical data and drawing conclusions from them only fragmentary bit by fragmentary bit seems aimless and blundering. The Japanese natural scientists are too well trained to violate the scientific method in their own technical specialties, but when they and others without adequate social science background venture into the unfamiliar field of social and political phenomena, they fall for the glittering comprehensive hypothesis which seeks to explain too much. The seemingly universal system of Marxism may be recognized by the experienced social scientist as an artificial conceptualization resulting from subjective mental gymnastics rather than accurate analysis of objective facts. But the very brilliance of the conceptual scheme, which should make one wary of it, leads many Japanese intellectuals, because of their predispositions rooted in their background, to regard it naïvely as the ultimate in sophisticated perception.

At the same time, it should be recognized that the Marxist inclination of the Japanese intellectuals is not solely the result of narrowness and naïveté; there are good and rational reasons as well. Many aspects of Marxian ideology are truly stimulating intellectually. Also, in view of the impotence of the liberal democrats throughout much of Japan's modern history, it is only natural for many Japanese intellectuals to conclude that only a precise and positive doctrine like Marxism could offer any hope of success against the forces of traditional conservatism. It is significant that Marxism exerts a strong influence upon the intellectuals of most of the democratic nations of western Europe; the Japanese intellectuals are not unique but share in the general world climate of intellectual circles. Perhaps it is the United States that is unique in its relative imperviousness to Marxian ideology. The Marxian impact on Japan may be more undiluted than on western European countries, however, because of the absence in Japan of countervailing forces, like the Christian Democratic movement, which exert a competitive pull on European intellectuals.

This does not mean that the Japanese intellectuals are Communist activists, for these academic radicals have had no occasion for direct contact with living communism. But because they fail to realize that modern communism as it operates ruthlessly in the contemporary world is very different from their own idealistic, bookish Marxism, they harbor a preconception which makes them receptive to the views of the Communists, whom they mistakenly believe to be kindred spirits, and conversely hypercritical of America and disdainful of American social science, which they assume to be hopelessly tainted with "capitalistic" and "bourgeois" bias.

Although many of the staunchest advocates of Western liberalism and democracy in Japan are found in the universities, the presence in the same universities of widespread Marxian influence makes the academic world an area of contention where the eventual outcome is by no means certain. While with very few exceptions Japanese intellectuals are professedly strongly "progressivist" or antitraditional, by no means are they predominantly supporters of democracy in the American or Western sense. The universities certainly are not now the centers of democratic leadership that they should be if democracy is to grow in Japan, and the Occupation succeeded in doing virtually nothing to bring about the desired situation.

If the universities are not living up to their potentiality as sources of leadership in democratic thought, at another level the newspapers, magazines, radio, and other media of mass communication are doing much better. For all its glaring shortcomings, the free press has come to be an important democratic influence in contemporary Japanese life, at least partly in consequence of the reforms wrought by the Occupation.

In fact, generally speaking, the press had long been a force for liberalism and democracy in Japanese life. This is not to say that the Japanese press was without serious faults. There had always been at least some measure of government censorship. In their concern for mass circulation, the newspapers had been prone to indulge in irresponsible sensationalism and scandal-mongering. Instead of a free competition for news, favored groups of reporters have maintained exclusive "press clubs" to monopolize certain pipelines to important news sources and to shut out competing reporters. A few of the minor newspapers were the mouthpieces of special interests, some of which were ultranationalistic and chauvinistic; some fly-by-night sheets were even instruments of organized black-mail. Finally, during the war all the newspapers and news agencies were rigidly controlled and regimented by the government. But for all these faults, up to the time it came under strict government control in the late 1930's, the press had in general been one of the few institutions in Japanese society that had been conspicuous for their democratic influence.

The reasons were several. Universal literacy made for tremendous mass circulation, so that highly profitable subscriptions rendered most newspaper companies quite independent of the influence of advertisers or of financial or political groups. Newspapers like the *Asahi* and the *Mainichi*, with national circulations of more than three million each, and the *Yomiuri*, which was not far behind, were powerful enough to be able to defy the pressure of almost any outside special-interest group. It was good business to cater to the inclination of the masses who preferred the vicarious thrill of reading audacious attacks on the government to reading dull official propaganda. By the very nature of their work, newspapermen tend to acquire a cynical disrespect for pretense and bombast, which makes them —if they are not wholly corrupt—the natural critics of most conventional authority. The newspapers and the magazines also offered an attractive field of activity for the nonconformist intellectuals to whom not many opportunities were open in the relatively closed and conventionalized society of Japan. As big vested interests themselves, the newspapers had no reason to be overly liberal; but as a relatively fearless and independent force in Japanese life they could usually be counted on to be fairly close to the front ranks in any attack on the authoritarian and restrictive elements of the established power structure. The newspapers thus tended to develop in their readers a questioning and critical attitude toward the government.

It is clear that the reactionary groups recognized the press as one of their most dangerous enemies, as evidenced by the censorship which conservative administrations imposed on the press. This censorship, however, had only limited effectiveness, for the ingenious newspapers often found ways of circumventing it, while in comparatively liberal periods like the 1920's the government found it expedient to keep the censorship extremely mild and even perfunctory. But with the rise to power of the military-fascists in the 1930's, the government set out with determination to tame the power of the press. The attitude of the military extremists was dramatically demonstrated at the time of the attempted military *Putsch* on February 26, 1936, when the insurgents broke into the *Asahi* building and smashed the press equipment in an attempt to stop the publication of this antimilitarist paper.

That same year the government established the Board of Information, which became Japan's closest approach to a ministry of propaganda. Organized, however, not as a ministry but as a sort of co-ordinating agency in which the army, the navy, and the Ministry of Home Affairs (representing the police) played the most important roles, the Board of Information was torn by the crosscurrents of interservice rivalries which often made its work confusing and inconsistent. But it did succeed in establishing strict controls over the press, especially after the outbreak of the war. Using as leverage its wartime rationing of scarce newsprint, it forced the more than 250 newspapers in the nation to consolidate into about 50. It also forced the merger of the two great rival news agencies into a single government-controlled news service. It not only tightened the censorship but issued increasingly detailed directives on how the news should be handled, until the newspapers found it virtually impossible—especially after the tide of war began to turn strongly against Japan—to print much more than the official press releases. Thus the entire Japanese press was finally reduced to reproducing with deadly uniformity and monotony the official propaganda line.

Such was the kind of press with which the Occupation had to deal. SCAP quickly decreed the freedom of the press and ordered the Japanese government to rescind all governmental controls over the press. But the Occupation itself immediately established a strict military censorship, exercised by the Civil Censorship Division of SCAP's Civil Intelligence Section, which also opened and inspected the Japanese mail. The Japanese press was ordered not to print any criticism of the Allies or anything detrimental to the objectives of the Occupation. Just what this included was interpreted differently at different times by the censors, depending on what happened at the moment to be the major concerns of SCAP. All copy had to be submitted to the censors in advance for their approval, first in galley proof and then in page proof, including at first even such materials as want ads, baseball box scores, and weather forecasts. This was a considerably tighter check than had been exercised by the Japanese military at the height of their wartime control.

During the first critical months of the Occupation, when the United States Army still had many experienced newspapermen in uniform who could be assigned to censorship duty, these men administered the censorship efficiently and sensibly with the minimum of bureaucratic red tape. After demonstrating their toughness for the first few days, they soon found that they needed to suppress very few items, for the Japanese press was generally highly co-operative and Japanese writers quickly sensed just what would and what would not be acceptable to the censors.

It is ironic that a year or two later, after the success of the Occupation had long been assured and the friendliness of the Japanese had long been proved, the censorship turned capricious and onerous. With the Occupation now transformed into a cumbersome semipermanent bureaucracy, the officers with newspaper experience had been demobilized and their places as censors had been taken by young second lieutenants who knew virtually nothing about newspapers. Often unsure of their own judgment, they would frequently refer decisions to superior officers in SCAP, whereupon a news story might pick up the O.K.'s of half a dozen colonels, but come back a week or more too late to be used.[3] Sometimes the censors would take issue with a story originating from a press relations officer of some American military unit; often stories would be held up while the censors thought up some petty correction, like the actual case of insisting on changing "heart attack" to "coronary

---

[3] On the newspaper of which the present writer was editor, during the first year of the Occupation the number of items held up by the censors averaged two a month; in the second year of the Occupation the number of items held up by the censors sometimes reached fifteen or sixteen in one day, although the majority were eventually approved after several days' delay.

thrombosis" in an account of the death of a SCAP official. Because Japanese writers quickly learned to exercise self-inhibition, most of the censored items were of American origin. Walter Lippmann's syndicated column—subscribed to by a few Japanese papers—was a frequent victim, and on one occasion Ripley's "Believe It or Not" cartoon was suppressed. More serious in relation to Occupation policies were such cases, previously alluded to, as the use of censorship to shut off public discussion of the new constitution and the Economic Deconcentration Law.[4]

Much speculation might be indulged in over the effect of this American censorship on the Japanese and over the paradox of a military occupation purporting to teach democracy to a subjugated populace. Japanese newspapermen in moments of irritation often complained that the American censorship was worse than the old Japanese military censorship, which was of course an exaggeration. Actually it left few serious ill effects. Practically all Japanese recognized that censorship was unavoidable in any military occupation; and although the censorship probably was continued longer than was really necessary, the Japanese were generally aware that it was never meant to be more than a temporary arrangement. Furthermore, however glaring were some individual cases, in relation to the total amount of materials on which the censors had to pass judgment, the ratio of foolish decisions was low. Moreover, unlike the arrogant and often vicious Japanese military censors, the American censors were nearly always personally kindly and sympathetic; and it was apparent that most of their mistakes stemmed from well-intentioned ineptness rather than from any fundamentally objectionable attitude. Before any serious permanent harm could be done, as the Occupation neared its end the censorship was sharply curtailed and then abolished altogether.

In the Occupation's influence on the Japanese press, far more significant than the censorship was the positive program undertaken by the Press and Publications Unit of SCAP's Civil Information and Education Section. Headed after the first several months by an elderly major who in civilian life had been

[4] See chaps. iv and viii.

a small-town newspaper publisher, this unit sought to reshape the Japanese press into an important instrument for the democratization of the nation. Some of the men of the great Japanese metropolitan dailies were inclined to smile condescendingly on this former small-town publisher who never could really comprehend the complexities of the mammoth Japanese newspaper industry, but, whatever his technical limitations, his innate kindliness, his absolute integrity, and his homely but uncommonly good sense eventually gained for him a universal respect and affection which enabled him to exert a wholesome influence on the Japanese press. By simple homilies and gentle persistence, he won over the Japanese newspapermen to a fairly faithful adhesion to a code of journalistic ethics which has put the general level of Japanese newspaper conduct on a reasonably decent level.

In the beginning of the Occupation, however, the outlook for the Japanese press did not seem encouraging. After several years of dictation by the government, the Japanese newspapermen had apparently forgotten how to exercise their initiative and originality and now looked to the Occupation for direction. They, in common with the rest of the Japanese populace, showed for a while an amazing lack of vitality. SCAP was concerned with infusing some life into the publishing business and with convincing the Japanese press that it was now free, within the comparatively broad limits of Occupation conditions, to do much as it pleased. Once the initial shock and bewilderment wore off, however, the Japanese press went headlong to the other extreme. As if on a jag after their long years of repression, many of the newspapers indulged in an outburst of undisciplined sensationalism, carelessly and irresponsibly mixing rumor with fact. In reaction to military-fascist wartime controls, they now often slanted their stories in a radical direction so that they fell in line with Communist propaganda. This was particularly true of the many new newspapers that now sprang into existence, but even the older, more reputable papers generally took a position well to the left of center. This tendency was aided by the fact that it coincided with the spectacular growth and leftward swing of the labor union movement[5] in

[5] See chap. ix.

which newspaper employees, including editorial workers as well as pressmen united in the same union, took a prominent part. When even the great newspapers of national circulation began hewing close to the Communist line, SCAP naturally became deeply exercised.

Matters came to a showdown in the spring and summer of 1946 over the case of the *Yomiuri-Hochi,* the third largest newspaper in the nation. Its employees' union, which was the first labor union to be organized after the surrender, demanded the resignation of the publisher, Matsutaro Shoriki, for supposedly having co-operated more energetically with the military than had appeared necessary. With his arrest on suspicion of being a war criminal, although he was eventually cleared and restored to high position,[6] his place as publisher of the *Yomiuri* was taken over by Tsunego Baba, an old-time liberal of unquestionable character. But in the confusion following Shoriki's ouster, the actual control of the paper was usurped by the managing editor, Tomin Suzuki, who turned out to be a strong Communist sympathizer if not an actual party member. Supported by the employees' union, Suzuki and his editorial assistants proceeded to turn out a paper which followed the Communist propaganda line in defiance of the moderate policy desired by Baba. This employees' mutiny against the management appeared to presage similar action in several other newspaper companies which were also experiencing turbulent labor-management relations at this time.

Within SCAP there were still some officials who encouraged such action on the part of the labor unions on the theory that a revolutionary overthrow of the former managers by the workers in any industry would be conducive to democracy. But other SCAP officials were already becoming alarmed over organized labor's inclination toward extremism and toward illegal resort to force. In the *Yomiuri* affair, not only was the dissemination of Communist propaganda by a major newspaper a serious matter, but SCAP saw that it involved a fundamental issue over journalistic principle. If freedom of the press was to be maintained, newspapers must be kept free from intimida-

[6] Shoriki eventually became the first chairman of Japan's Atomic Energy Commission.

tion not only from the government but from any group that might seek to impose its will by force. A newspaper enterprise must be free to determine its own editorial policy without interference from whatever source, whether from the government, from reactionary terrorists, or from a radical union of its own employees. Thus SCAP, despite some disagreement among its own officers, finally made it clear that it officially sided with the *Yomiuri* management.

Baba then mustered enough courage to discharge Managing Editor Suzuki and five of his associates, and thus attempted to assert control over his own paper. The complications that ensued need not be detailed. In brief, Suzuki refused to consider himself discharged; some of the employees went on strike in support of Suzuki; for a time a nationwide sympathy strike of newspaper and radio workers appeared imminent; demonstrations and riots swirled in and around the *Yomiuri* building almost daily for a while; repercussions occurred in intensified labor-management disputes in several newspaper companies; unions quarreled and split up over the affair; the conflict within SCAP flared up anew; and even Soviet Russia became involved when its representative in the Allied Council for Japan made a thinly veiled attack on SCAP's handling of this affair. But in the end the *Yomiuri* management was sustained, and the radical unions suffered a decisive setback.

The *Yomiuri* affair proved to be the turning point. Although many of the newspapers continued with their radically inclined editorial policies for some time, the pressure from extremist unions waned. Gradually the more balanced and moderate elements gained the upper hand in both management and the unions, and the newspapers settled down to a condition of sensible normalcy. In some ways the newspapers have returned to their prewar condition. Competing vigorously for mass circulation, they have regained all their old-time alertness and ingenuity. While some represent the conservative point of view and a few represent the radical, most of them—including the largest and most influential ones—follow a middle-of-the-road policy. As a mass organ, the press comes close to reflecting accurately the character of the general Japanese public, although it probably leans somewhat more toward the progressive urban portion of the population than toward the conservative rural portion.

But in many ways the Japanese press today is far better than it ever was in the past. It is a truly free press, governing itself by a code of professional ethics bequeathed to it by the Occupation, and no longer subject to any external controls. With the great resources provided by its mass circulation, which totals about 34,000,000, and spurred by relentless competition, it shows great enterprise in providing its readers with a remarkably rich coverage of both news and features. While it still has its full share of flamboyant and frivolous characteristics, it seems to have gained perceptibly in maturity and responsibility as compared with even the best of its prewar years. In the atmosphere of free and vigorous clash of ideas which characterizes the contemporary Japanese society in ferment, the newspapers provide an effective forum for the airing of all points of view. In this sense, the press is functioning well as an indispensable instrumentality for the democratic process. Furthermore, freed now from external controls, newspapermen are indulging more uninhibitedly than ever in their natural proclivity for exposing and attacking abuses of power in high places. The newspapers have been in large measure responsible for stirring up the popular outcries which have hampered the efforts of the conservatives to nullify the Occupation-inspired reforms in such fields as civil liberties, police organization, and education. Thus the press has come to be the chief watchdog for the protection of Japan's new democracy.

In most respects, what has been said about the newspapers can also be said about the magazines. But the magazines have some special characteristics. Able to aim at smaller and more specialized groups of readers than the mass circulation dailies, the widely varied magazines reflect a wider spectrum of interests and points of view than the newspapers, running the gamut from extreme right to extreme left, from pornography to religion, from horse racing to nuclear physics, from hairdressing to international politics. But, while the largest number of magazines naturally cater to popular tastes, it is highly significant that "high-brow," "intellectual" magazines enjoy surprisingly large circulation. These are the opinion-molders in the influential sectors of Japanese society. Written largely by professional "intellectuals," their articles represent the kind of thinking which quite closely resembles that which prevails in university circles as described earlier. This means that, while conservative and moderate points of view are often capably presented, the Marxist point of view generally tends to receive more prominent representation. These magazines are quick to take up all the major social, economic, political, and intellectual issues that are the concerns of the moment throughout the world, and in this respect they keep their readers well posted on the outside world; but when these matters are filtered through the unique, highly theoretical interpretations of the Japanese Marxists, they often emerge in a form quite different from the reality as perceived by Western thinkers.[7]

In this respect, some of the Japanese magazines are doing a disservice to the public. Although the fad for hypercritical leftist interpretations of American attitudes has abated considerably in the past few years as compared with the period immediately following the end of the Occupation, the serious magazines too frequently still reflect the unrealistic, academic Marxian bias of many of their writers. Thus like the universities, the most thoughtful of the magazines are failing to live up to their full potentiality in providing the kind of intellectual guidance that would best serve the interests of democracy as conceived by the democratic peoples of the West.

The radio today in its characteristics resembles much more closely the newspapers than the magazines, but its early history was very different from either. From the beginning, radio broadcasting was a government monopoly. Operating under the jurisdiction of the Ministry of Communications, which was more interested in the engineering aspects of broadcasting than in its program content, the Japanese radio suffered from

[7] For example, according to some Japanese writers, the lesson to be derived from the Hungarian uprising of 1956 was that, if the Hungarians were justified in rising up against the Marxist—and therefore benevolent—Russians, the Japanese should be inspired to throw out the non-Marxist—and therefore exploitative—Americans from Japan. Also, the equivocal attitude of the P.E.N. (Poets, Essayists, Novelists) Club of Japan toward the Pasternak affair caused the novelist Arthur Koestler, when he visited Japan, to engage in bitter controversy with the Japanese writers.

not many more restrictions than the private newspaper industry. But as a bureaucratic enterprise not subject to the stimulus of competition, the radio could afford to refrain from pandering to low mass tastes, but it also had no incentive to offer programs of distinction. Respectable mediocrity was therefore its chief characteristic. When after 1936 the Board of Information began to exercise increasing control over the press, the radio came to be subjected to the same kind and about the same degree of control. The entertainment value of the radio steadily declined as more and more of its time was taken over by slanted news and unimaginative, didactic propaganda.

With the beginning of the Occupation, SCAP apparently chose the radio as the chief medium for widely disseminating its propaganda, euphemistically referred to as "re-education for democracy." It was a logical choice, for the centrally controlled broadcasting system was easy to manipulate, and the ratio of one radio set to every 1.4 families meant that Japan had more radios than any other country in the world except the United States. Quickly the air was filled with news, commentaries, and dramatizations, written by the officers of CI&E's radio unit and hurriedly translated into Japanese, designed to impress upon the Japanese that their past conduct had been evil and that only the acceptance of democracy offered the hope of their redemption. Much the same material was also fed into the Japanese newspapers, although the impact over the radio was much greater. The impact, although great, backfired. After their defeat the Japanese were in a mood to engage in soul-searching and to accept advice from the Americans, but the Japanese wanted to do it in their own way—in a mood of quiet, sorrowful reflection. The technique of the Americans—with its slam-bang, high-pressure, now-it-can-be-told, "March of Time" manner with strident sound effects and crude overdramatizations—struck a false note, and the Japanese snapped off their radio sets in disgust over what appeared to them as juvenile propaganda.

The Americans soon perceived their mistake, and CI&E changed its policy to that of letting the Japanese radio writers set their own pace, giving them encouragement to develop their own initiative after the years of stultifying control. To enhance the entertainment value and thus to spur listener interest, the Japanese radio was encouraged to copy popular American programs. The Americans also eventually gave much advice of good technical quality with respect to program planning. The entertainment features of the Japanese radio soon showed spectacular improvement. As for its handling of news and public affairs features, the Japanese radio kept very close pace with the developments in the newspaper field. Together with the newspapers, the radio went through a period of extreme gyrations and then eventually settled down to a generally high level of performance.

An important landmark was the removal of radio broadcasting from direct government operation through its transfer to a public corporation. Finally, with the authorization of private broadcasting, a host of commercial stations and networks have come to offer keen competition to the network operated by the public corporation. The same system of competitive organization prevails with respect to the television industry, which has been experiencing phenomenal expansion since its inauguration in 1953. In consequence, in both radio and television, despite the continued existence of a public corporation, the pace is set by commercial competition as in the case of the newspapers. Like the newspapers the competition has made for ingenuity, flexibility, and progressiveness. While the emphasis in radio and television is on entertainment, in their handling of news and educational features they supplement the newspapers and perform the same public functions in very much the same manner and spirit. Thus, like the newspapers, they have become an important instrumentality for the conduct of the democratic process. Although the direct effects of the Occupation actions on broadcasting were relatively minor, the American influence on Japanese radio and television can hardly be exaggerated.

All these activities in the fields of education and mass communication obviously exercise a profound effect on the shaping of public opinion. SCAP, from the outset, was naturally anxious to gauge the changing temper of Japanese public opinion, and for this purpose various units in SCAP headquarters, particularly those in the Civil Intelligence Section, turned out a steady stream of digests of translations of Japanese publications for their own perusal. These digests, however, were mostly hurried and haphazard samplings, with wide variations in accuracy, made by inexperienced officers whose primary interest was in other matters. A small group of professional social scientists comprising the Public Opinion and Sociological Research Unit—later expanded into a Division—existed within CI&E, but its relatively meager resources were sufficient to conduct only a very limited number of thorough studies.

In the meantime, the Japanese themselves quickly developed an almost compulsive fascination with their own changing public opinion. A large number of public opinion agencies sprang into existence. Some of the most extensive and useful of the public opinion polls were conducted by the large newspapers, which utilized their great resources to good advantage. To keep its finger on the public pulse, the Japanese Cabinet sponsored the establishment of a National Public Opinion Institute. Interest in the techniques of polling resulted in the formation of the Association of the Science of Public Opinion. These developments were encouraged and aided by SCAP's Public Opinion and Sociological Research Division. Many important projects were planned within this division in close collaboration with the National Public Opinion Institute and then farmed out to various Japanese agencies for execution. This division also employed several Japanese social scientists, who, after acquiring training and field experience under American experts, were later absorbed into the various Japanese agencies to act as a leaven. As the result of the stimulus provided by this close collaboration, the science of opinion polling and analysis in Japan has been developed to a high level. Not only is there now in existence a prodigious collection of data which is constantly being added to, but this information, as it is fed back to the public, undoubtedly has the effect of further stimulating social change. Such great concern with what the public thinks is another manifestation of the democratic trend of postwar Japan.

In summary, at the highest level of producing democratic

leaders and in influencing opinion, the universities and the intellectual magazines still leave much to be desired. The Occupation's achievements were negligible as far as they were concerned. At the popular level of a working democracy among the masses, however, the newspapers, popular magazines, radio, and television have come to play a most significant role in helping to preserve and facilitate the practice of democracy. The widespread preoccupation with public opinion itself is also evidence of a concern with democracy. In all these fields except television, which came later, the Occupation was most successful in promoting and nurturing the latent Japanese proclivities in the desired direction.

CHAPTER XII

Social Change

The Process of Democratization

The crux of the problem of the democratization of Japan lies in social change. Whatever may be the reforms instituted by the Occupation in the political, legal, economic, or educational fields, these institutional changes must necessarily remain merely formal and superficial until the nature of Japanese society becomes sufficiently compatible with their aims as to give them real substance. The question therefore is whether the development of Japanese society has in fact become sufficiently set in the direction of permanently sustaining the changes wrought by the Occupation.

Democracy is premised on the essential equality of all individuals and on the right of the individual freely to exercise his own choice. As has repeatedly been implied earlier, the reforms sponsored by the Occupation were intended to accord with this basic principle of democracy—although not all of them actually did so. Thus the new constitution was based on the doctrine of popular sovereignty whereby essentially equal individuals freely choose to be bound in contractual political relations with one another. The various political, administrative, and legal implementations of the constitution spelled out in detail this basic democratic principle. The economic reforms were designed to provide an environment favorable to this principle, and the educational reforms were designed to promote appreciation of it. As has already been noted, these reforms have proved in the main to be more successful than had generally been expected and in some respects conspicuously so. But at the same time there are obviously reasons for misgivings.

Traditionally, the Japanese state had been conceived of as a great patriarchal family, comprised in turn of countless lesser families. In such a society, the family rather than the individual was the basic unit. So basic was the collective entity of the family as the working unit of society that, in circumstances and for functions where the natural family was obviously unsuitable, artificial collective entities like guilds, gangs, secret societies—generally referred to generically as *kumi*—tended to take the place of the family, patterning not only their operating processes but even their organization, their internal relationships, and the ritual which symbolized the norms of their value system, upon those characteristic of the natural family.

This did not mean that ritual kinship groups, strictly speaking, were a particularly ubiquitous or conspicuous feature of Japanese society, but they did exist; and even where they did not exist, as in the more informal and tenuous relations between associates in most occupational and social groups, certain characteristics similar to intra-family relations nevertheless were manifest in some measure. In such relationships the participants were seldom equals, each free to make his own individual choice. The individual found his justification and his life fulfilment only in performing his proper role and in occupying his proper status within the structure of his group. His individual will therefore was subordinated to the prescribed obligations of his relationship to the other members of his group.

Obviously such a social system was not democratic. Yet neither was it wholly authoritarian, for, despite the rationalization provided by Confucian ethics—or rather by a Japanese interpretation of Confucian ethics—the Japanese family differed significantly from the patriarchal Chinese family, in which the father was the absolute, though benevolent, autocrat. It is true that the father in aristocratic Japanese families somewhat resembled the Chinese father, for the privileged position of many aristocratic families rested on the patrimony which the father held from his overlord. Hence the father was all-important and the other members of the family were wholly dependent upon him. But among commoners, particularly among the peasants, the family farm and the subsidiary household activities required the co-operative labor of all the members of the family. The father could not be the absolute autocrat, for he was as dependent on the services of the other members of the family as they were on his services. Thus, in accordance with the task assigned to each member of the family, each person had a unique status with corresponding rights and duties. Although the individual had little independent existence apart from the basic family unit, within the family he did have rights as well as duties which the father usually could not arbitrarily override.

These intra-family relations did not stem wholly from the moral authority of the father as in the true Confucian family, nor from spontaneous and voluntary affection as in the inter-personal relations of individuals in the American family. In the Japanese family, although elements of both authority and spontaneous affection existed, the relations partook somewhat more of the nature of contractual obligations. The relationship between parent and children, or between husband and wife, was not of dominance and submission purely, but there was a strong element of reciprocity—as of repayment of debt owed to one another.

Professor Takeyoshi Kawashima,[1] the foremost Japanese authority on the family, characterizes the relationship in the Chinese Confucian family between the patriarchal chief and the other members of his family as a "master-slave" relationship. Ideally the master is benevolent, but, benevolent or not, the other members of the family have a general obligation to serve and honor the master. In contrast, says Kawashima, the Japanese family is more feudal than patriarchal. The inferior members of the family have specifically defined "rights" which they can expect from the superior members, in return for which there is reciprocation of specifically defined "duties." In the feudal system a vassal receives land from his lord, and only because of this grant, or fief, does the vassal owe allegiance to the lord. Similarly, to state it somewhat baldly and exaggeratedly, in the feudalistic family the children owe allegiance to

[1] In his *Nippon Shakai no Kazokuteki Kosei* [*The Familistic Structure of Japanese Society*] (Tokyo: Nippon Hyōronsha, 1948).

the parent only by virtue of the parent's bestowal upon them of benevolence. There is no generalized, absolute loyalty or unconditional piety; there is only conditional, specific obligation.

However, inasmuch as the aristocrats had historically shaped the making of laws and had been the more articulate, and they were the ones most interested in maintaining absolute authority, the standards of the aristocratic family had become the official norms. Thus the official interpretation of the Meiji Constitution, if not its formalized institutions, inclined toward authoritarianism and patriarchal paternalism. The pre-Occupation Civil Code accorded legal recognition to the pre-eminence of the family, bestowed distinctive powers upon the head of the family, and provided for the perpetuation of the family headship through primogeniture. The subordination of the individual to the family was particularly reflected in the legal status of women, for, under the old Civil Code, while a spinster who was the head of her individual household had the same legal status as a man, a married woman had virtually no legal competence separate from her husband and had distinctly inferior and limited rights as compared to her husband with respect to such matters as inheritance and ownership of property and right of divorce. Thus the individual was legally subordinated to the family as represented by its titular head.

In actual operation, however, the contractual rather than the authoritarian aspects of interpersonal relations were more important than the official norms might indicate. This was particularly true in quasi-family relations wherein, for instance, a teacher would feel obliged to extend a father-like benevolence over his disciple, while the disciple would feel obligated to repay the debt of favor with perpetual loyalty, or wherein an employer would feel an obligation to accord paternalistic protection to his employee while the employee would feel obliged to reciprocate with faithful service. This was the "feudalistic" *oyabun-kobun* system—literally "father-like"–"child-like" system—of reciprocal obligations between liege lord and vassal, between boss and henchman, between patron and protégé, which pervaded almost all aspects of Japanese life. Such a relationship was not necessarily arbitrary, autocratic, or exploitative, for, not only did both sides possess socially sanctioned rights as well as obligations, but the intimate and subtle relations between the two often made each of them highly sensitive to and appreciative of the interests of the other. But such a relationship, however beneficent, was not democratic in the Western sense of according free play to the individual wills of essentially equal persons.

In view of such a social background, it might well be questioned whether the democratic reforms of the Occupation could go beyond a superficial form. Would not the Japanese continue to behave in accordance with their accustomed traditional social patterns so as informally to circumvent and nullify in practice the democratic institutions set up by the Occupation?

In the summer of 1947, a SCAP spokesman declared that a vast and insidious network of feudal forces threatened the democratic policy of the Occupation. As reported by American correspondents, the impression was created that SCAP had uncovered an "invisible empire" engaged in a conspiracy to subvert the Occupation. The Japanese were puzzled and resentful, for they knew of no such movement and could not imagine what the Americans were talking about. Even Socialist Prime Minister Tetsu Katayama, mild and docile though he usually was, protested vigorously that he knew of no feudalistic underground. It eventually became clear that the SCAP officials were not referring to any subversive political movement but were merely referring to the racketeering gangs operating on the border zones of legality. The picturesque language of exaggeration used to describe them resulted from the amazement of the SCAP officials as they came to realize fully what they had heretofore only vaguely suspected, namely, that the extensive power and influence and discipline of the gangs rested largely on the tight and elaborate web of *oyabun-kobun* relations between boss and henchmen.

Although the gangs worked in such lowly fields as the black market and the protection racket among small shop and street-stall keepers, the illicit working arrangements which they apparently had with the police suggested a powerful influence which might penetrate up into much higher levels of the government. If such influence was based on an age-old and deeply rooted traditional pattern of social relationships, would not the whole structure of the new responsible, representative government be rendered impotent? It is understandable that some Occupation officials thought of the possible ramifications of the unfamiliar *oyabun-kobun* influence in nightmarish terms.

Actually these gangs did not differ much from the underworld gangs of American cities with respect to either their activities or the dynamics of their power, although the strength and extent of the *oyabun-kobun* relationships gave them some unique features. Furthermore, although such gangs had had a very long and often romanticized history in somewhat the spirit of the Robin Hood legend, the extent of the gangs' influence which so amazed the Occupation officials was largely, though not entirely, a postwar phenomenon. Amid the administrative and economic breakdown following the surrender, when the authorities were unable to look adequately after the hordes of demobilized soldiers and repatriates, gangster bosses had set up well-organized black-market businesses and petty rackets as well as legitimate businesses which provided—in exchange for a regular assessment—a livelihood for those who would otherwise be unemployed. In one sense it was extortion, but it was a well-regulated extortion which seemed to many willing "victims" a reasonable fee to pay for the opportunity to make a living. The boss provided an essential social service; the beneficiaries paid him tribute and counted themselves his henchmen. When rival gangs resorted to violence in their competition, or when a boss used his strong-arm squads to discipline recalcitrant henchmen, the resulting scandal was embarrassing; but the local police and administrative authorities were understandably tempted to view the gangs with indulgence for performing in their own rough way many useful functions which otherwise would have had to be assumed by the overburdened authorities themselves. This tacit farming-out of public functions was of course not regular, but in itself it was not a much greater threat to the new democracy in Japan than the indulgence of the police in some American cities toward certain gangster activities is to American democracy.

Some Occupation officials were also greatly disturbed over their discovery of the labor-boss system in which day laborers belonged to permanently organized gangs held together by *oyabun-kobun* ties under a boss who exacted a percentage of their wages but who saw that they were supplied with jobs or looked after them when times were bad. It was embarrassing and frustrating to the Occupation officials preaching democracy and individual freedom to find that the only labor the United States Army could hire for work on constructing military housing or for stevedoring military stores had to be contracted through labor bosses who held a feudalistic control over the workers.

But while the actual menace of the racketeering gangs and the exploitative authoritarian nature of the labor-boss system were imagined in an exaggerated form by some Occupation officials, the insidious implications of the *oyabun-kobun* system to the democratic process in government could not be ignored. While the *oyabun-kobun* system could often operate as a quick and effective channel of communication to transmit the wishes of those at the lower levels to those in power at the top to the mutual benefit of both, it could also operate to hold together a tightly disciplined political machine more efficiently than the use of simple patronage of the type familiar in American politics. Japanese politicians, associating originally for the inevitable "back-scratching" and "log-rolling" familiar in politics everywhere, might inevitably become enmeshed in a web of mutual obligations and tied into exclusive cliques whose members would be permanently bound by a socially sanctioned sense of intense loyalty to one another in all circumstances. Such a relationship, while perhaps not so different in motivation and in essential nature from the shifting and temporary exchanges of favor among Western politicians, could be quite different in the degree of its perniciousness. If the actions of a politician or a voter should be determined by his obligation to a group rather than by his own individual free will, then obviously democracy would be endangered.

From one point of view, as has already been discussed at length,[2] the constitutional and political reforms instituted by the Occupation are quite significantly breaking down the traditional patterns of group control of politics and giving rise to independent individual politicians whose power rests directly

[2] See chap. vii.

on popular support in their constituencies. At the same time, factionalism and the interplay of special interest groups based on ties of obligation to collective entities continue to be features all-too-prominent in Japanese politics.

In the field of intra-family relations, which is of probably more basic importance than political relations in setting the general pattern of interpersonal relations in Japanese society, the situation seems equally confusing. The new Civil Code, which implements the equal individual rights guaranteed by the new constitution, seems to be making possible the emancipation of the individual from the social controls exercised by the family. Nowhere is this tendency more dramatically manifested than in the changing position of women, as evidenced by the entrance of women into political activity, by the increase of career women in business and in the professions, by the increase in the number of love matches in which the marriage partner is not selected by the parents, by the increase in the number of divorce suits initiated by women who no longer feel much inhibition about taking the offensive against men, and by the increasing number of husbands who help their wives with the grocery shopping or sometimes even help with the dishes. On the other hand, such emancipated individuals are still undoubtedly in the minority, though a growing minority, and even where they are in substance abandoning traditional practices they usually feel it expedient for the sake of social respectability to go through the forms of the conventional practices. Thus young people who have independently made their own choice of marriage partner usually call on their parents to go through the motions of fixing a family-arranged match according to the traditional form, or the wife who in the privacy of their home makes her husband wash the dishes meekly waits hand and foot on him when guests are present. Traditional standards are thus persistent in form, even where they are crumbling in fact.

In this confused situation abounding in highly divergent and contradictory evidences, one can quite easily see whatever one wants to see and draw whatever conclusions one is predisposed to draw. Some are impressed with the magnitude of the changes and feel sure that Japan is in a transitional period in which most of the reforms instituted by the Occupation are on the way to becoming permanently established. Others are impressed with the tenacity of traditional attitudes and feel that once the impetus of the Occupation dies down Japan will essentially lapse into her traditional way of life.

A balanced and consistent appraisal and interpretation of these apparently contradictory evidences can perhaps be made by analyzing the nature of social change in Japan. On reflection it appears that the change which has taken place in Japan in the postwar period is not basically different in kind from the change which has been going on in Japan ever since the beginning of her modernization and so-called Westernization. The tempo of this change has fluctuated from time to time. The Occupation obviously represented a vast stepping-up of the tempo for a while; today there has come to be a slowing-down and even a reaction in some sectors of Japanese life. But over the years the process of change has been going on, and while the postwar years represent a difference in degree, they do not represent a different kind of historical phenomenon from that which has long been going on in Japan.

European nations underwent modernization as part of a gradual historical evolution. Non-Western societies are undergoing modernization in consequence of Western influence, but different non-Western societies undergo this process in different ways. Non-Western societies of a relatively primitive sort undergo modernization as a consequence of colonization and economic exploitation by the West. In such societies the impact of the West causes the native cultural order to disintegrate, then to be replaced by elements of Western civilization. The content of the change is largely determined by the nature of the Western influence that is directed upon the native society. But in a complex, civilized, non-Westernized society like Japan's, the impact of the West does not result in the disintegration of the native cultural order and in the bodily substitution of elements of Western culture. Although the Western impact is impelling enough to cause change in the native society, the national culture strongly persists; and it is native cultural ends rather than the character of the Western influence that largely determine what new techniques and what new ideas will be accepted for adaptation and utilization. Here change and modernization may be very rapid and extensive rather than otherwise, because the full force of the national culture itself—using traditional as well as newer means of social control—can be directed toward promoting the desired change.

Modernization in Japan is thus neither a spontaneous evolutionary process nor a process inexorably imposed from the outside, but the result of ends and means more or less consciously formulated by the Japanese themselves. In other words, in terms of applicability to the problem of understanding the changes in postwar Japan, the key should be sought not in the Occupation reforms so much as in the objectives and plans of the Japanese.

Knowledgeable analysts of social change in Japan have pointed out that the Japanese, in their conception of their objectives from the time of their first contact with the West down to the present day, have tended to divide into three distinct groups, which might be termed: those who hold to the "conservative hypothesis," those who hold to the "liberal hypothesis," and those who hold to the "pragmatic hypothesis."[3] Although such labels are somewhat misleading because of unintended but inescapable political connotations, and although wide variations and inconsistencies in individual behavior cause the three groups to appear to overlap greatly, these labels do quite clearly identify the three distinguishable orientations as to attitudes among the Japanese.

The "conservative hypothesis" contends that successful and desirable modernization for Japan depends on maximum continuity with Japanese cultural tradition. Those who hold to this view welcome modern Western technology and even many aspects of modern Western social and political organization, but only as instruments for giving effect to traditional cultural values. The businessman who adopts modern labor-saving

[3] The present writer is indebted to his former anthropologist colleague, Professor John W. Bennett, for suggesting the theory and the typology of the groups determining social change in Japan. See John W. Bennett and Robert K. McKnight, "Approaches of the Japanese Innovator to Cultural and Technical Change," *Annals of the American Academy of Political and Social Science*, CCCV (1956), 101–13, for a much more detailed and refined analysis than can be given here.

machines in his office so that he can have more time to indulge in his hobby of ceremonial tea which gives him supreme spiritual satisfaction, or the neo-Shinto cult that maintains a radio station to broadcast appeals for a return to the worship of the Sun Goddess, are crude and obvious examples of adherents of the "conservative hypothesis." The *genro* Ito, who went to Europe to find the model of a constitution for the purpose of reviving traditional imperial authority, is a more apt historical example. However much they may adopt specific aspects of Western technology, members of this group do not welcome the introduction of Western cultural values or social behavioral patterns and regard technical change as a separate or independent process which ought to take place without changing the original cultural base.

The "liberal hypothesis" contends, on the other hand, that successful modernization for Japan depends on introducing into Japanese society all the changes brought about in Western society through "natural" historical evolution. While the purpose may be similar to that of the conservatives—namely, to enhance the power and glory of Japan—this group believes that the adoption not only of Western technology but of a Western cultural and institutional model as well would be to the benefit of Japan. Communists, syndicalists, some Socialists, some Christians, and other non-conformists who completely model their life styles and preferences on Western standards obviously belong to this group. But men like Yukichi Fukuzawa, the famous founder of Keio University, who all his life avoided political controversy and remained on a basis of intimate and respected relation with those in power, was also an adherent of the "liberal hypothesis" in that he unobtrusively but consciously nurtured the growth of liberal Western ideology through his educational and writing activities.

The "pragmatic hypothesis" contends that neither traditional values nor Western models are suitable to meet the complex and unique needs of modern Japanese life, that human beings are not capable of infallible judgment on such matters anyway, and that successful modernization for Japan should be based on the common-sense policy of coping with specific and immediate situational problems as they arise. Under this theory, as under the others, the Japanese would exercise deliberate control over the changes to be introduced, but would strictly limit their goals and plans to short-term ones which could easily be seen as appropriate to immediately obvious needs instead of projecting comprehensive plans to accord with preconceived ideological schemes or models. This is the hypothesis which, for reasons to be discussed presently, appealed strongly to most of the Japanese.

Given the circumstances of the Japanese historical and social background,[4] it was probably inevitable that the "conservative hypothesis" should be more popular among those who exercised political power and enjoyed social influence. Thus the "conservative hypothesis" was usually regarded as the orthodox line, and there developed the view—quite prevalent in the West—that the so-called Westernization of Japan was but skin-deep, that Japan merely adopted Western technical tools while retaining essentially traditional standards in her social and spiritual life.

A closer analysis of the historical record will undoubtedly reveal, however, that in fact the "conservative hypothesis" did not usually prevail. While the conservative, the liberal, and the pragmatic schools never lost their respective theoretical orientations, in practice both the conservative and the liberal groups came to approximate the pragmatic group. It is true that in some periods either the conservative school or the liberal school was clearly dominant. Prior to the 1880's and again during the early stages of the Occupation, the liberal school enjoyed great vogue. Throughout the 1930's and until the surrender in 1945, the conservative school—particularly an extreme and bigoted section of that school—wielded dominant power. But during most of Japan's modern history, while the conservative school outwardly appeared dominant, it was the pragmatic course of action that actually prevailed, with consequences that are very significant to an understanding of the Occupation period.

The reasons for the prevalence of pragmatic conduct are not hard to understand. The conservatives soon found that Western technology very often could not be made to work effectively

4 See chap. iii.

without changes in the social and cultural attitudes and in the pattern of interpersonal relations of those who would make use of it. Of course, as many observers have pointed out, it is true that there are innumerable examples of traditional social organization and group dynamics successfully harnessed to run modern technical operations; the result is not only an extremely rapid and smooth assimilation of modern technology to the existing social environment but also the revitalization of traditional values. But it is equally true that there are innumerable examples where Western technology has been found to work best—or to work only—in a social milieu quite different from the traditional Japanese one. Hence, while refusing to abandon their theoretical goals, the conservatives often found it necessary to accept much more from the West than they had originally bargained for.

Many of the conservatives thus found it expedient to put at least part of their cultural goals in temporary cold storage and, like the pragmatists, to concentrate on short-term situational needs. Also, in order to make use of the talents of the liberals, which were sometimes sorely needed, the conservative leaders compromised with them on the short-range, *ad hoc*, pragmatic programs. Thus, while continuing to pay lip service to the "conservative hypothesis," those who wielded power in Japanese public life became more and more indistinguishable in action from those who held to the "pragmatic hypothesis."

In a somewhat similar manner, those who held the "liberal hypothesis" also tended to approximate the actions of the pragmatists. Inasmuch as the conservatives usually occupied positions of power in Japanese society, the liberals found that they had to disguise their beliefs if they were to escape being relegated to oblivion. Therefore, while holding to ultimate liberal goals, many of them found it expedient in their outward conduct to conform to the conservative pattern of behavior and to work together with the conservatives wherever they could find a common meeting place on the neutral ground of a short-range pragmatic program. Thus, while the pragmatic program was regarded by the conservatives as a temporary concession to expediency, and by the liberals as an entering wedge for something more extensive, both nevertheless joined to make the pragmatic line of conduct the prevalent one. Lack of space precludes a documentation of this interpretation here, but detailed study of the great formative years of the Meiji period in modern Japanese history makes it amply clear that the major changes, while deliberately fostered and manipulated by the elite leadership group, were developed in the pragmatic manner rather than in accordance with any comprehensive preconceived ideological scheme.

The willingness of so many conservatives and liberals alike to temporize on a pragmatic program instead of holding out for their beliefs in defiance of consequences, as indeed a comparatively few extremists on both sides did, points to what might be regarded as a relative lack of principle or lack of dogmatism on the part of most Japanese. Although exceptional individuals and exceptional periods have not infrequently been seen in Japanese history, generally the Japanese have shown a preference for conformity to widely acceptable middle positions. Whether it stems from a paucity of logical philosophic thinking, or from the "situational ethics" discussed early in the book, or from a social system which emphasizes an equilibrium of contractual relations, the Japanese tend to seek easy accommodation to circumstances. In view of such characteristics, even more important than the willingness of conservatives and liberals to compromise is the weight of the majority of the people, who are temperamentally attuned to the pragmatic position and favor it for itself without conscious thought of expediency. A plodding advance over the road of practicality, rather than soaring flights of idealism or principle, seems to be the genius of the Japanese, just as "muddling through" is of the British.

This interpretation needs to be carried one step further. Although both the conservatives and the liberals adopt the pragmatic line of action as a matter of temporary expediency, continuation of this expediency in the long run works slowly to undermine the conservatives more than the liberals. Even narrowly technical innovations, once adopted, are likely to have ultimate effects beyond those intended by the planners. Modern technology, and widespread industrialization based upon it, tend to bring in their train an insidious transformation of many non-material aspects of life as well. While indoctrination and propaganda may delay the effects for a while, there develop rational habits of thinking, new forms of administrative organization and procedures, greater social mobility, recognition of individual ability with consequent respect for individual worth, new types of social relationships, and changed standards of values—such as the substitution of a universalistic ethic for the old particularistic ethic—wherever the old culture is found to be unsuitable in these respects to the needs of technology. While they may perhaps come about far too slowly and too haphazardly to satisfy the liberals, these changes threaten to get out of hand as far as conservative goals are concerned. Even conservative innovations thus contribute to the growth of a cultural medium in which there can be advance toward liberalism.

This does not necessarily mean the ultimate victory of the "liberal hypothesis" over the "conservative hypothesis," for there may be no conscious abandonment of traditional cultural standards and no conscious adoption of a Western model. But innovations deliberately instituted for pragmatic—or even conservative—ends almost always generate a chain reaction whose cumulative effect in the long run is a changed cultural environment in which the limited conservative goals are eventually discovered to be no longer relevant and are left behind. To the extent that Japan adopts modern technology and engages in modern industrial activity, the basic conditions that govern her national life will tend to resemble those of Western nations. As this happens, her cultural environment will also undergo change, and in the same direction. Finally, although a considerable time lag is to be expected and although because of historical differences Japan can never exactly duplicate the West, there may eventually evolve a transformed Japanese cultural pattern in which political, social, and spiritual values fairly comparable to those of the West will be more truly expressive of Japan's own new national life than the traditional standards of her fading past.

At the risk of unduly repeating much material already discussed at length in earlier chapters, this interpretation might profitably be applied, by way of example, to the appraisal of certain specific Occupation reforms.

Take the matter of responsible government, which is the key element in political democracy. The Meiji Constitution, with its glorification of the position and theoretical authority of the Emperor, appears to be a manifestation of the "conservative hypothesis," namely, the adaptation of the Western technical device of a written constitution and of Western governmental forms to buttress the ancient political myths and to serve the ends of a traditionalist oligarchy. The new constitution, with its emphasis on popular sovereignty, appears to be a manifestation of the "liberal hypothesis," namely, the adoption of a Western model of a democratic political theory. Yet, an examination of the historical background would seem to indicate that the change from the old constitution to the new constitution was not an abrupt change from the clearly conservative to the clearly liberal, for the old constitutional system had been evolving in a pragmatic manner into something with even some liberal implications. It will be recalled that the ruling oligarchy which had formulated the Meiji Constitution in conformity with the "conservative hypothesis" soon found it imperative to make pragmatic compromises. While the oligarchy had no desire to share power with the popular political parties, and indeed while the real intention of the oligarchy was to blunt the opposition of the political parties, individual oligarchs found it expedient to join political parties and, as party leaders, to attempt to manipulate the parties in the direction of the policies of the oligarchs. However subordinate the role of the parties, this represented some concessions to the distinctive function of parties in the governmental process, and to that extent it meant a diluting of the oligarchy's monopoly on authority.

While the conservatives thus compromised to the extent of working in some degree through the political parties, many of the liberals on their side also compromised to the extent of seeking limited gains within the framework of the conservative-dominated government instead of directly opposing the government. Minobe's "organ theory" was a theoretical rationalization of the pragmatic point of view which the compromising liberals could accept. Unlike the more uncompromising of the liberals who frankly espoused some Western model of government and were consequently hounded by the authorities, the pragmatically inclined liberals accepted the conservative constitutional system as a starting point. But while purporting to be loyal to this conservative system, they tried to give it the most flexible interpretation possible. While starting from a seeming acceptance of the traditional sovereignty of the Emperor, they led gradually from authoritarianism to increasingly responsible government. In all this, probably few of these compromising liberals were aware that they were making a compromise. Undoubtedly most of them were unconsciously manifesting the native predilection for moderate ideas of a practicable and gradualistic nature.

While the liberals were never able to take over power completely for themselves, it is significant that the oligarchs were forced to make more and more pragmatic compromises, until by the 1920's something close to responsible party government had come to prevail. While very imperfect and feeble by Western standards, it represented a great change and advance from the government originally intended by the conservative authors of the constitution.

This change and advance in the government came about only in part through the conscious effort of the liberals. More important was the fact that, while the conservatives and the liberals were engaging warily in short-range pragmatic co-operation with each other, the basic conditions of Japanese national life were undergoing modification in a direction unfavorable to the conservatives. As modern industry supplanted agriculture, the traditional bases of the power of the oligarchy became increasingly irrelevant to existing conditions; the immediate and specific situational problems calling for solution involved the new social classes and new vested interests created by the industrial economy, and the base of political power had to be broadened to include these new elements. Pursuit of even short-range pragmatic programs thus brought about a succession of changes which in the end went far beyond the limits envisaged by the conservatives.

This analysis might seem to be refuted by the rise of the

militarists in the 1930's and the loss of all the democratic achievements made up to that time. But actually the validity of the interpretation is not affected. Admittedly the democratic gains had not yet been consolidated and intrenched to the point where they could successfully resist determined assault, but the fact that the opponents of the democratic changes felt impelled to resort to violent and forcible counteraction only attests to the reality of the democratic changes that provoked them. When the anachronistic reaction should spend its force, as it was bound to do eventually because it was fighting against the inexorable march of time, the pragmatic trend toward more change and modernization was bound to be resumed.

It is against this background that the postwar constitutional change needs to be evaluated. Defeat in war had discredited the reactionaries; the liberals apparently stood vindicated. It was now obvious that Japan still had much to learn from the victorious West; the "liberal hypothesis" thus came to enjoy great vogue. When the Occupation imposed upon Japan the Western model of popular sovereignty in the postwar constitution, it therefore received considerable measure of sincere acceptance, for it was in line with the ideology of those who subscribed to the now popular view. But despite the temporary vogue of the liberal position, the conservatives and pragmatists were still very much alive. As the initial reaction to the defeat wore off and the Occupation drew to an end, the liberals who had waxed brave under the protective wing of the Occupation found that they could not continue their program alone. They had to take into account the existence of the conservatives and pragmatists. Moreover, while many conservatives whose self-confidence had been shaken by the effects of the war had gravitated easily into the pragmatic camp, comparatively few of them could make the jump all the way to the liberal camp. The practicable course for all, therefore, was to compromise again on the basis of short-range pragmatic programs.

It was the realization of the practical desirability of the pragmatic course from the beginning that caused so many who believed in ultimate liberal goals to feel consternation over the crudely "liberal hypothesis" basis of the "MacArthur Constitution." Thus the present movement for the revision of the new constitution and for the modification of many of the political reforms of the Occupation period does not necessarily represent a trend toward complete repudiation of democracy and reversion to traditionalism. It represents the reassertion of the historic tendency toward pragmatism. Even many liberals are willing to support this movement in the belief that the way to make solid progress toward democracy lies in short-range pragmatic compromises, relying on gradual modifications in the general cultural environment to make possible further successive steps toward the ultimate goal. Such a compromise is not the result of deliberate stratagem; it represents the genius of most Japanese to incline toward gradual changes rather than toward a rigid status quo or a cataclysmic revolution.

Just one other example might be briefly drawn, namely, in the social sphere with respect to the change in the status of women. As already mentioned, under the prewar laws women did not have the right to vote; women generally—with some technical exceptions—did not have property rights separate from their husbands; women—again with some technical exceptions—did not succeed to the family inheritance; and women were entitled to fewer grounds for divorce than men. Here was a manifestation of the "conservative hypothesis," the use of the modern technical device of a system of codified law, based in large part on the model of the Code Napoléon, to perpetuate the traditional subordinate position of women in Japanese society.

Under the postwar constitution, women are guaranteed exactly the same rights as men; and through the new laws implementing the new constitution, women enjoy the right to vote, they may own property as individuals separate from their husbands, they succeed to exactly the same share of the family inheritance as their brothers, and they enjoy exactly the same grounds for divorce as their husbands. This would seem to be a manifestation of the "liberal hypothesis," the improvement of the position of women through the adoption of modern Western standards as well as of the Western legal technology. It has therefore become quite common to attribute to the Occupation, and specifically even to the informal example of the American G.I.'s treatment of women, the chief influence for bringing about the change in the status of women in Japan.

Such a view, however, is most superficial. The change was not a simple change from the clearly traditional to the clearly liberal. If the change had been introduced primarily as an imitation of American example, it would not have taken hold; the reforms in the law concerning women would have remained paper reforms only. To the extent that the legal reforms have been accepted in practice, they reflect a real change that has been taking place in Japanese society from within, and this change has been going on since long before the Occupation.

Even while the old laws were in effect, which supposedly embodied the "conservative hypothesis" upholding the traditional subordinate status of women, the pragmatic requirements of an increasingly technological Japanese society had been affording increasingly greater educational opportunities to women, had been affording increasingly greater vocational opportunities to women, had been increasingly freeing women from traditional social controls as industrialization gradually broke up the collective authority of the extended rural family and substituted the greater social mobility and individual independence of the nuclear urban family. This tendency was particularly pronounced during the war—paradoxically supposedly a reactionary period—when as the result of the manpower shortage women flocked into industry in larger numbers than ever before. Women ran the streetcars and the railway and subway trains, women handled much of the food-rationing, women conducted much of the fire-fighting activities during the air raids, and women generally took over much of the work formerly considered to be solely the province of men. Women came to play a new role in Japanese life, and with the new role came a new status and new socially sanctioned rights.

If the women are now divorcing tyrannical husbands—as they are doing in increasing numbers—it is not because the Occupation-sponsored law says they can, but it is because husbands are no longer their only available meal ticket. If the women are now attaining public office—as they are doing increasingly—it is not because the new law says that they now have the same political rights as men, but it is because there are now more women with experience in industry and in business and in labor unions and in civic organizations who are capable of holding their own against the men at their own game. The new status of women is resulting not so much from a conscious adoption of Western standards as from the internal changes in Japanese society developing out of pragmatic responses to a succession of immediate situational needs.

The same sort of examples can be drawn in almost any field. Modern industry, adopted by the zaibatsu originally as a mere technical instrument, has called into being the countervailing force of an organized labor movement and a Socialist party powerful enough to challenge the zaibatsu dominance over the nation's economy. Western technology with its demand for professional technical competence has also been causing the zaibatsu organizations to fall increasingly under the control of a professional managerial class whose career interests become a countervailing force against the original traditional, exclusive family character of the zaibatsu system. It is these forces arising out of pragmatic adjustments to immediate situational needs, rather than the American model of trust-busting legislation, which are slowly but surely transforming the character of the zaibatsu.

The same sort of process is causing the labor boss system to wither away in areas where governmental social security measures and public employment agencies are beginning to offer day laborers greater benefits than the paternalistic favors labor bosses can offer to members of their gangs, is causing the peasants to break loose from the undue influence of the rich man of the community as his money-lending function withers away with the growth of credit co-operatives, and is causing individuals to cut loose from family controls as job opportunities induce the children to leave the family farm and live by themselves in factory towns. These changes are pragmatic responses to changing social situations rather than an ideological conversion from traditional loyalties to new models of ideal behavior.

Social change in Japan has not been seriously hampered by loyalty to old standards, nor has it been particularly inspired by new Western models. The generally non-doctrinaire, pragmatic inclination of most Japanese has resulted in neither a status quo nor a sweeping revolution but in a succession of gradual changes in response to specific situations, producing over the years a significant transformation in the nature of Japanese society. The postwar period has added nothing essentially different to this historic pattern of change, although the Occupation vastly speeded up the tempo of change for a short while. Such a pattern of social change would seem to indicate that the Japanese response to the stimulus of the Occupation is having gradual but profound long-range consequences. There was no immediate wholesale adoption of the American example; attempts to foist such an example bodily on the Japanese were quietly resisted or circumvented. But neither was there a blind and stubborn clinging to the past. The changes stimulated by the Occupation will undoubtedly be all the more permanently assimilated into Japanese life insofar as they were accepted by the Japanese of their own volition as suitable to their situation.

From one point of view, this interpretation would seem to minimize very greatly the importance of the influence of the Occupation on the general course of Japanese history. Even though the impact of the Occupation was such as to throw the Japanese quite off balance for a while, they were never completely swept off their feet and they never fully lost control over the direction of their progress. Thus, even though the Occupation program bore some aspects of wholesale change which justify in a sense its characterization as an induced revolution, there was not a true revolution in the sense of a complete destruction of the old and the bodily replacement by something totally alien. Even where there was a large degree of a destruction of the old, the Japanese managed to retain some elements of continuity. The Japanese have even been sloughing off some of the measures which they once accepted under the Occupation but which they have now come to consider unsuitable and undesirable. These facts may cause some to conclude that the Occupation has been largely ineffective in its permanent effects.

From another point of view, however, these same facts can be seen to point up the notable success of the Occupation. If the Occupation had been a completely extraneous intrusion into Japanese life, imposing changes by sheer force alone, then the Japanese might have been expected to reject all the Occupation-sponsored reforms as soon as the force was removed. But insofar as the Occupation represented just another situation—albeit an unprecedentedly big one—of the kind the Japanese had been reacting to in a pragmatic way for a century, they reacted to this situation as they had always tended to do. This meant that, although they accepted only a part of what was offered, what they did accept they accepted through their own decision about what was practicable for them. They may even reject some things which they once accepted, but what they decide to keep will probably be all the more firmly held for being the result of their own decision. The changes which the Japanese decide to retain may appear quite limited and modest; but even a seemingly minor measure, taken in response to an immediate exigency, can set in motion a chain reaction which may lead to an ultimately great change. It would seem that such a gradual process is the only way by which substantive social change in the direction of democracy, as distinguished from superficial institutional changes, can be soundly brought about. It would also seem, from the way most of the key reform measures of the Occupation period are being continued by the Japanese with not too much dilution, that such a process of social change is now actually working toward the steadily increasing democratization of Japanese society.

In this connection, it might be helpful in clarifying the problem to recall the question, posed in the early part of this work, of what is to be considered as constituting democracy.[5] If democracy is taken to mean specific ideals and practices, it is clear that the Occupation's program of effecting specific institutional reforms has been attained only in part and the results might therefore be called disappointing. If democracy is considered a way of doing things through public decision, then the evidence is that this is just what the Japanese are doing—deciding, for instance, through the free interplay of their own ideas what changes they will accept—and insofar as the Occupation contributed significantly to this result, it succeeded in its objective of stimulating democracy in Japan. Of course, in

[5] See concluding portion of chap. ii.

common usage democracy means both of these things and the Occupation, without much self-analysis or insight, tried to promote democracy in both aspects without distinguishing very clearly between them, necessitating consideration of each of them and adding to the confusion in appraisal. But if the two are viewed separately, the Occupation did comparatively poorly—but even then, not too badly—with respect to the first meaning of the term, and did remarkably well in the second meaning of the term, which is the more essential.

Japan still remains so different from the West that comparison might easily leave the impression that Japan has undergone no fundamental change. But a comparison of the Japan of today with the Japan of a hundred or fifty or even ten years ago cannot fail to reveal the highly significant social and cultural change that has taken place, even though much of it remains veiled behind the façade of traditional forms. In contributing the stimulus, even if not the direct control or motivating power, for the most rapid and intensive period of such change, the Occupation exercised an influence on Japanese history which can hardly be exaggerated. In stimulating changes which, however modest, set Japan on vitally important steps in the direction of further sound democratic development, the Occupation for all its shortcomings must be judged on balance as a magnificent success.

Unfortunately, however, it is not possible to end on a note of unqualified optimism. No matter how successful the Occupation and how soundly established the present Japanese trend toward democracy, there can be no assurance that democracy will prevail in Japan. The Japanese are not entirely masters of their own destiny; their own proclivities may not decisively shape their fortunes. Whatever their own desires, in this age of global conflicts and international interdependence, it is not likely that they could long hold out as a beleaguered democratic outpost if powerful nations and extensive areas in their general neighborhood should fall to militantly antidemocratic regimes which would exert upon Japan strong pressures—whether military, economic, ideological, or psychological. The problem of Japan, like that of all countries today, is no longer a national but a world problem.

Bibliographical Notes

No formal bibliography is presented because this work is largely a personal account based on the author's direct observations while engaged as editor of the *Nippon Times* of Tokyo during the years under discussion. Most of the interpretations in the book are distillations of views expounded, or occasionally only discreetly inferred, in the editorials of that paper which the author wrote almost every day from 1945 to 1949. These views took shape from the countless interviews, conversations, and arguments in which he engaged with both Americans and Japanese—with the proverbial man-in-the-street as well as with important personages, and particularly with Japanese colleagues encountered in the course of daily newspaper work.

Upon looking over the files of his old editorials, the writer notes that his basic interpretations have changed surprisingly little with the passage of time. The many books he has had occasion to consult since forsaking journalism for an academic life have, however, helped him to sharpen the focus of his earlier views and to set them off against a wider perspective. The books which most usefully supplement his account are listed below.

Basic to any study of postwar Japan is Edwin O. Reischauer, *The United States and Japan* (rev. ed.; Cambridge, Mass.: Harvard University Press, 1957). This is a deceptively short and seemingly simple book which, however, constitutes a most comprehensive, judicious, and authoritative appraisal of Japanese life and national characteristics. *Japan since Recovery of Independence,* edited by Kenneth E. Colton, Hattie Kawahara Colton, and George O. Totten, a special number of the *Annals of the American Academy of Political and Social Science* (Vol. 308, November, 1956), while uneven in quality as is almost inevitable with such collections of articles, is a useful summary.

The following are some of the more important general books on the American Occupation concerned with many of the same topics as the present book but with some notable differences in point of view. Baron E. J. Lewe van Aduard, *Japan: From Surrender to Peace* (New York: Frederick A. Praeger, 1954), is a concise and lucid account by a Dutch diplomat formerly stationed in Japan; while its treatment of the Occupation itself is conventional, it is unsurpassed for its treatment of the interrelations between domestic events and the international politics leading to the peace treaty. Harry Emerson Wildes, *Typhoon in Tokyo* (New York: Macmillan Co., 1954), provides the most authentic "feel" of Occupation activities, but it makes little effort to analyze systematically the underlying social forces involved, though its episodic and detailed treatment is often rich in astute insights. W. Macmahon Ball, *Japan: Enemy or Ally?* (New York: John Day Co., 1949), written by the Australian member of the Allied Council for Japan, intelligently and penetratingly raises some legitimate questions concerning the fundamental nature of Occupation policy, but some of the particular views expressed by the author reveal how insulated a person in such a position was from the realities of Japanese life as well as from the workaday problems of the Occupation. Robert B. Textor, *Failure in Japan* (New York: John Day Co., 1951), is a discerning criticism of Occupation policy from the point of view of an Occupation officer at the local level; although the author himself would undoubtedly admit today that some of his conclusions were out of balance, the book remains valuable for its perceptive details.

Edwin M. Martin, *The Allied Occupation of Japan* (Stanford, Calif.: Stanford University Press, 1948), and its sequel, Robert A. Feary, *The Occupation of Japan, Second Phase: 1948–1950* (New York: Macmillan Co., 1950), present an unexciting but accurate account from the official Washington point of view. Major General Charles A. Willoughby, *MacArthur, 1941–1951* (New York: McGraw-Hill Book Co., 1954), and Brigadier General Courtney Whitney, *MacArthur: His Rendezvous with History* (New York: Alfred A. Knopf, 1955), are illuminating but hardly objective memoirs by two high Occupation officials who were very close to General MacArthur. Among the official publications of Occupation headquarters, the most generally useful is SCAP, Government Section, *The Political Reorientation of Japan* (2 vols.; Washington: Government Printing Office, 1950).

Of the journalistic works, Mark Gayn, *Japan Diary* (New York: William Sloane Associates, 1948), is perhaps the most interesting but also the most unreliable; despite its popularity with Japanese readers who were titillated by its purported exposé of Occupation shortcomings, it contains erroneous information and distorted conclusions derived in considerable part from Japanese Communist informants. Russell Brines, *MacArthur's Japan* (Philadelphia and New

York: J. B. Lippincott Co., 1948), while superficial and often inconsiderate of the Japanese point of view, is a generally accurate and comprehensive account. William Costello, *Democracy vs. Feudalism in Post-War Japan* (Tokyo: Itagaki Shoten, 1948), is a thoughtful and conscientious work, marred however by somewhat distorted interpretations stemming from inadequate knowledge of the historical background.

In addition to the general works mentioned above, numerous books are of value in supplementing the present author's treatment of the specific topics of the several chapters.

Chapter i, while based almost solely on personal observation, finds considerable corroboration from Ruth Benedict, *The Chrysanthemum and the Sword* (Boston: Houghton Mifflin Co., 1946). Although this book must be used with caution because of its sometimes fanciful overgeneralizations, it is a valuable pioneering work which uses the techniques of the cultural anthropologist to open up a highly suggestive new approach to the understanding of Japanese traits and attitudes. John W. Bennett, Herbert Passin, and Robert K. McKnight, *In Search of Identity: The Japanese Overseas Scholar in America and Japan* (Minneapolis: University of Minnesota Press, 1958), vastly refines and enriches this approach in its study of the attitudes of Japanese intellectuals and of the influences that have played upon them; this work has far wider significance than its title might indicate, for it offers a comprehensive, well-balanced, carefully documented theory in explanation of the attitudes underlying the process of social change in modern Japan.

Chapter ii can best be supplemented by the general works on the Occupation mentioned above and by the voluminous official publications of GHQ, SCAP.

Chapter iii is a personal interpretation of some pertinent selected aspects of the Japanese historical background. Standard works dealing with this general period, some of which disagree with the present author's point of view, are: Sir George B. Sansom, *The Western World and Japan* (New York: Alfred A. Knopf, 1950), a brilliant account by the acknowledged master of the subject; Chitoshi Yanaga, *Japan since Perry* (New York: McGraw-Hill Book Co., 1949), which is rich in factual detail; and Hugh Borton, *Japan's Modern Century* (New York: Ronald Press Co., 1955), a thoughtful and balanced presentation. More specialized works dealing authoritatively with certain aspects of the historical background are: E. Herbert Norman, *Japan's Emergence as a Modern State* (New York: Institute of Pacific Relations, 1940); Delmer M. Brown, *Nationalism in Japan: An Intro-*

ductory Historical Analysis (Berkeley and Los Angeles: University of California Press, 1955); Nobutaka Ike, *The Beginnings of Political Democracy in Japan* (Baltimore: Johns Hopkins Press, 1950); and Robert A. Scalapino, *Democracy and the Party Movement in Prewar Japan: The Failure of the First Attempt* (Berkeley and Los Angeles: University of California Press, 1953). Despite its difficult style, Robert Bellah, *Tokugawa Religion* (Glencoe, Ill.: Free Press, 1957), is worth reading for its close analysis and interpretation of the dynamics of the historical process of Japan's modernization.

Chapter iv deals with a subject which has been written about voluminously by many Japanese writers. The most important of these works are discerningly analyzed and evaluated by Robert E. Ward in "The Origins of the Present Japanese Constitution," *American Political Science Review*, Vol. L, No. 4 (December, 1956). Harold S. Quigley and John E. Turner, *The New Japan, Government and Politics* (Minneapolis: University of Minnesota Press, 1956), contains a good section on the constitution.

Chapter v is based virtually wholly on personal experience but can be corroborated by numerous accounts in Japanese newspapers and magazines. Somewhat more formal samplings of popular attitudes toward this subject can be found in the many public opinion polls such as those frequently taken by the large newspapers on various aspects of this apparently perennially fascinating subject; the National Public Opinion Institute, Tokyo, has been responsible for conducting or supervising the best of these surveys. Jean Stoetzel, *Without the Chrysanthemum and the Sword* (New York: Columbia University Press, 1955), in its study of the changing behavior pattern and character traits of postwar Japanese youth, presents some interesting but not altogether convincing material on attitudes toward the Emperor.

Chapters vi and vii concern subjects usually dealt with at considerable length in almost all standard works on the government and politics of Japan. Among the most notable of these are: Harold S. Quigley and John E. Turner, *The New Japan, Government and Politics*, previously mentioned, particularly good for the constitution and the political parties; Burks's section on Japan in Paul M. A. Linebarger, Djang Chu, and Ardath W. Burks, *Far Eastern Governments and Politics* (2d ed.; Princeton, N.J.: D. Van Nostrand Co., 1956), an incisive and stimulating summary; Nobutaka Ike, *Japanese Politics* (New York: Alfred A. Knopf, 1957), a cohesive, neat, and logical presentation; and Chitoshi Yanaga, *Japanese People and Politics* (New York: John Wiley & Sons, 1956), a more loosely constructed presentation which, however, renders more justice to the nuances and inconsistencies in Japanese political life. Among works dealing with specialized aspects, notable are John D. Montgomery, *Forced To Be Free* (Chicago: University of Chicago Press, 1957), on the "purge"; the articles on local government by Kurt Steiner in various journals; and the highly discerning reports on recent political developments by Lawrence Olson of the American Universities Field Staff.

Chapter viii deals impressionistically with many of the topics introduced by Jerome B. Cohen in the last chapter of *The Japanese Economy in War and Reconstruction* (Minneapolis: University of Minnesota Press, 1949), and further developed in *Japan's Postwar Economy* (Bloomington: Indiana University Press, 1958). T. A. Bisson, *Zaibatsu Dissolution in Japan* (Berkeley and Los Angeles: University of California Press, 1954), is a thorough study of the zaibatsu problem whose value is not impaired by the fact that some of the author's conclusions are highly controversial.

For chapter ix also, the works of Jerome B. Cohen, mentioned above, are helpful. Solomon B. Levine, *Industrial Relations in Postwar Japan* (Urbana: University of Illinois Press, 1958), is a careful study of the labor problem in relation to the general Japanese economic background. James G. Abegglen, *The Japanese Factory* (Glencoe, Ill.: Free Press, 1958), deals with some narrower aspects of labor relations. Laurence I. Hewes, Jr., *Japan—Land and Men* (Ames: Iowa State College Press, 1955), is the most complete account of the land reform. R. P. Dore, *Land Reform in Japan* (New York: Oxford University Press, 1959), is the latest and most thorough study of both the historical background and the effects of the Occupation's land reform. A. F. Raper, T. Tsuchiyama, H. Passin, and D. L. Sills, *The Japanese Village in Transition* (GHQ, SCAP, Natural Resources Section, Report No. 136, November, 1950), is a detailed sociological study of some of the effects of the land reform; it, however, badly needs to be brought up to date. Irene B. Taeuber, *The Population of Japan* (Princeton, N.J.: Princeton University Press, 1958), is a formidable but authoritative treatment of the population problem.

Chapter x should be compared with the account in *Education in the New Japan* (2 vols.; Tokyo: GHQ, SCAP, Civil Information & Education Section, May, 1948), which is the official report. An essential reference is the *Report of the United States Education Mission to Japan* (Washington: Government Printing Office, 1946). Robert K. Hall, *Education for a New Japan* (New Haven, Conn.: Yale University Press, 1949), is a not too objective account by a former education officer in SCAP. Walter C. Eells, *The Literature of Japanese Education, 1945–1954* (Hamden, Conn.: Shoe String Press, 1955), suggests additional reading.

For chapter xi, the same references cited for the previous chapter are useful. In addition, William J. Coughlin, *Conquered Press* (Palo Alto, Calif.: Pacific Books, 1952), presents an excellent account of the "MacArthur Era" in Japanese journalism.

Chapter xii draws heavily from wide personal contacts experienced during a journalistic career. For the theoretical interpretations, the author has been greatly influenced by Professor John W. Bennett and his research associates, whose writings should be closely consulted, particularly John W. Bennett and Robert K. McKnight, "Approaches of the Japanese Innovator to Cultural and Technical Change," *Annals of the American Academy of Political and Social Science*, Vol. 305 (May, 1956); and John W. Bennett, Herbert Passin, and Robert K. McKnight, *In Search of Identity: The Japanese Overseas Scholar in America and Japan*, mentioned previously in connection with chapter i. The books on the general historical background cited in connection with chapter iii may also be profitably consulted in connection with chapter xii.

Works dealing with the period subsequent to that covered in the present book may profitably be read to bring the account up to date. Probably the most convenient is Hugh Borton *et al.*, *Japan between East and West* (New York: Harper & Bros., 1957), written under the auspices of the Council on Foreign Relations. The older work, Edwin O. Reischauer (ed.), *Japan and America Today* (Stanford, Calif.: Stanford University Press, 1953), is still useful in many respects. Admirable specialized works, based on sound research, have been appearing in increasing numbers in recent years; the annual bibliographical number of the *Journal of Asian Studies* should be consulted.